Number One: Environmental History Series

MARTIN V. MELOSI, *General Editor*

American Environmentalism

American Environmentalism

Values, Tactics, Priorities

By

Joseph M. Petulla

WITHDRAWN

Texas A&M University Press
COLLEGE STATION AND LONDON

Library of Congress Cataloging in Publication Data

Petulla, Joseph M
  American environmentalism.

  (Environmental history series ; no. 1)
  Includes bibliographical references and index.
  1. Human ecology—United States—Philosophy.
2. Environmental policy—United States.
3. Conservation of natural resources—United States—
Philosophy. I. Title. II. Series.
GF21.P43   304.2'0973   79-5278
ISBN 0-89096-087-9

Manufactured in the United States of America
FIRST EDITION

Contents

Preface

THE term *environmentalism* has historical precedents which are not necessarily connected to its present usage. It has referred in the past to the many varieties of geographical determinism. Sorokin wrote more than fifty years ago:

There scarcely is any physical or psychical trait in man, any characteristic in the social organization of a group, any social process or historical event, which has not been accounted for through geographical factors by this or that partisan of this school. Distribution of the population on the surface of the earth, the density of population, racial differences, the character of economic, political, and social organization, the progress and decay of nations, the character of religious ideas and beliefs, the forms of the family and of marriage, health, fertility, intelligence, crimes, suicides, cultural achievements, the number of men of genius, the traits of literature, poetry, and civilization, the movement of economic and social life, in brief, almost all social phenomena have been attributed to geographic influences.[1]

As early as 1788 Lord Kames complained about the "endless number of writers who ascribe supreme efficacy to climate." Not only the climate but also the stars and countless other physical conditions have been perceived as influencing or determining everything from the individual personality to the rise and fall of empires. That is, environment has been seen as all-powerful, while culture and human nature have been viewed as plastic and easily shaped. Hundreds of important

[1] P. A. Sorokin, *Contemporary Sociological Theories* (New York: Harper and Row, 1928), pp. 100–101.

thinkers throughout history are associated with environmentalism.[2] Needless to say, their theories have often been refuted, but the environmentalist arguments persist to the present day, even to a renascent interest in astrology (like the "scientific" computer astrology) and somewhat less obviously in folklore and more obliquely in the contemporary environmental movement.

The treatment in this book does not propose to make any connections between old and new meanings of the word *environmentalism*. Instead, its purpose is to note that the usage is quite different today from what it was a generation or two ago. Indeed, Edward Hyams, when writing the new preface to the 1976 edition of his *Soils and Civilization*, itself classifiable as "environmentalist" literature since it draws a causal connection between soil productivity and the strength of a civilization, claims that in 1952 when the book was first published the term *environmentalism* was not yet coined. His point is that the contemporary meaning of the word had not yet been developed.

Now the term *environmentalism* has a more positive connotation, referring to the ideas and activities of those concerned with the protection or proper use of the natural environment or natural resources. Thus in 1977 the American Sociological Association sponsored a session on the "Social Roots of Environmentalism" at its annual conference. Earlier, Donald Worster's anthology, *American Environmentalism: 1860–1916* included writing from principals of the first conservation movement and original American exponents of urban planning, applying the modern meaning to an earlier era. Environmentalism still can refer to external influences on behavior (as opposed to genetic influences), as it does in the debate over testing for IQ. The word has firmly established itself, however, as referring principally to questions concerning the physical environment.

What is of importance is the environmental argument today, the issues with which it is involved, and the priorities and values which are established in the national consciousness. Because this book is concerned with the ideas, activities, values, and priorities of modern environmentalism, it is necessary to sort out the assumptions of the

[2] Ibid., pp. 99–193. See also the extended treatment of this idea in C. J. Glacken, *Traces on the Rhodian Shore* (Berkeley: University of California Press, 1967).

traditions and data commonly presented to prove arguments. Often environmentalists (and antienvironmentalists) present problems or ask questions with built-in assumptions which come from quasi-religious or methodological commitments. Therefore the data which are selected often point to predetermined conclusions or moral absolutism. It is not surprising that ensuing environmental contests turn into miniature holy wars instead of rational public policy debates inspired by the real values of people.

Some of the material in this book has been presented in various forms in a course at the University of California, Berkeley, entitled Environmental Philosophy and Ethics. Those engaged in the philosophical enterprise attempt to verify the truth claims of a discipline, activity, or body of knowledge. In this case we examine the tenets of contemporary environmentalism. Environmental philosophy is particularly concerned with ideas which clarify values—often values in conflict are used as a means to the understanding of environmental issues so that judgments can be made about the resolution of apparent contradictions.

Thus, an environmental philosophy is an activity of exploration, examination, and elucidation of ideas rather than a set of principles or directives indicating the best way to live. Of course some conclusions should be derived from the philosophical effort. They might lead to norms of behavior and possibly to a better vision of the meaning of the total natural environment beyond the fragments of knowledge that come from the many disciplines which speak of the environment. If an approach to environmental philosophy is presented here, it is because I am making an effort to promote rational and critical discussion or conceptual exploration about the assumptions, methods, unexplained language and data, truth claims, and propositions of all those who speak about this increasingly important subject. Even conflict groups have to live with each other in nature—that is, in the natural world. And that natural world must be understood by human reason.

All of these purposes spurred this volume into print. My former book, *American Environmental History* (San Francisco: Boyd & Fraser, 1977), was written to show how historical events surrounding the exploitation of natural resources have led to contemporary environmental problems. There the emphasis fell more on economic history and the history of technology than on the political, social, and conservation histories that played related roles, because the path to economic development has in large measure led to progressively greater pollution, ecological disruption, and exponential depletion of natural resources.

The roots and scope of contemporary environmentalism, along with the values which inspire it, are much more subtle than I was able to illustrate in a generalized historical account. For example, following the traditional division of the conservation movement into the preservationists (of wilderness) and the utilitarians (of natural resources) in *American Environmental History*, I omitted the influential role of the development of ecological science, which has provided an intellectual basis for and a predominant role in the leadership of the contemporary environmental movement. Mostly, however, I could only touch slightly on the significance of the values and assumptions which have supported both the thrust of "progress" in the United States and the various reactions to it. These notions could not be fully developed in *History* but only scattered through several chapters, mainly the last two. They have been redesigned and amplified for the present volume. Here I have begun with the importance of values, showing how they fit into a social system and how they are shaped by the social structure.

I have attempted to sort out and clarify the many qualities and values mixed into what is known as the environmental movement and to reflect on them critically. I have examined their historical roots, assumptions, goals, methodologies, struggles, successes, limitations, and trends, and finally the priorities brought to the national consciousness through them. This project, then, can be described as a summary interpretive history of the modern environmental movement.

Part I sets up the problem and the description of environmental values and conflicts, their contemporary importance, and a model of the ideological traditions of conservation in the United States. Part II describes the contemporary blossoming of those traditions—the biocentric, ecologic, and economic—indicating the contributions of each to the success of today's movement. Part III takes a step back for a critical look at environmentalism's sometimes absolutist assumptions and methodologies—their limitations as well as their contributions in highlighting dangers of unquestioned growth and blind risk. Part IV discusses some public policy priorities, trends, criteria, and ethics for the directions suggested by the values of environmentalism.

The book starts with the idea of values and the environmental traditions which are derived from three sets of values. Next, in Part III, "critical issues" are examined. I assumed when I began to work on that section that I could trace definite lines from one or more of the environmental traditions to specific issues which are the major areas of contemporary concern. In some cases I found obvious connections between past traditions and present issues, but more often the complex interactions among modern value systems (in business, labor, the spectrum of middle-class perceptions, minority subcultures, religious beliefs, and so on) have tended to combine to form qualitatively new formulations of older definitions.

It seems to me that the environmentalist traditions still form the substructures of present ways of looking at environmental issues, but our understanding of environmental problems also includes newer scientific, economic, and philosophical notions about these issues. Thus "environmentalism" embraces disparate issues, which come from a complicated web of ideologies, and the bridge between the specific environmental traditions I set forth in the first half of the book and the issues I discuss in the second half is not as obvious as I had originally suspected. In my attempt to focus on the important variables of environmental thought, I was not able to lay out a simple, neat model which would explain wide divergences of thought and argument. Yet if the job sometimes seems to be a bit untidy, I would plead that historical events make it so.

Simply stated, I am trying to make sense out of American environmentalism in general and the American environmental movement in particular. As Sheldon Novick, former editor of *Environment* magazine, put it, "One of the most serious problems that faces anyone trying to grapple with 'environment' issues is the difficulty of disentangling the various disparate ideas and movements which have been lumped together by the media as a 'movement.'"[3] I hope that this piece of work will assist the disentangling process, though the job is admittedly far from done.

The disentangling, or clarifying, process involves political impli-

[3] D. L. Sills, "The Environmental Movement and Its Critics," *Human Ecology* 3 (1975): 2.

cations and judgments about the recent directions of the environmental movement. Again, the themes and conclusions of my *History* seem to have dispirited some environmentalists, students, and others, mainly because the book did not adequately cover the upbeat possibilities of modern environmentalism. Here I try to sort out what has been done, what can be continued quite easily because of the momentum of environmentalist traditions, and what important issues will be difficult to raise politically or implement practically because of the systemic weight of American institutions and values (for example, some issues surrounding questions of growth and risk). If these issues are to be effectively dealt with, a wider ethical understanding and political basis of support will need to be established.

I am especially grateful to former colleagues at the University of California, Berkeley—Joseph Hancock, Clarence Glacken, Arnold Schultz, Michael Hanneman, Douglas Greenberg, and Richard Walker —whose comments and criticisms on the early draft were very helpful to me while I was attempting to clarify basic notions of the book. Discussions with two very competent graduate students, Nancy Litterman and Nicholas Sundt, also acted as wonderful catalysts during the project. Students in my course Environmental Philosophy and Ethics have at once been challenging to and representative of viewpoints presented in the book; Aileen Alfandary from that class was an especially perceptive critic. I am also very grateful to Adrienne Morgan for providing the text with informative maps. In all, the book has been a collegial effort; I am thankful to many in the environmentalist community.

PART I
PROBLEM AND BACKGROUND

1

Environmental Values

MOST people who think about environmental crises make some general assumptions about values. And one of those assumptions will be that questions of environmental values will be simple ones. Environmentalists lament what they think are universal attitudes of waste and economic values which reward despoilment of the natural environment. Even representatives of offending corporations, many labor unions, churches, and perhaps land developers will agree, adding their own moderating provisos. Government agencies fall in line with the peculiar jargon of official documents. If we listen to environmental debate, it will appear that there is even some kind of consensus regarding values.

Yet when you scratch the surface, when individuals—executives, labor officials, factory workers, teachers, professional workers, farmers, traveling salesmen—begin to tell you their own life stories, their hopes, needs, feelings, and opinions, you get a glimpse of the complexity of the problem of values. Very often the same person holds contradictory attitudes. Values seem to arise from economic interests, yet many of the oldest and most deeply embedded ones, like those prevalent for centuries in religious thought, enjoy an existence virtually independent of economic conditions. Attitudes toward waste can be understood as only a small cluster in the vast constellation of values coming from hundreds of cultural sources—family, religion, economic beliefs, even personality and character. Values are learned early in life and strengthened, lost, renounced, and compounded as

individuals are nurtured by social, economic, and political institutions. They can be derived, therefore, from class position, but also
from political or social ideals as well as from religious heritage.

The Role of Values

Interest in environmental values has recently been strengthened
by writers who have attempted to demonstrate that religious beliefs
and values determine in large measure how the people of a particular
culture will view and act toward nature. The commentators therefore
prescribe a new ethic for the society or culture as a prerequisite for
changing old behavior. Historian Lynn White, for example, focuses on
the Judeo-Christian belief that nature is both separate from man and
also created for human use and service. He thus presents the thesis
that western religion is at the root of the contemporary ecological
crisis: "The artifacts of a society, including its political, social and
economic patterns, are shaped *primarily* by what the mass of individuals in that society believe, at the sub-verbal level, about who they
are, about their relation to other people and to the natural environment, and about their destiny. Every culture, whether it is religious
or not, is shaped primarily by religion. . . . The religious problem
[now] is to find a viable equivalent to animism [i.e., worship of the
spirits of nature]" (my italics).[1]

Lewis Mumford makes a similar statement: "For its effective
salvation mankind will need to undergo something like a spontaneous
religious conversion: one that will replace the mechanical world picture with an organic world picture." Rene Dubos hopes for a new
"common faith"; Charles Reich dreams about "Consciousness III . . .
an attempt to gain transcendence"; Theodore Roszak looks to a "visionary commonwealth." These writers see, in the human capacity for
visionary experiences, the hope for a common set of values, a new
ethic, that will transform not only religion but also other cultural

---

[1] "Continuing the Conversation," in *Western Man and Environmental
Ethics*, ed. I. Barbour (Reading, Mass.: Addison-Wesley, 1973), pp. 57–62.
The quoted item was written a few years after White's original article, "The
Historical Roots of Our Ecologic Crisis," in *Science* 155 (1969): 1203–1207,
also included in Barbour, *Western Man*.

institutions. The transformation, coming from good intentions, will lead at last to a society that is responsible to environmental needs.[2]

There are two problems connected with this kind of hopeful thinking. The first is that it assumes that value systems automatically follow from conversions. It also assumes that "new" value systems really are new. But such new systems derive support from the institutions they challenge, and it assumes that private experience will be able to change whole societies. It is true that conversion experiences sometimes do lead to new value systems. But we must not rest our faith on conversion alone. To do so is to forget the power that established institutions have to incorporate new values and attitudes. It may take some time for values to take root or die, but some may settle and become strong if the institutions themselves remain. This phenomenon has been described by Max Weber in *The Protestant Ethic and the Spirit of Capitalism* and by R. H. Tawney in *Religion and the Rise of Capitalism*.[3]

Weber and Tawney both showed how the religious ideas of Calvinism were linked to the development of new capitalist financial and economic institutions. These institutions replaced the loose discipline of Roman Catholicism. Weber was interested in rationalization, which has characterized western society more and more as it has evolved. The Protestant ethic is a special kind of rationalism which sanctifies economic activity to such an extent that personal material progress affirms the religious values of Calvinism and other branches of "ascetic Protestantism." Both capitalism and Calvinism demanded a "calling" to work in an assiduous, systematic manner, and that calling emerged in the rational climate provided by the Reformation.

Another, newer study, by Norman Gottwald, traces the social/environmental development of "liberated Israel."[4] Gottwald shows

---

[2] L. Mumford, *The Myth of the Machine: The Pentagon of Power* (New York: Harcourt Brace Jovanovich, 1970), p. 413; R. Dubos, *So Human an Animal* (New York: Scribners, 1968); C. A. Reich, *The Greening of America* (New York: Random House, 1970); T. Roszak, *Where the Wasteland Ends* (Garden City: Doubleday, 1972).

[3] M. Weber, translated by T. Parsons (New York: Scribners, 1930); R. H. Tawney (New York: Harcourt, Brace, 1926).

[4] *The Tribes of Yahweh: A Sociology of Religion of Israel 1250–1000 B.C.* (Maryknoll, N.Y.: Orbis Books, 1979).

how systems of production and distribution, social and political organization, and even such technological elements as improved iron tools
and watertight cisterns all influenced and were influenced by changes
in the religion of Israel. Gottwald's remarkable work shows the institutions of Israel to have been in constant flux as the tribes sought
autonomy within a Canaanite society through egalitarian forms of
sociopolitical organization, economic production, and resource use.
At the same time, Gottwald delineates the continual interplay among
societal structures and religious beliefs. The point of his and other
works is simply that a new ethic is not born in a vacuum. That is,
a social system often generates values which motivate individuals.
Changes in individuals presuppose group value systems coming from
traditions or institutions.

The second difficulty which stems from the wish that environmental values might in themselves change the direction of a society
for the better is that contemporary cultures contain dozens of conflicting sets of values. During former ages when communities tended to be
nuclear and isolated, it might have been possible for the entire society
of an area to function harmoniously for a limited period of time. A
set of values could support a compatible social system and vice versa.
Yet even very early cultures changed rapidly as new technologies or
religions or economic institutions were introduced, any one element
of which could throw the entire societal system into a state of dysfunction until a new equilibrium was achieved. There probably was
never a completely harmonious society for very long.

Subcultures as Cultural Environments

In contemporary society the variety of ideas in circulation, types
of social classes (and their respective values), religions, personal belief systems, occupations, political ideologies, economic institutions
(and supporting values), even psychological needs all thrive in subcultures. These subcultures and other cultural groups develop or receive
peculiar languages; pursue unique goals; and share common attitudes,
symbols, opinions, values, and commitments in special constellations
of meaning.

In American society economic or political interest groups can be considered such subcultures. Some groups follow the laws, habits of thought, roles, codes, and standards of the larger society. Some do not. Many harbor several sets of values. These cultural groups develop familial ties since often they are reference points regarding self-identity, purpose, and meaning in life. They offer a diverse richness to their larger cultures, and a measure of complexity, and of course most people derive attitudes, language, and behavioral patterns from a variety of such reference groups.

Although the larger society exercises a special power over the smaller cultural groups since it dictates the economic and political rules of the game, the groups themselves enjoy much latitude in determining their private value structures and behavior. The economic, political, and social structures of the larger society do not require uniform life-styles, political or religious beliefs, or even economic consumption patterns, the forces of advertising notwithstanding. Subcultures can also act as counter-structures through which a population can act out changing roles and commitments, sometimes in conscious opposition to established structures. As anthropologist George Park has pointed out in another context, "Culture has many voices."[5]

These "voices" often become ideologies of the cultural groups. Ideologies do not necessarily take the form of propaganda, but the people who hold to them tend to use the ideologies to justify their way of life. Ideologies can mirror the beliefs of religions, political parties, or voluntary groups. Corbett, in *Ideologies*, defines their content as "any intellectual structure consisting of: a set of beliefs about the conduct of life and the organization of society; a set of beliefs about man's nature and the world in which he lives; a claim that the two sets are interdependent; and a demand that those beliefs should be professed, and that claim conceded, by anyone who is to be considered a full member of a certain social group."[6]

Of course subcultures develop ideologies according to their own interests. Some might encourage or promote positive environmental values. Some are completely unconcerned about the natural environment. Some groups feel their economic interests are threatened by environmentalists. Environmentalists find it difficult to overcome the

[5] *The Idea of Social Structure* (New York: Vintage, 1975).
[6] P. Corbett, *Ideologies* (London: Hutchinson, 1965), p. 12.

hostility of those who oppose their views most strongly. As it is, when they carry on discussions with opposing groups they tend to concentrate on winning over those who are still uncommitted to environmental causes. The voices of subcultures have their own imperatives, their own agendas. Thus it is not certain that education or an increase in environmental information will in themselves promote favorable attitudes toward the environmental movement.[7]

At the beginning of the 1970s the environmental movement concentrated its forces on a widespread educational campaign through hundreds of newly formed environmental groups in local communities and college campuses.[8] At that time these groups received widespread local support from the media, business and professional groups, and the public at large. However, as the issues became more specific and their educational campaigns remained unproductive, environmentalists turned more to power strategies such as litigation, boycotts, legislation, injunctions, and lobbying and away from participation strategies such as education, voluntary recycling, and urging life-style changes.[9]

The change in tactics naturally precipitated opposition groups from some corporate, labor, and even minority groups. Education has retained a paramount role in the environmental movement, but because of dwindling human and financial resources in environmental organizations, proportionately less time and money are spent on it in the face of more pressing legal demands. It has long since been clear that the early unity of the modern environmental movement has given way to conflicts of value and behavior.

[7] C. E. Ramsey and R. E. Rickson, "Environmental Knowledge and Attitudes," *Journal of Environmental Education* 8 (1976): 1. Ramsey and Rickson found that the results of environmental education and information are variable, sometimes exercising little or no impact on the receivers.

[8] For a good summary of the activity of the environmental movement during this period, see D. E. Morrison, K. E. Hornbeck, and W. K. Warner, "The Environmental Movement: Some Preliminary Observations and Predictions," in *Social Behavior, Natural Resources and the Environment*, ed. W. R. Burch, N. H. Cheek, and L. Taylor (New York: Harper and Row, 1972), pp. 259–279.

[9] Ibid., pp. 264–265. The authors use the power-participation distinction suggested by L. Killian, "Social Movements," in *Handbook of Modern Sociology*, ed. R. E. L. Faris (Chicago: Rand-McNally, 1964), pp. 436–455. See also R. E. Dunlap and D. A. Dillman, "Decline in Public Support for Environmental Protection," *Rural Sociology* 41 (1976): 382–390.

Conflicts of Value

It took only a few years for polarization of interest groups and cultural groups over environmental issues to occur on both eastern and western seaboards. By 1975 a half-dozen powerful antienvironmental groups composed of representatives of industry, labor, developers, and politicians had been formed in the Pacific Coast states and many more parts of the country.[10] On the other hand, environmental organizations like the Sierra Club increased their membership two- and threefold, including large numbers from middle-class groups which place a premium on the values of the natural environment. Some labor unions, under the not-so-gentle nudging of an environmentalist labor leader, Anthony Mazzocchi of the Oil, Chemical, and Atomic Workers Union, perceived that industrial health and safety were ultimately environmental problems.

Environmental groups, moreso individuals in organizations, tended to stress different issues. Some stayed exclusively with wilderness preservation and protection of wildlands from development; others, many with a scientific emphasis, were concerned more with ecological disruption or issues of environmental health; environmentalists in government agencies tended to consider environmental resource use in economic terms. A cultural, aesthetic, scientific, or economic background and a related conceptual framework or methodology often determined an environmentalist's perspective and commitment.

Much has been made of the fact that the membership of the modern environmental movement has been largely composed of people from the middle, upper-middle, or upper classes, and thus the movement's values have been seen as determined by the interests of these classes.[11] Most studies about social issues indicate that middle- or upper-middle-class people—generally educated people—tend to be more concerned than others about community welfare and societal issues. These classes embrace millions of people. (It has not been

---

[10] D. E. Morrison, "The Environmental Movement: Conflict Dynamics," *Journal of Voluntary Action Research* 2 (1973): 81. Morrison predicted the phenomenon in 1972.

[11] J. Harry, R. Gale, and J. Hendee, "Conservation: An Upper-Middle Class Social Movement," *Journal of Leisure Research* 1 (1969): 246–254. See also R. Neuhaus, *In Defense of People* (New York: Macmillan, 1971).

determined which environmental issues the different segments of these classes care most about and why.)

The patterns of local or regional environmental conflicts during the first years of "power strategies" were similar. When the building of an industrial complex, a dam, a pipeline, or a subdivision was proposed, sooner or later the project would be challenged in the courts or public agencies. The struggle more and more became centered on sheaves of paper called environmental impact statements (EISs) detailing tens of thousands of bits of information. The more intense the controversy, the more thousands of pages would be added to the reports, each one required for any project that significantly affects the environment. (Now it is not unusual for an environmental contest to last many years and to cost millions of dollars.)[12]

So long as the battles were waged through unreadable technical reports instead of public debates, where values could be explained, they were destined to polarize and antagonize rather than enlighten. Robert Socolow summed up the problem of values in such an environment in an essay entitled "Failures of Discourse: Obstacles to the Integration of Environmental Values into Natural Resource Policy," a subsection of which is entitled "Analyses Are Not What People Care About."[13] The book in which the essay is included is an attempt to separate and weigh conflicting values and to penetrate the "failures in discourse" while studying only one environmental controversy—the proposed and now seemingly defunct Tocks Island Dam project on the Delaware River. Socolow's opening statement is important enough for this subject to be quoted at length:

> Major environmental decisions have a way of getting stuck and staying stuck. The decisions about whether to undertake substantial transformations of natural areas—to bring about new power plants, dams, airports, pipelines, deep water ports—have several pathologies in common. A cluster of detailed technical analyses accompanies the formulation of the program and its initial rush onto the stage; the proponents of the project imply, and generally believe, that all one could reasonably have expected

---

[12] S. J. Diamond, "Reports on Ecology—A New Industry," *Los Angeles Times*, January 6, 1977, p. 1. Diamond refers to EISs in terms of "pure paper tonnage."

[13] In *When Values Conflict*, ed. L. H. Tribe, C. S. Schelling, and J. Voss (Cambridge, Mass.: Ballinger, 1976), pp. 1–33.

has been done, both to justify the program and to anticipate its pitfalls. As after a carefully planned transplant, the reaction of rejection is slow in coming but grows relentlessly. The analyses are shown to be incomplete, and new analyses starting from different premises are eventually produced by those who wish to stop the program. But, contrary to what one might naively expect, the existence of disparate analyses does not help appreciably to resolve the debate. Rarely are the antagonists proud of their own analyses; more rarely still are they moved by the analyses of their opponents. The combatants on both sides have been constrained by mandated rules of procedure as well as by the tactics of compromise. Understandably the politicians in a position to determine the outcome conclude that their time is not well spent pondering the available analyses, even though they may commission still more of them.

The failure of technical studies to assist in the resolution of environmental controversies is part of a larger pattern of failures of discourse in problems that put major societal values at stake. Discussion of goals, of visions of the future, are enormously inhibited. Privately, goals will be talked about readily, as one discovers in even the most casual encounter with any of the participants. But the public debate is cloaked in a formality that excludes a large part of what people most care about.[14]

Socolow admits that "analyses are part of the formal debate" but appeals for a wider public discussion which would include reflection over values and goals and the possible alternative futures which would affect all groups. This kind of discussion would perhaps clarify values in general, particular environmental values, and ethical reflection (what should be the proper course of action). Presumably such clarification would take place in the context of any proposed change in the environment of a region.[15]

Values as Subjective or Objective Norms

In the discussion above, the term *values* has been used in the sociological sense (following Durkheim) of moral support of a social system, or "societal values." That is, types of social, economic, and

---

[14] Socolow, "Failures of Discourse," pp. 1–2.

[15] There is an implication in Socolow's statement that it might be possible to obtain a consensus about primary goals, visions of the future, or other major societal values if these questions were discussed in public debate. As I indicate below, such consensus does not seem to be possible, but clarification might be helpful.

political activity are undergirded by a set of shared norms which reward, sanction, and orient behavior in a particular direction. The rules are learned in the family, in school, from religion, and from laws. Cultural codes tell the members of a society what kinds of activity make good or bad members of the group.

Until the end of the nineteenth century the philosophical study of value was not independent, but instead was subsumed under the study of ethics or aesthetics. Then because of the influence of religious, philosophical, and scientific individualism; capitalist economics; and attempts at democratic government, values also came to be understood as *properties of individual human beings* rather than as part of objective systems which contain the true, good, and beautiful in themselves.

People probably always had their own preferences despite shared social values, but until societies were reorganized after feudal times, and mobility of land and labor was demanded by new capitalist institutions, few *value* options existed. Values of various cultures were spread abroad (and marketed) under the impetus of modern capitalist ideologies, although the clusters of values still had to be nurtured in social or cultural environments within capitalism. When value theory was first discussed, mainly by pragmatists in the United States, values tended to be reduced to subjective experiences. They said in effect, *De gustibus non est disputandum.* The principle that people not argue about their private tastes (since they are completely subjective) was applied to value judgments. "You might like forests, but I prefer redwood paneling in my living room; let's not argue about tastes."

The argument over values still has more than a trace of the old objective-subjective debate. In any given situation it may appear, for instance, that a small group of environmentalists is forcing its opinions (which is to say its subjective values and questionable tastes) onto an unsuspecting public. Thus, environmental goals and values in such situations would not be seen by opponents as objectively good or valuable (thus attracting those who are made aware of these values), but rather as the subjective desires of a group of people who seek to make their private tastes into public goals. The opposition's chagrin is compounded as the general financial burden increases—for pollution control equipment, catalytic converters, land for wilderness preservations, and the like. Incidentally, the opposition also responds negatively to the environmentalists in such situations because it tends to perceive them as a small, vocal, powerful, and probably dangerously disruptive group.

The response of the environmentalists to the challenges of opposition groups has been to spend more of their human and financial resources on power strategies in the courts and legislatures, to learn the tricks of the EIS game, and to take on opposing parties in every arena, knowing that they will win some battles and lose some, so they might as well oppose development everywhere if the money is available to do so. Although environmentalists believe their cause(s) to have a solid base in ("objective") ecological and scientific truth, and although they seem to have few alternatives in an adversary system of law, their tactics seem to preclude a rational setting of priorities.

What Socolow refers to as the "failure of discourse" points up the increasing polarization of the vocal parties in environmental disputes. Established groups follow a pragmatist tradition in arguing that environmentalists threaten to slow down the economic growth necessary for jobs and housing, especially for minorities. They also maintain that environmentalists push inflationary pressures to a dangerous level and indirectly allow the erosion of what they think of as American economic supremacy. Whenever antienvironmental groups define the issues, they see traditional American (individualist, subjectivist) values under unwarranted attack.

On the other side, environmentalists seek a new objectivist ethic, one based on respect for the natural environment rather than its exploitation for little more than increased profits. Thus, their values support what they believe to be an alternative ethical system.

Interests and Institutions

It is not possible to analyze all the values and the interests of the conflicting parties. It is useful, however, to suggest how difficult it can be to keep track of people's interests. Consider these points:
1. Belief systems, ideologies, values, goals, commitments, and modes

of behavior *contain* or *express* interests.[16] Thus, a person who believes in personal property, who has a commitment to providing for his family, and who is working to send his children through college will probably attach high value to earning money. He may adopt a behavior pattern stressing hard work. That person's interests may well include protecting his job, gaining advancement, and the like.

2. Belief systems do not necessarily lead to group action. Many people share what Talcott Parsons calls *attitude systems* without organizing themselves. They do not form what Ginsberg calls *definite groups*.

3. We can therefore say that people who share interests without doing anything to forward their interests have *latent interests*. As soon as the people organize to put forward an interest, that interest becomes a *manifest interest*. And of course those who stand to lose if the present way of doing things is changed are said to have *vested interests*.

Suppose a group forms to carry out an interest—to change it from a latent interest to a manifest interest. The group tries to bring in others with the same latent interest. Or it tries at least to get support from the general public. It recruits.

Both parties to environmental conflicts have tried to use the media to convince others that their cause is right. In doing so, they have appealed to what they perceived as the latent interests of Americans: maintaining a good quality of life, getting and keeping jobs, and providing health care for the poor, for example.

So we have environmental struggles. The actors are groups. The groups are fighting for their interests; some are protecting vested interests. Others are trying to push the cause of their manifest interest and appealing to people for support by playing on the latent interests of the general public.

---

[16] See R. Dahrendorf, *Class and Class Conflict in Industrial Society* (Stanford: Stanford University Press, 1959), pp. 157ff. Dahrendorf's treatment is a critical analysis of the topic of class from the time of Marx, but it also applies to our discussion. He uses the terms *latent interest, manifest interest, quasigroups,* and *interest groups* from M. Ginsberg, *Sociology* (London and New York: Oxford University Press, 1953).

What kinds of interests drive the environmental battles? In nearly every one, the real economic interests and personal belief systems lie just beneath the surface of the debate. On that surface, though, the groups are arguing about other subjects.

For example, an industry-favoring group of county commissioners in Pittsburgh placed a referendum on a local ballot for the voters to decide whether "elected officials should fight to change federal environmental laws in order to preserve existing jobs in the steel industry." (Not unexpectedly it passed, two to one.) As environmental and union representatives pointed out, foreign steel competitors, not environmental regulations, were threatening jobs. The ballot summary, "Change federal environmental laws to preserve existing jobs, yes or no," was at best misleading and at worst dishonest.[17] The issue really should have been stated in terms of modernizing ancient, polluting, inefficient steel mills instead of laying off workers to maintain profits, according to critics of the commissioners.

For their part, the environmental organization Group Against Smog and Pollution (GASP) proposed to put their own question on the ballot for the following year: "Should elected officials work to enforce environmental laws which work to protect the health of the public?" A different perspective, reflecting different values, phrased in ethically different terms.

Occasionally an environmental group constructs an abstract ethical system or proposes an ethical system of a previous age. People are expected to accept such systems uncritically. The main difficulty with uncritical acceptance of such systems is that they are not attached to societal or cultural structures. The reverse may also be true; that is, people are sometimes asked to hold to ethical mysteries that do not fit a changing world situation. For example, prohibitions against birth control made good, practical sense at a time of high infant mortality and higher demand for labor, either on a feudal manor or in an early

---

[17] See V. Pappas, "Vote to Save Steel Jobs by Changing Laws on Pollution Stirs Row," *Wall Street Journal*, November 11, 1977. For another kind of confusion, see the results of a similar problem in northern Illinois in N. C. Sharma, J. E. Kivlin, and F. C. Fliegel, "Environmental Pollution: Is There Enough Public Concern to Lead to Action?" *Environment and Behavior* 7 (1975): 455–471.

capitalist village. Religious rules were even elevated to the status of natural law. However, today most infants live. Overpopulation will become a serious problem, so the proscription against birth control now becomes a demand that is illogical; it must now be accepted on blind faith. It does not fit into the common experience and the understanding of ordinary people, nor does it reflect either the contemporary needs or latent interests.

A parallel complaint can be made about the construction of systems of environmental ethics which for any reason are not grounded in legal, economic, and cultural institutions or related to the personal experience of the members of a society. Lynn White's suggestion that Judeo-Christian doctrines about nature—for example, that nature was created for human exploitation—be replaced by a modern version of animism is unrealistic, even if one accepts his questionable assertion that all Judeo-Christian cultures hold an exploitative view of nature. Into what existing cultural structure or environment would such a new animistic ethic fit? Would White expect us all to assume the traditional culture of the American Indian? At the 1977 meeting of the American Association for the Advancement of Science (AAAS), Vine Deloria, the prominent American Indian leader and author, pointed out that an animistic ethic does not even fit every traditional American Indian culture, and it certainly does not suit the culture of urban Indians today.

Much support has developed among environmentalists for Aldo Leopold's *land ethic*, which suggests that animals, plants, rocks, and the natural world in general be regarded on an ethical plane with humans. Leopold writes, "A thing is right when it tends to preserve the integrity, community, and beauty of the biotic community. It is wrong when it tends otherwise."[18] But until institutions which will support the operation of his maxim are developed, it will remain meaningless (at worst, facetious) to most people.

The process of institutionalizing environmental values has already begun in American society. Since 1966 and the Endangered Species Act, an entirely new legal thinking has been introduced into the courts, one that was defined by the 1969 National Environmental Policy Act (NEPA) so "that presently unquantified environmental amenities and

[18] A. Leopold, *Sand County Almanac* (New York: Oxford University Press, 1949), pp. 204, 221, 224–225.

values may be given appropriate consideration in decision-making along with economic and technical considerations." The Laboratory Welfare Act of 1970 goes even further. It places laboratory animals under "the human ethic that animals should be accorded the basic creature comforts of adequate housing, ample food and water, reasonable handling, decent sanitation, sufficient ventilation, shelter from extremes of weather and temperatures."

Rare and endangered species around the country—the furbish lousewort in Maine, the snail darter in Tennessee, the desert pupfish in Nevada, and others—have stopped or delayed the construction of dams and other huge projects because of newly institutionalized environmental values. Because of the Marine Mammals Protection Act, a federal judge halted the tuna industry in southern California for several weeks because its methods of catching tuna also killed porpoises. Even the strip mining laws which require mining companies to restore lands to their original contour represent a different way of thinking about the landscape—different, that is, from the way the strip mining operators have thought in the past.

Others would go further in this direction. For example, environmental lawyer Christopher Stone has proposed that objects of the natural environment such as trees, rivers, lakes, and mountains should be granted legal rights in somewhat the same way that corporations have rights in this country. Through a guardian, natural objects would have standing in their own right so that they would be allowed to institute legal actions and report their injuries; damages would be assessed according to their unique natural "hardships," and they could be the recipients of rewards for themselves.[19] Stone points out that those agencies which are responsible for protecting the environment often neglect their duties in that they do not provide for the individual entities in the environment.

Conservative and Progressive Traditions

In acting as a spokesman for environmental concerns, the environmentalist often plays the curious double role of conservative (in

---

[19] C. D. Stone, *Should Trees Have Standing?* (Los Altos, Calif.: William Kaufman, 1974).

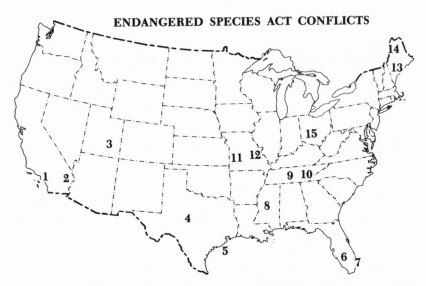

ENDANGERED SPECIES ACT CONFLICTS

1. El Segundo blue butterfly—expansion of airport
2. Brown pelican, peregrine falcon—space shuttle
3. Black-footed ferret—power plant
4. Red-cockaded woodpecker—timber management
5. Whooping crane—bomb testing
6. Florida Everglades kite—airport
7. Manatee—nuclear power plant
8. Mississippi sandhill crane—highway construction
9. Mussels and snails—dam
10. Snail darter—dam
11. Gray bat—dam
12. Higgins-eye pearly mussel—dredging of river
13. Clam larvae—power plant
14. Furbish lousewort—dams
15. Indiana bat—river channeling

A mighty weapon in the hands of the environmentalists has been the Endangered Species Act, a law passed by Congress in 1973 with nearly unanimous support. Soon afterwards, however, because of its successful employment in development cases, the law became the object of derision, hostility, and continued efforts to weaken it. The act requires that good-faith efforts be made to resolve conflicts before a project is halted. Of the five-thousand-odd cases presented to the Department of the Interior by mid-1978 for consultation before legal action, all but three were resolved, practically all of them within a period of a few hours.

matters of scientific understanding and social and environmental change) and radical (in matters that challenge conventional assumptions about progress, growth, and other accepted concepts of economics and politics). It should not be surprising that the day-to-day critical and ethical reflections of those who are concerned with environmental matters often take an uncertain course.

Part of the reason for the dual and occasionally paradoxical values of environmentalism lies in the origins and history of their expression. Three sources of environmental traditions inspire most environmental groups; in this text they are called biocentric, ecologic, and economic. The first, or biocentric, tradition stems from primitive feelings which led ancients both to fear and to respect nature and the power of *mana*—the unknown creator and destroyer of life—within nature. Mana was the extraphysical force which gave plants, animals, and other objects of nature both their individuality and their ability to act in behalf of or against humans in the maintenance of order in the universe.

The tradition has been refined over many millennia by the forces of civilization. It changed its expression in the religions of biblical lands, India, China, and Japan. Eventually it was modified by Christianity, and it remains among us today in both a progressive and a conservative form. Just as the ancients played it safe when it came to dealing with the caprices of nature, and medieval Christians tended not to trespass into or touch those regions of wilderness which were thought to be the domain of the devil (or alternatively because they represented the unapproachable handiwork of God), so in our day many moderns warn against tampering with nature lest all manner of evil befall us. Or they say that nature should remain inviolate because it is valuable (godly) in itself. This very sensitivity can become a progressive force, a reaction against those in society who interpret nature only in terms of resources for commodities.

The second, or ecologic, tradition has evolved from ancient Greco-Roman theories of natural law which have come to us through the Christian interpretations of teleology (investigation of the purposes and final ends of nature) of the medieval Scholastics, and from them through the natural philosophies of the eighteenth-century Enlightenment, ending finally in what we know as modern science. The pursuit of knowledge from the early natural-law philosophers to contemporary scientists has been characterized mostly by the desire to uncover predictable "laws of nature" and to use those laws according to the prevailing religion, ideology, or dominant class interests. In some cases such "laws" are even used for the benefit of those who would speak against the dominant culture. For example, natural laws were used to develop a natural moral law which could undergird the Christian faith when paganism dominated. They were also called upon to conquer the "universal enemies of mankind," including hunger, disease, and debilitating labor. Natural laws were used to devise new products and justify them for the market, even to understand the laws so that people might better "follow nature" (because "nature knows best"). The tradition cuts in both conservative and progressive directions. It aids and furthers the purposes of modern capitalism because it encourages people to find methods to exploit the natural and synthetic worlds. It demands processes which will overcome the pollution that manufacturing causes, or it leads to development of new materials to replace the depleted supply. This second tradition also publishes those ecological laws and principles which illustrate the ill effects of "progress" both on nature and on human health.

The third tradition, the economic, is relatively modern. It grew out of the need to make efficiency a virtue in early capitalist society. Max Weber and R. H. Tawney have made a strong case illustrating the connections between the principles of Calvinism, Puritanism, and other religions on the one hand and the development of the middle class in early capitalism on the other.[20] The strong community consciousness of the medieval world broke down when individual, personal, conscientious habits of thrift, industry, and honesty were needed in a period of capital formation. Individualistic religions—that is, religions that focused on the individual rather than the particular church —appeared to offer both the mark of holiness and eternal rewards as well to those who, with strict self-discipline, lived up to their societal duties. The individualistic virtues replaced social solidarity, fraternity, and sympathy when "economic man" was born in the grand alliance between the bourgeoisie and organized religion.

It then took just one short step for moral and political leaders to support economic theories of "the invisible hand" in which the common good of all could be reached by individual competition. Finally, goodness became identified with efficiency (that is, economic efficiency) and elimination of waste so that even monopoly consolidations and "economic planning" could be touted as more efficient and therefore morally superior. Urban "efficiency" planning at the turn of the century also was viewed in terms of progressive morality, which in turn justified political moves intended to clean up corruption in city government, poverty in the slums, and filthy cities generally.

Thus could the discipline of economics aid business and govern-

[20] Weber, *Protestant Ethics*; and Tawney, *Religion and Capitalism*.

ment alike to achieve higher and higher levels of (economic) efficiency. But economics has not only bolstered the cause of capitalist enterprise in progressively greater resource exploitation; it has also called attention to the alarming rate of natural resource depletion, to "inefficient pollution," and more recently to the rapid loss of significant natural environments.

Thus, all three traditions have both progressive and conservative tendencies which have enabled different conflict groups to feed from different kinds of religion or ideological nourishment.

Value Changes and Public Policy

In this account, environmentalist groups are seen as playing an important role in precipitating mostly positive value changes in their society, certainly not only because they offer new ethical ideals, nor only because of scattered success in the courts and legislatures around the country, nor even because their ruckus-raising must eventually lead to rational debate and planning, but especially because their activity forces social, technological, and economic alternatives to established courses of action which they perceive as dangerous. Such conservative radicalism—not acting in the established way, therefore acting in a theretofore unimagined manner—contains within it the seeds of value change. New social or technological substitutes are injected into a social system to replace previous elements and to throw the older system into dysfunction ever so slightly. For example, if nuclear power plants or highly polluting coal-fired plants are not built, either alternative forms of energy must be found or a new conservation consciousness must take hold in a society. In both cases the character and values of societal structures are changed.

Value change is not possible without structural adjustments within societal institutions along with alternative images embodying new values. When the supply of gasoline was limited and prices were raised by the oil companies during the 1974 oil embargo, and during a similar oil drought in 1979, Americans adopted a fuel-conservation life-style for many months. They drove less, observed fifty-five-mile-per-hour speed limits, and inaugurated car-pooling arrangements in hundreds of cities throughout the country. Nor was there much public outrage, except perhaps against the oil companies. But after people became accustomed to paying more for gasoline, fuel supplies were restored and the conservation ethic was forgotten. No structural change—such as extra taxes for further development of public transportation, a rationing system, or even a government energy corporation—accompanied the alleged crisis to stabilize and internalize the new consciousness in the national psyche.

Graphic images which explain and clarify the environmental values of new institutions are as important as the structural changes themselves. Clear images were lacking in President Carter's energy plan, which did attempt to legislate the beginnings of an institutional framework supporting conservation consciousness. Although the president proposed measures like a tax on gas-guzzling autos (a weaker provision eventually was passed by Congress), a tax on motor fuel, a tax on crude oil, a tax on business uses of oil and gas, and utility rate revision, he was not clear about the problem itself (people could not believe that we were running out of oil when there was so much of it available) despite solemn and dramatic television appearances. Nor did he challenge the source of the problem, a pervasive culture based on automobiles, by presenting the appealing image of a society less dependent on the auto.

Images and schemes such as experimental communities with inexpensive alternative technologies encourage the national and regional environment debate to focus on values which support institutional arrangements. That is, in the case of energy, since the problem has to do with declining energy supplies coupled with a polluting, energy-intensive society, the image should be focused on new institutions and life-styles which are not energy-intensive and polluting and which positively contribute to a higher quality of life. The images often have the power to pull society to their fulfillment, or at least give some direction to an alternative realizable future.[21]

The reason that much criticism is directed at environmentalists is that their proposals demand a change in behavior, and with it an acceptance of new values. The urgency of public debate on environmental questions occurs not only because technical studies are ineffec-

[21] See F. Polak, *The Image of the Future*, trans. and ed. E. Boulding (San Francisco: Jossey-Bass, 1973).

tive, but also because spokespersons for any new ethic must have a forum to explain their positions in an open public debate. They need a way to present desirable, yet realistic, alternatives. In short, environmental change is not possible without both change of institutions and change of perceptions. A few provisions of Carter's energy plan were eventually enacted by Congress in 1978 and 1979, and these could lay the foundation for further legislation. Without continued struggle for more substantial measures, these beginnings will be strangled by established economic forces.

Ethical positions, as we have seen, are in large measure determined by group value systems, that is, the latent but real values of quasi-groups which, though unorganized, are capable of affecting public policies. Their values stem from countless traditions, environmental or not, which may be manipulated by means of the powers in the legislatures, agencies, courts, and media by interest groups (and their manifest corporate or environmental interests).

For example, the very traditions that nourish environmentalism can offer ammunition against it. The argument that people should be preferred over natural objects is as religious as the "land ethic." The scientific tradition can provide a strong counterattack to any ecological proposal and simultaneously claim to alleviate human suffering (while only secondarily devastating the natural environment). And of course the efficient, economical use of natural resources first of all means that they should be *used*—processed, bought, and sold rather than preserved.

The following chapters indicate that the environmental movement is far from monolithic. The underlying assumptions, social commitments, methodologies, and viewpoints of its members are far from uniform.

Therefore, an attempt must be made to understand something about the roots of environmentalism as well as the recent history and successes and failures of the movement and what kind of viewpoints its members represent. Then it might be possible to let its argument unfold as we establish priorities and propose alternatives in the light of a clarified value structure. Public policy should transcend the values and ethics of closed interest groups—even those representing environmentalism—and be purified and tempered in the forge of critical discussion and alternative traditions.

2

Traditions of Conservation

GIVEN the frenetic pace of American economic development, it is not surprising that individuals or cultural groups should rise to challenge what was considered to be the wanton destruction of the natural environment or at least the unseemly waste of natural resources.[1] The leveling of forests hardly went unnoticed by those who loved, and came to need more and more, a walk in the woods and also by those leaders of the nation who were gripped by fear of timber famine. No one in colonial times denied that trees were often an obstacle to settlement; it was the speed of their demise that shocked great numbers of Americans and foreign travelers alike. Yet for a hundred years before and after the Revolution Americans were cutting down trees with increasingly efficient methods and tools. By the twentieth century, the gasoline engine and portable chain saws signaled the possibility of massive forest harvesting—and with it, complete destruction of a natural resource that at one time had seemed inexhaustible.

A score of travelers to the North American colonies during the 1700s had already complained about American waste of soil and land. Peter Kalm, a Swedish botanist, marveled over how little care was given the soil. He wrote of "careless agricultural practices . . . owing to a slight respect for natural history." George Washington was embarrassed by the way his fellow farmers ("if they can be called farmers," he complained) treated the land, but he admitted that land was cheap

[1] J. M. Petulla, *American Environmental History: The Exploitation and Conservation of Natural Resources* (San Francisco: Boyd & Fraser, 1977).

and labor expensive. It takes much extra work, time, and money to manure and fertilize fields, rotate crops, protect against erosion, and otherwise conserve the soil.

Public lands, on which forests grew, were treated even more poorly by timber or railroad companies and a multitude of other trespassers, who pillaged, despoiled, and stole the timber for steamboat fuel, railroad ties, and personal use. The laws were made for quick settlement, not for conservation, during the eighteenth and nineteenth centuries. By the end of the 1880s, when the frontier closed, the federal government had lost what control it had over its best land, and since the public land fell into private hands, its owners could then do with it what they wanted.

The economic imperative risked land despoilment or waste in the search for other natural resources. Fifty or more years of strip mining for coal left the lands of Appalachia in ruins by the middle of this century. Oil was important for lamps during the last century, but millions of barrels of it were wasted. The oil drained into rivers and streams, caught fire, or evaporated in open containers and dams mainly because, like everything else in the country, there seemed to be plenty of it. Natural gas was used to push oil to the surface—the market did not justify its containment—so every day for decades billions of cubic feet were lost.

For quick profits many hundreds of species of wildlife were exterminated, decimated, or depleted: beavers, fur seals, sea otters, whales, buffalo, passenger pigeons, and many other species of wild birds. It was inevitable that a reaction should set in because of the despoilment of nature, that a conservation movement should spring up. When it came, the response arose from people and groups embodying a number of diverse values and interests. Just as the viewpoints and values of environmentalists today encompass a variety of interest groups and subcultures, so did those of their earlier counterparts in conservation movements. In fact, the past and present thought patterns are linked by such values and interests. Then as now, of course, people accepted the value orientation of more than one emphasis but at the same time tended to develop an interest in conservation or environmentalism from primarily one cultural or interest group. Theodore Roosevelt, for example, loved the outdoors for itself, but he was more concerned about economic aspects of conservation for future generations.

Here, three value typologies or traditions are specified: the biocentric, the ecologic, and the economic. Those who look at the natural environment from the biocentric point of view concentrate value in nature for and in itself, apart from human uses of it. They would follow Aldo Leopold's land ethic, which assumes equal rights for humans and beings of the natural world. They also would tend to agree with the charter declaration of Britain's Society for the Prevention of Cruelty to Animals (SPCA): "We do not accept that a difference in species alone can justify wanton exploitation or oppression in the name of science or sport, or for food, commercial profit or other human gain. We believe in the evolutionary and moral kinship of all animals and that all sentient creatures have rights to life."

The ecologic emphasis is derived from a scientific understanding of interrelationships and interdependence among the parts of natural communities. The important ecological concept for the group is a model of a stable community made up of plants and animals (preferably rich and diverse) and a traceable flow of energy which may be disrupted by natural phenomena or, more commonly, by human activity.

Finally, the economic perspective, sometimes more broadly called the utilitarian approach to conservation, focuses on the optimal use of natural resources for the longest period of time or, more recently, the assignment of costs to those who take away public environmental amenities. Almost a century's worth of urban and resource planners fit into this tradition because of their interest in the highest level of efficiency for the benefit of the tax-paying public. Thus the interest of economists, agency officials, or decision makers in economic values has not necessarily removed them from an active defense of the natural environment, nor has it disqualified them from a lively participation in the environmental movement.

Historically the attitudes and values of interest groups have been defined by leaders, founders, or thinkers who have given contemporary or later organizations their concepts and principles—in some cases even their programs of action. The people listed and described below represent currents of thought of the quasi-groups in the larger society who might have reacted in similar ways to changes wrought in the natural environment. The leading thinkers described provided Americans with a "system of values for the pursuit of which human beings organize."[2]

The leaders usually both reflected attitudes of their time and acted as catalysts for new organizations embodying new systems of ideas. The writers are presented here to indicate the fermentation of society at particular periods and the gradual refinement of thought to the present day. The three perspectives should not be considered as existing completely independent of one another, however; that is, the three traditions are not mutually exclusive. They overlap in content and practice.

The Biocentric Perspective

Though a sensitive appreciation of the value of nature has found expression in primitive religions of the world as well as in the writers of western culture for centuries,[3] the notion comes through first most strongly in America in the transcendentalism of Emerson and Thoreau. In his *Journals* Emerson points up the connections between his philosophy of nature and "the Dangers of Commerce." He says, "This invasion of Nature by Trade with its money, its credit, its Steam, its Railroads, threatens the balance of Man, and establishes a new, universal Monarchy more tyrannical than that of Babylon or Rome." He and other transcendentalists saw America as ready to be overcome by a "material interest," which is at once "sensual" and "avaricious."

Thoreau's *Walden* is also an essay against materialistic commercialism written as an apology for the simple life: "If a person does not join the general scramble and pant with the money-making street, we deem him spiritless and lacking in ambition." Only the uncluttered mind which has taken a stand against a pervasive American materialism will find God where Emerson, in *Nature*, depicts Him: "behind Nature, throughout Nature."

The test of the Transcendentalist is the value he or she placed in

---

[2] B. Malinowski, *A Scientific Theory of Culture and Other Essays* (Chapel Hill: University of North Carolina Press, 1944), p. 52.

[3] C. J. Glacken, *Traces on the Rhodian Shore: Nature and Culture in Western Thought from Ancient Times to the End of the Eighteenth Century* (Berkeley: University of California Press, 1967).

the glories of Nature itself. Not for human use, still less for commercial exploitation, not even for study, Nature remains beyond the grasp of human understanding as Emerson himself preached:

> The method of nature: who could ever analyze it? That rushing stream will not stop to be observed. We can never surprise nature in a corner; never find the end of a thread; never tell where to set the first stone. The bird hastens to lay its egg: the egg hastens to be a bird. . . . If anything could stand still, it would be crushed and dissipated by the torrent it resisted, and if it were a mind, would be crazed. . . . The beauty of these fair objects is imported into them from a metaphysical and eternal spring. In all animal and vegetable forms, the physiologist concedes that no chemistry, no mechanics, can account for the facts, but a mysterious principle of life must be assumed, which not only inhabits the organ but makes the organ. . . . [Nature] will not be dissected, nor unravelled, nor shown. Away profane philosopher! seekest thou in nature the cause? This refers to that, and that to the next, and the next to the third, and everything refers. Thou must ask in another mood, thou must feel it and love it, thou must behold it in a spirit as grand as that by which it exists, ere thou canst know the law. Known it will not be, but gladly beloved and enjoyed.[4]

If Emerson taught the Transcendental doctrine, it was John Muir who lived it to the utmost. Emerson and Thoreau perceived the value of nature or wilderness in itself; Muir experienced the fact, and his newspaper accounts, journal articles, essays, and letters are filled with a passionate expression of that experience. He knew the mountains, rivers, and valleys of California probably as no one else did. He also knew many more places: Wisconsin, Florida, Nevada, Utah, Arizona, Alaska, Cuba, Panama, the Amazon, the Nile, the Black Sea, the Caucasus Mountains of Russia, Siberia, Manchuria, Korea, the foothills of the Himalayas, China, Japan, Australia, New Zealand, the Philippines. In such places and regions Muir filled his soul with the Spirit that strengthened his faith in Nature: "I go to the mountains as a particle of dust in the wind."

Muir preached his religion with zealous fervor, writing for such magazines as the *Overland Monthly*, *Scribners*, the *Century*. He or-

---

[4] R. W. Emerson, "The Method of Nature," in *Complete Works*, vol. I, *Nature, Addresses and Lectures* (Boston: Houghton Mifflin, 1893), pp. 181–213; reprinted in *The American Transcendentalists*, ed. P. Miller (New York: Doubleday, 1957), pp. 54–55. This address was delivered in 1841 in Waterville, Maine.

ganized the Sierra Club to protect the beauties of Nature. Mostly, however, he lived a life that has inspired countless exponents of the wilderness mystique.[5] He praised nature in its many shapes and colors, most often beckoning his fellows to the wilderness for the renewal of their spirit: "Climb the mountains and get their good tidings. Nature's peace will flow into you as sunshine flows into trees. The winds will blow their own freshness into you and the storms of energy, while cares will drop off like the autumn leaves."[6]

The Transcendentalist faith itself is perhaps best summed up in a passage from Muir:

> The world, as we are told, was made especially for man—a presumption not supported by the facts. A numerous class of men are painfully astonished whenever they find anything, living or dead, in all God's universe, which they cannot eat or render in some way what they call useful to themselves. . . . Now it never seems to occur to these . . . that Nature's object in making animals and plants might possibly be first of all the happiness of each one of them, not the creation of all for the happiness of one. Why should man value himself as more than a small part of the one great unit of creation?[7]

Although Emerson, Thoreau, and Muir can be described as the early pillars of the American biocentric perspective, their own values were shaped by thousands of people and hundreds of prominent nineteenth-century figures.[8] John James Audubon's *Birds of America* (1827–1838) fed a growing appetite for natural history, while at the same time Audubon was lamenting the "destruction of the forest" and consequent loss of thousands of wild birds and animals. Joining him in his criticism were James Fenimore Cooper (especially in *The Prairie*), painter Thomas Cole, writer Washington Irving, poet William Cullen Bryant, essayist Charles Lanham, traveler-historian Francis Parkman, and artist George Catlin (who first proposed the idea of establishing national parks).

[5] L. M. Wolfe, *Son of the Wilderness: The Life of John Muir* (New York: Knopf, 1945).

[6] T. H. Watkins, "Why a Biographer Looks to Muir," *Sierra Club Bulletin*, May, 1976, p. 18; published originally in D. Jones and T. H. Watkins, *John Muir's America* (Menlo Park, Calif.: American West, 1976).

[7] "Why a Biographer Looks to Muir," p. 18.

[8] R. Nash, *Wilderness and the American Mind* (New Haven: Yale University Press, 1967). This book is the standard reference which chronicles this movement from early American times to the present.

By the turn of the century Muir and the others were joined by educators in questioning the moral supremacy of man over other parts of nature—such persons as Germanist scholar Edward Evans, in "Ethical Relations between Man and Beast" (1894), and Harvard geologist Nathaniel Shaler, in *Man and the Earth* (1905), from whom Aldo Leopold gained insight into the need for an ecological ethic.[9] David Brower, executive director of the Sierra Club (1952–1969) and since then director of Friends of the Earth, spoke in the stream of a hundred-year tradition when he proclaimed, "I believe in wilderness for itself alone. I believe in the rights of creatures other than man."[10]

Without that tradition Christopher Stone's proposal that natural objects be given legal standing in their own right could not have received such widespread legal attention. When a case regarding development at Mineral King, California, *Sierra Club* v. *Morton* (which Stone hoped to influence with his essay), was reviewed by the Supreme Court in 1972, Justices Douglas, Blackmun, and Brenner endorsed Stone's concept in their dissent, and Senator Philip Hart of Michigan entered the article (originally published in the *Southern California Law Review* in 1972) into the Congressional Record. Justice Douglas, who had read Stone's article, endorsed the idea that a guardian (in this case the Sierra Club) should be able to speak "in the name of the inanimate object about to be despoiled, defaced, or invaded by roads and bulldozers and where injury is the subject of public outrage."

The Ecologic Perspective

The conceptual difference between biocentric and ecologic viewpoints lies in the commitment of the viewer, whether to the rights of nature in itself or to a model of scientific understanding of how nature orders itself. If conservationists of ecologic persuasion are concerned about widespread destruction of forests or the plowing of the prairies or, more recently, the use of chemical pesticides, their alarm stems from a perception of the need for stable (or at least the natural) func-

[9] D. Worster, ed., *American Environmentalism: The Formative Period, 1860–1915* (New York: Wiley, 1973). Selections from these writings appear under a section Worster entitles "The Biocentric Revolution." I have adopted and extended somewhat his use of the term *biocentric* in this treatment.

[10] J. McPhee, *Encounters with the Archdruid* (New York: Ballantine, 1972), p. 65.

tioning of ecosystems rather than necessarily from the placement of value in each natural component of those ecological systems. The distinction is often blurred in practice, though. Muir, for example, often spoke of interrelationships in nature and the need to preserve the harmony of natural balance; but the larger measure of his commitment fell on the side of the intrinsic worth of nature. The same can be said of Emerson and Thoreau, who, despite their devotion to nature, occasionally engaged in more or less scientific studies of nature.

Although the ecologic tradition goes back at least as far as natural-law theories of the Stoics and Scholastics and the later beginning of modern science, George Perkins Marsh, whose early training in languages opened up to him the scholarly works in a dozen or more languages, including the writings of Alexander Von Humboldt (who combined an aesthetic appreciation of nature with a scientific understanding of it and who showed the influence of man on vegetation) and Carl Ritter (who also described relationships between man and nature), sought to understand biological laws which explain successional processes and balance in nature. Marsh enlarged the title of his classic *Man and Nature* (1864) to *The Earth as Modified by Human Action* in a later edition, an indication of the focus of the book.[11] He was fascinated by the damage man could do to the earth by overcutting, overgrazing, and thoughtless agricultural practices. He had noted such devastation in Mediterranean countries while he was the U.S. minister to Turkey from 1849 to 1854 and to Italy from 1861 to 1862. He made thoughtful connections between what had happened in older civilizations and what was happening in his own country, based on what he had observed in his native Vermont.

The scientific presumption in Marsh's writings is that nature enjoys a self-regulating balance, even under the stress of great natural catastrophes, which enables it to restore itself to a kind of primordial harmony as long as human activity does not interfere with the process irreversibly. Marsh starts with the Roman Empire and shows how human intrusions through plant and animal domestication and clearing of forests caused erosion and other damage. Thus were lush forests and fields transformed into "an assemblage of bald mountains, or barren, turfless hills, and of swampy malarial plains."

[11] *Man and Nature*, ed. D. Lowenthal (Cambridge, Mass.: Harvard University Press, 1965).

Early ideas expressing the notion of balance in nature in American thought seemed to be derived from Marsh, or perhaps from Charles Darwin, who independently developed the web-of-life concept about the same time. Marsh's notions indirectly influenced American public policy through Franklin Hough, follower of Marsh and first head of the Division of Forestry under the commissioner of agriculture, and Charles S. Sargent, professor of arboriculture at Harvard and an active member of the American Forestry Congress, founded in 1882. Marsh's thought was even influential through the famous conservationist head of the Forest Service under Theodore Roosevelt, Gifford Pinchot.

The development of ecology as a science, however, came from Darwin through Ernst Haeckel, who coined the word *oecologie* and spoke of "Nature's Economy" (1866) with reference to interrelationships and interactions among competing organisms in a community. In the United States the first ecological studies were done on plant communities by Frederic E. Clements and Henry Cowles as early as 1898. Clements was working in the midcontinental grasslands around and in Nebraska, where he taught, and Cowles studied the sand dunes of Lake Michigan. Clements and Cowles had great influence on the beginnings of the science of ecology, especially through their students (Weaver, Cooper, Nichols, Transeau, and others). By 1915 enough ecologists were doing research to found the Ecological Society of America.

Ecological studies were broadened to include animal populations by Englishman Charles Elton, who, beginning in the 1930s, popularized many of the concepts still used in the field: food chains and the food web, producers and primary or secondary consumers, reducers and decomposers, pyramid of numbers and biomass, territorialism and niche. In 1935 A. G. Tansley introduced the term *ecosystem* as the system resulting from the integration of all the living and nonliving factors of the environment. Tansley continued a trend begun by Edgar Transeau, who attempted to quantify the energy flow of a system into manageable components.[12]

[12] J. M. Petulla, "Toward an Environmental Philosophy: In Search of a Methodology," *Environmental Review* 1 (1977): 14–43. See this source for a further discussion of the significance of early ecological and social scientific methodologies with reference to environmental literature, and see also D. Worster, *Nature's Economy* (San Francisco: Sierra Club Books, 1977).

Aldo Leopold met Elton in 1931 at the Matamek Conference on Biological Cycles. Leopold went to the conference with a background of practical work in wildlife protection in the American Southwest, and Elton's research confirmed his experience. Wildlife had been the subject of a variety of public policy decisions, including the protection of threatened species from extinction, with little understanding of ecological relationships between predator and prey, area size, and type of vegetation. For example, some species at the time, such as Kaibab deer, no longer had natural predators to control their numbers, because stockmen had systematically wiped out wolves, coyotes, and pumas to protect their cattle and sheep. With greatly increased numbers, the deer encroached upon the Grand Canyon National Game Preserve and proliferated until they consumed the vegetation they themselves needed to eat as well as that for the protected bison and bighorn sheep. Thousands of animals died.

Leopold's *Game Management*, published two years after the conference, applied ecology to biological systems management. Although his ecological ethic seems to give him mainly a biocentric focus, his life work of wildlife management was more concerned with the practical problems of ecological balance of game and vegetation. Therefore, he cultivated predators along with the species more popular with humans: One "cannot love game and hate predators," his biocentrically oriented *Sand County Almanac* affirmed.[13]

It is significant to note the ecological inspiration and parallels between game management and the early Malthusian rule of "breeding against the means of sustenance." Long after Malthus, who lived at the very beginning of the Industrial Revolution, American commentators used ecological concepts to point out that through science and technology—steam power, gasoline engines, electricity—mankind was exploiting nature up to the brink of catastrophe. Even during the economic boom years of the twenties, E. N. East, in *Mankind at the Crossroads* (1923), and E. A. Ross, in *Standing Room Only* (1927), warned of imminent doom because of limited resources, rapid exploitation, and skyrocketing population rates.

In the 1940s two more writers, natural scientists Fairfield Osborn, in *Our Plundered Planet* (1948), and William Vogt, in *Road*

[13] A. Leopold, *Sand County Almanac* (New York: Oxford University Press, 1949), pp. 130–132.

to Survival (1948), had much the same message. They noted the lack of ecological balance between human populations and the natural resources on which mankind depends for survival as well as the devastating impact humanity was having on the land. This latter theme was close to the mid-nineteenth-century thought of George Perkins Marsh.

These writers are the links to the present and biologists like Paul Ehrlich and Garrett Hardin, who also applied the ecological perspective to man-land relationships. Ehrlich's *The Population Bomb* (1968) predicted that "hundreds of millions" of people would starve in the 1970s because of overpopulation and the lack of resources to feed them. Garrett Hardin's tone was more measured and his argument more strictly ecological in *Exploring New Ethics for Survival* (1972), but his doomsday forecasts and prescriptions for zero population growth followed established precedents. Hardin's book stemmed from his popular earlier essay, "The Tragedy of the Commons," which referred to the carrying capacity of the common grazing areas in medieval English villages.[14] If some unscrupulous villagers increased their herds, they would gain in economic advantage, but since the commons were limited in size and vegetation, eventually the entire system would collapse because of lost resources. The story was applied to the world population problem, where Hardin saw voluntary measures as inadequate solutions; he proposed coercive methods in *Exploring New Ethics for Survival*.[15] His ecological reasoning was carefully constructed.

The ecologic perspective is solidly entrenched in the contemporary environmental movement. Two other influences, Rachel Carson and Barry Commoner, will be discussed in a later chapter.

The Economic Perspective

Those who espouse the "wisest," most efficient use of natural resources over the longest period of time have generally been considered to belong to the "utilitarian" wing of the conservation movement. In the past this group has been perennially associated with the federal government and more recently with a new breed of environmental economists; there is also a connection with the new middle class asso-

[14] G. Hardin, "The Tragedy of the Commons," *Science* 162 (1968): 1243–1248.

[15] (New York: Viking, 1972), pp. 199–202.

ciated with the beginnings of capitalism, as was pointed out in chapter 1. Economists are as interested in efficient use of natural resources as they are interested in use of other factors of capital and labor.

As early as 1877 the newly appointed secretary of the interior under Rutherford Hayes, Carl Schurz, emphasized in his annual report that forests should be preserved and managed for the long-term use of the American people. Not until 1891, however, did the president receive power from Congress to set aside forest reservations. By the end of Theodore Roosevelt's administration, almost 170 million acres of land had been set aside as national forests and parks.

The person who was largely responsible for the forest reserve clause, Bernhard Fernow, spent much of his tenure as head of the Division of Forestry from 1886 to 1898 attempting to wrest funds from Congress to manage the forest reserves. In an effort to stop further forest reservations in their home states, western Congressmen managed to prevent funding for the forests already under executive control. Trained in forest management in Germany, Fernow was in the Forestry Division long enough to establish policy directions, and his *Economics of Forestry* (1902), published a few years after he left government service, clearly indicates the public values of economic conservationists: "The natural resources of the earth have in all ages and in all countries, for a time at least, been squandered by man with a wanton disregard of the future, and are still being squandered wherever absolute necessity has not yet forced a more careful utilization. This is natural, as long as the exploitation of these resources is left unrestricted in private hands; for private enterprise, private interest, knows only the immediate future—has only one aim in the use of these resources: namely, to obtain from them the greatest possible personal and present gain."[16]

Fernow argues for government responsibility in limiting the rights of private parties over natural resources and managing them for the long-term public good of society; thus, he outlines proposals for the economic management of natural resources in general and of forest resources in particular.

[16]Quoted in Worster, *American Environmentalism*, pp. 73–74. See also the biography by A. D. Rodgers, *Bernhard Edward Fernow* (Princeton: Princeton University Press, 1951).

Gifford Pinchot received Fernow's legacy. He has been recognized as the embodiment of the values of early economic conservationism. Steward of Theodore Roosevelt's Progressive conservative program, Pinchot publicized the "all things to all men" approach of the conservation movement in his famous *The Fight for Conservation* (1910): "The first great fact about conservation is that it stands for development . . . [not just] husbanding of resources for future generations . . . but the use of natural resources now existing on this continent for the benefit of the people who live here now. . . . In the second place conservation stands for the prevention of waste. . . . The third principle is this: The natural resources must be developed and preserved for the benefit of the many, and not merely for the few. . . . Conservation means the greatest good for the greatest number for the longest time."[17]

The values of economic conservation in the Roosevelt era rested on the traditional economic doctrines of scarcity enunciated by the classical economists—Malthus, Ricardo, Mill—that increasing scarcity of natural resources would lead to increasing competition and eventually to social disaster. (The connection with Darwinian thought can be seen when one considers Malthus's predictions. In the face of overpopulation, humans will be reduced to Darwinian struggle for survival.) Spokesmen for the conservation movement eschewed the laissez-faire approach to natural resource use, pointing out that it was the duty of governments to regulate the inherently inefficient, short-term economics of private businesses by devising public policies with the future needs of society in view,[18] even though in practice they aided large corporations in their program to weed out small, "inefficient" industries.

Because of this approach to conservation and a general disillusionment with the behavior of big business, the conservationists in government allied themselves with the Progressive movement and the incipient city planning movement at the turn of the century, with all three groups holding faith in the ability of government to bring effi-

---

[17] In *The American Environment: Readings in the History of Conservation*, ed. R. Nash (Reading, Mass.; Addison-Wesley, 1968), pp. 59–61.

[18] H. J. Barnett and C. Morse, *Scarcity and Growth* (Baltimore: Johns Hopkins, 1963), pp. 72ff.

cient, non-wasteful economic order out of the chaos of laissez-faire. The conservation movement also assimilated other "progressive" notions, especially the multiple-use idea of WJ McGee, who convinced Pinchot and the president that government could rationally regulate a variety of present and future uses of the natural environment at the same time, especially in the "conservation" of water. (It did not always work out so ideally.)

Franklin D. Roosevelt took up the theme of the need for government intervention to control the "havoc" which had historically characterized U.S. natural resource use and allocation.[19] Roosevelt had a long-time interest in conservation, but it was increased by the effects of the Great Depression and a severe drought. Government intervention for the public economic good had been played down during the Republican Coolidge and Hoover administrations (although it was accepted when their corporate allies deemed it necessary). By 1930 the pitiful state of the American economy rekindled public distrust of laissez-faire economics, and FDR used this widespread sentiment to justify stronger government controls over the economy and spending government money for conservation projects.

The precedent of Roosevelt's intervention, as well as the publication of John Maynard Keynes's *The General Theory of Employment, Interest and Money* (1936), bolstered by U.S. growth and spending during and after World War II, all changed the character of the conservationist economists. Keynes's theory, eventually accepted throughout the western world, held that capital investment, and therefore economic growth, depended on the prior economic demand or consumption habits of a population, and that governments could keep employment high and the economy strong by stimulating consumption. The salutary effect of government activity, in Keynes's opinion, through expenditures, tax incentives, and borrowing, would stimulate capital investment, increase national income, and raise employment levels. Keynes was not directly concerned with the distribution of the elevated national income, with class poverty, or with economic power.

Whether from the unwilling application of Keynesian economics or from the vagaries of history or both, the U.S. economy took off at

[19] Ibid., pp. 19–20.

a meteoric rate after World War II, with a correspondingly high rate
of consumption habits, waste, pollution, and heightened resource extraction. Just as this historical development affected environmentalists
with biocentric and ecologic perspectives according to their own world
views, so did environmental economists develop their viewpoints from
the tradition of twentieth-century economics.

The inspiration of their outlook came from another Englishman,
A. C. Pigou, who founded "welfare economics," mainly concerned
with an equitable distribution of the national income Lord Keynes
was so determined to increase.[20] Pigou's *The Economics of Welfare*
(1920) also touches on another facet of the irregularities between
private and public interests. He recognized that very often an economic transaction affected third parties unintentionally. This was an
idea that economists later called "externalities"—services (external
economies) or disservices (external diseconomies) that were not an
intended part of the economic enterprise and could not be billed or
given recompense for easily. (It should also be noted that as far back
as 1890, English economist Alfred Marshall pointed out that economists should be concerned with forces outside conventional economic
analysis.)

Pigou cited worn-out roads or construction of buildings that
degrade a neighborhood environment and suggested that the state
sometimes regulate such "divergences" between public and private
goods or tax in such a way that the offending party would bear the
cost of the social difficulty. Later, the economic regulations would be
referred to as "internalizing" the externalities. Thus, one large task
which the new environmental economists have taken upon themselves
has been that of calculating the costs of economic growth in general
and of specific projects which cause air, water, and noise pollution,
wilderness disruption, and the like.

Again, it should be emphasized that few people in the environmental movement would fall exclusively into one group described
above. The groupings represent traditions and ideas which can be
traced through American history and which remain strong in the contemporary discussions of environmental groups. The strong middle-

[20] D. Fleming, "The New Conservation Movement," *Perspectives in American History* 6 (1972): 66–68.

class basis of the traditions should be mentioned again, though this characteristic should not necessarily be construed as a criticism. Concern for the natural environment need not militate against the interests of the poor even if conservationist objectives have been coopted in the past by monopolistic or middle-class morals.

Results of Traditions

Next it is necessary to tell of the struggles and some eventual successes of contemporary environmentalists who come out of these traditions. Recent history attests that some environmental groups have won significant victories in behalf of the larger forces of environmentalism. Thus, it should not be necessary to prove that these groups have exercised a measure of political power. Nor is it enough to analyze the leaders or membership of the groups to make academic points which prove theories of pluralism or elitism. Both approaches admit what seems obvious to both participants and outsiders of the struggles: that though small groups or coalitions may do the work of organizing and confronting, they and their opponents need the political support of wider constituencies. That is, interest groups, with ethical or non-ethical arguments, appeal to quasi-groups to implement their program, stop a project, or carry out other activities. In so doing they draw on common democratic or environmental traditions which they maintain will justify their behavior.

Recent history not only shows the power which environmentalists have wielded in the public arena, but also indicates the traditions which have inspired them.

PART II
STRUGGLES AND SUCCESSES

3

Friends of the Wilderness

IT seems that the biocentric ethic waxes strong in the United States in proportion to the increase of affluence. Ironically, the trappings of wealth have both separated Americans from the workings of nature and made the natural world accessible. At the same time, industrial production has wreaked havoc on the natural environment. Modern civilization offers people the tools—automobiles, roads to wilderness areas, leisure time, education, even lightweight camping gear and freeze-dried food—with which they can appreciate and enjoy the wonders of nature about which Muir spoke so glowingly. Thus, capitalism both takes its severe toll on the environment and offers commodities through which nature can be enjoyed.

In the abundance generated by the aftermath of World War II, the first great modern awakening to wilderness values took place on the occasion of an environmental struggle. The call was given to stop the damming of the Green River at Echo Park in the 320-square-mile Dinosaur National Monument on the Colorado-Utah border. The area, designated by Woodrow Wilson as a national monument in 1915 because of prehistoric dinosaur fossils, also was blessed with the kind of deep, narrow gorge at Echo Park that hydraulic engineers seek out for dams, especially in the West.[1]

During the 1940s the federal Bureau of Reclamation began a comprehensive plan to develop a ten-dam Colorado River Storage

---

[1] R. Nash, *Wilderness and the American Mind* (New Haven: Yale University Press, 1967), pp. 209–220. This work contains excellent bibliographical information in its footnotes.

Project to meet the growing water needs of the burgeoning Southwest. Fights over water in the West had become common by that time, but the Echo Park controversy is noteworthy because it was one of the first widely publicized recent contests—since Muir's battle to save Hetch Hetchy Valley in Yosemite—in which the values of wilderness in itself were at stake. Another important fact about the event was that during the 1950s, when the Echo Park discussion occurred, extremely powerful political and public support existed for more and bigger dams in the West. The Colorado project was viewed as the West's great hope for economic independence, even supremacy. It was also undergirded by the enthusiasm which usually accompanies new capital expansion and by the attention of corporate enterprises looking for new development projects.

Secretary of the Interior Oscar L. Chapman held a public hearing on the Echo Park Dam in 1950 and quickly recommended that "in the interest of the greatest public good" Echo Park be included in the project. However, since the entire Colorado project had to be approved by Congress, opponents of the dam retained some hope that they could have it struck from consideration. In the half-dozen years that followed Chapman's public hearing, wilderness defenders learned the tactics of modern political advocacy which have served them quite well since that time.

Besides mounting an effective national campaign through articles in publications such as *Life, Newsweek, Saturday Evening Post,* and conservation magazines, the Sierra Club, the Wilderness Society, and other groups initiated a direct-mail campaign and took out full-page ads in newspapers like the *New York Times* to encourage wilderness supporters to write to their congressmen and the secretary of the interior. Although their message was not the complete biocentric argument that wilderness is valuable in and for itself (this idea was just below the surface, however), it was striking in its attack on purely economic or materialistic values at that very period of U.S. history when big capital was flexing its muscles after a wartime transfusion.

The wilderness coalition mostly used arguments like those employed by Muir himself:[2] "Wilderness areas have become to us a spiri-

---

2 Ibid.

tual necessity; an antidote to modern living"; they are needed "for our spiritual welfare"; they present a prehistoric "reservoir of stored experiences in ways of life before man"; "we deeply need the humility to know ourselves as the dependent members of a great community of life."

The western establishment—chambers of commerce, politicians, developers, and representatives of cities and utilities—countered with appeals that the good American life should be cultivated in the West. "Beautiful farms, homes, industries and a high standard of civilization are equally desirable and inspiring," one western congressman declaimed. The debate was heated, both in and out of Congress, until the very hour a final vote was taken on the Colorado River Storage Project.

Because of the strenuous efforts of the preservationists, Echo Park Dam was taken out of the project bill, and the intention of Congress was stated "that no dam or reservoir constructed under the authorization of the Act shall be within any Park or Monument." The bill became law in April, 1956. The success of wilderness advocates in saving the monument was quite remarkable, even if it was true that Echo Park represented only a crumb—one small dam out of dozens possible—offered by the political powers of the day, for it gave preservationists the kind of momentum only victory can supply.

The Wilderness Act

The practice of preserving an allotted amount of wilderness was a long-standing policy of the U.S. Forest Service—justified by their multiple-use philosophy—as a result of the work of men like Aldo Leopold and Robert Marshall in the 1920s and 1930s. Their idea was that some federal agency should protect wildlands from roads, settlements, and economic development. But without permanent legislation, what was wilderness on Sunday could become harvestable timber or a dam or a mining site on Monday simply by administrative decree. And occasionally such changes did occur. The same problem of protecting some areas of development existed in national parks and monuments.

Therefore, elated and spurred by the national support of Echo

Park preservation, Howard Zahniser of the Wilderness Society immediately sought to revive an old idea of a national system of wilderness protection. Such legislation would have the advantage of establishing a national legal principle in behalf of the value of wilderness, thus avoiding arguments based on need for growth in particular regions.

Zahniser worked with other conservation groups to prepare a bill to take wilderness protection out of the hands of the Forest Service (who therefore originally opposed the bill) as well as to designate additional wilderness areas within the National Park System (whose administrators also opposed the bill, mainly because they preferred the development of more recreational park lands).[3]

The general opposition, who began to take wilderness advocates seriously, campaigned and lobbied intensely against the bill; again, they were western politicians and their mining, oil, grazing, lumber, power, and irrigation allies. Although they eventually supported a draft bill with compromises, the Forest Service and the National Park Service never gave the bill strong support. It took nine years, about sixty-five rewritten bills, eighteen hearings—twelve outside Washington—and a ton or more of transcripts before a final bill could be enacted. The congressional debate was primarily concerned with who would have the authority to add lands to the wilderness system, how much or little economic development would be permitted in the areas, and how much land would originally be set aside. Preservationists repeated arguments they knew best and doggedly attempted to keep public opinion on their side. Thousands of letters were sent in behalf of the bill.

President Kennedy endorsed the concept of a wilderness system, but Representative Wayne Aspinall of Colorado, as chairman of the House Interior and Insular Affairs Committee, had the power to call hearings on the bill. Aspinall, who represented the interests of western development, could and did delay and weaken the proposed legislation. The Senate passed a strong wilderness bill as early as 1961;

[3] Ibid., pp. 220–226. D. V. Mercure and W. M. Ross, "The Wilderness Act: A Product of Congressional Compromise" in *Congress and the Environment*, ed. R. A. Cooley and G. Wandsforde-Smith (Seattle: University of Washington Press, 1970), pp. 47–64. See also M. McCloskey, "The Wilderness Act of 1964: Its Background and Meaning," *Oregon Law Review* 45 (1966): 288–321.

Aspinall's committee members, coming mostly from western states, rewrote it in terms that no conservationist could accept.

Finally, Aspinall and his foes came to a compromise that included these points: mining would be allowed for nineteen years in wilderness areas (until 1984); only Congress, not the president, could add to the system; the Forest Service lost authority to declassify wilderness lands; and all the lands already classified as primitive areas in the national forests were put into the system—over nine million acres in fifty-four units, with another five and one-half million acres to be brought in later. The bill was diluted from its original strength, especially since all new areas to be added to the wilderness system had to go through the maze of congressional committees and approvals. This process put an enormous financial burden on conservationist groups each time they wanted to have more land added to the system. But passage of the Wilderness Act was a significant milestone for friends of the wilderness. President Johnson signed the bill on September 3, 1964, "To preserve for the American people of present and future generations the benefits of an enduring resource of wilderness . . . [to be] administered . . . in such a manner as will leave them unimpaired for future use and enjoyment as wilderness, and so as to provide for the protection of these areas, the preservation of their wilderness character."

The Dam Struggles

The Dinosaur Battle, as the Echo Park Dam conflict has come to be known by insiders, was probably the beginning of the modern phase of the biocentric movement, and the Wilderness Act was no doubt a success of genuine legal importance, but subsequent history has proved that wilderness advocates could hardly rest on their laurels. They have had particular difficulty with the dam builders, the Army Corps of Engineers and the federal Bureau of Reclamation. As David Brower has remarked, "You have to stop dams from being built over and over. You only have to put them up once and they stay there forever." (Brower has also been quoted as saying, "The Bureau of Reclamation engineers are like beavers. They can't stand the sight of running water.")

The bureau and the corps are given ample layman support from a nationwide lobby organization founded in 1901 called the National River and Harbors Congress (NRHC), which includes a variety of contracting firms, dredge-and-fill companies, recreational interests, chambers of commerce, from local to federal levels of government agencies, congressmen, and corps employees themselves as *ex officio* members of the group. The purpose of the NRHC lies in promoting such water projects as dam building and irrigation regionally and nationally. They do not suffer from a lack of public relations funds; they work at maintaining contacts with friendly politicians on all levels of government, particularly in the growth-minded West, where such projects tend to enjoy public support anyway.

Biocentric preservationists love the sound and sight of undammed, wild, free-flowing, foaming rivers. They spend much of their time trying to keep them free-flowing, especially in areas they consider uniquely beautiful, such as the Grand Canyon. As early as 1950, Bridge Canyon, within the Grand Canyon, was given Senate authorization as a dam site, but the bill was defeated in the House. Interest in the use of the Grand Canyon for dams goes back to the last century. Marble Canyon, also in Grand Canyon, had been considered a prime target area, and both sites were eligible for dams because the act which created Grand Canyon National Park authorized the secretary of the interior to permit dam construction wherever he deemed it necessary in the park. Interest in preserving the areas increased as reclamationists eyed sites for dam projects in the Grand Canyon from the beginning of the century onwards. When Secretary of the Interior Udall unveiled the Bureau of Reclamation's Pacific Southwest Water Plan in 1963, while the Wilderness Act controversies were beginning to untangle, horrified preservationists found dams planned for Bridge Canyon and Marble Canyon.[4]

Their horror was compounded during the same year when they realized that just upstream from the Grand Canyon on the Colorado River, in a region of breathtaking beauty far removed from roads and other trappings of civilization, water was backing up behind the newly built Glen Canyon Dam. And their emotions turned to anger and grief when they found that Lake Powell behind Glen Canyon Dam would

[4] Nash, *Wilderness*, pp. 229ff.

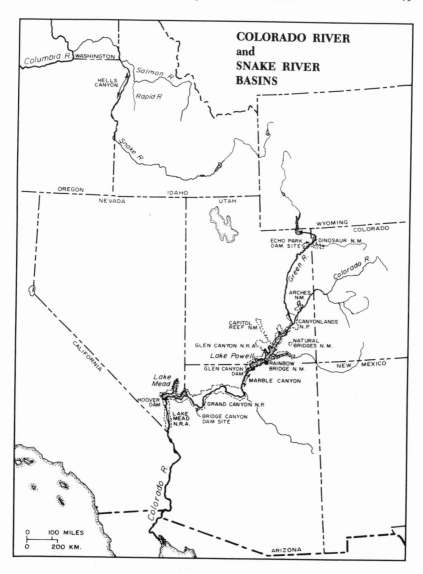

COLORADO RIVER
and
SNAKE RIVER
BASINS

Although American environmental history is largely a story of the variegated methods devised by an ingenious population in order to tame and market a seemingly limitless and hostile wilderness, recent environmental struggles have begun to reverse the trend, especially in the West. In 1964, Congress passed the Wilderness Act to preserve a small part of the remaining natural wild landscape from roads and development.

reach all the way to Rainbow Bridge National Monument despite legal stipulations to the contrary in the Colorado River Storage Project Act.

Preoccupied with the Dinosaur Battle and the Wilderness bills, preservationists had simply overlooked Glen Canyon because it was not already a park or a monument. But those who knew the region told of its beauties loud enough for all to hear. David Brower made a film of Glen Canyon's gorgeous canyons, pools, grottoes, wild flowers, ferns, and gorges—"the place no one knew." Now the preservationist guns had to be leveled at invisible dams inside the Grand Canyon itself.

An enraged David Brower and a tiny army of supporters took out full-page ads in the *New York Times, Washington Post, San Francisco Chronicle*, and other newspapers at great expense, headlining them with such attention-grabbers as: "SHOULD WE ALSO FLOOD THE SISTINE CHAPEL SO TOURISTS CAN GET NEARER THE CEILING?" and "NOW ONLY YOU CAN SAVE THE GRAND CANYON FROM BEING FLOODED . . . FOR PROFIT." This ad concluded, "there is only one simple, incredible issue here. This time it's the Grand Canyon they want to flood. *The Grand Canyon*."

Tens, perhaps hundreds of thousands of people again responded with letters of protest, telegrams, and telephone calls to Washington offices. When the Internal Revenue Service took the tax-deductible status away from the Sierra Club, the protest spread because of the seemingly unjust punishment of a group performing what appeared to be a public service—that of informing the public. The Sierra Club never regained tax-exempt status, though a foundation was formed within the organization to achieve the same results.

On the other side were the endorsements of President Johnson and Secretary Udall, not usually unfriendly to environmentalists, for the entire project. Furthermore, the Bureau of Reclamation claimed that the dams would not even be visible from most viewing areas on the rim of the canyon. Under increasing criticism, the bureau removed Marble Canyon Dam from the project but kept in the Bridge Canyon Dam. This maneuver brought more ads, a film, omnipresent bumper stickers ("Save Grand Canyon") and a book published by the Sierra Club on the beauties of the free-flowing river in the Grand Canyon. Filled with biocentric convictions (Zahniser's "Out of the wilderness has come the substance of our culture") and breathtaking color photos, Francois Leydet's text described a trip down the Colorado; the book indirectly summarized the case against the dam.

The public continued to respond in great numbers against the dam. Secretary Udall and the president changed their minds about the Grand Canyon dams, and by the middle of 1967 both dams had been deleted from the Senate approval of the Pacific Southwest Water Plan bill. Even Representative Aspinall, still chairman of the House Interior and Insular Affairs Committee, who seemed ready for a fight over the dams, could not get enough support from his colleagues to carry on the skirmish. Not only were the Grand Canyon dams deleted from the bill, but so was the construction of any dam theretofore prohibited between the Hoover and Glen Canyon dams, that is, within the entire Grand Canyon. The bill was signed into law by President Johnson on September 30, 1968.

Three days later the president signed a related, also very important, bill for wilderness advocates, one which established a National Wild and Scenic Rivers System: "The established national policy of dam and other construction at appropriate sections of the rivers of the United States needs to be complemented by a policy that would preserve other selected rivers." The law followed the pattern of the Wilderness Act of 1964 and protected the "free-flowing condition" of eight selected rivers, a number that was intended to grow, as it has done slowly but significantly year by year.

Advocates of the biocentric ethic took advantage of the momentum generated by Earth Day in 1970 to enlist new support for further federal legislation. In 1972 the Marine Mammal Protection Act was passed and signed, protecting seals, sea otters, sea cows, whales, porpoises, and polar bears. Soon afterward, in 1973, the Endangered Species Act was signed into law. The legal idea that a listed nonhuman resident of the United States is guaranteed, in a special sense, life and liberty has shocked countless human residents, but the discontent of the latter has not changed hundreds of legal decisions which have stopped at least two major water projects and forced relocation of many more developments or highway projects. (The nature lovers, it appears, are not so naive or politically unsophisticated as their opponents have wanted to believe.)

Hells Canyon and Tocks Island

At the end of 1975 the famous Hells Canyon Gorge on the Oregon-Idaho border was designated as part of the National Wild and Scenic Rivers System. It included the headwaters of the Rapid River and a one-hundred-mile stretch of the Snake River within the newly created seven-hundred-thousand-acre Hells Canyon National Recreation Area. It is also a region of incredible geologic and geographic beauty, with perhaps the deepest river gorge in North America (a maximum of 7,900 feet compared to the Grand Canyon's maximum of 5,500 feet), an ample variety of wildlife, fish populations, and a turbulent, free-flowing river.

By this time it was not surprising that against great odds preservationists had outlasted their opponents and won a battle that had begun twenty years earlier. In the 1950s the private utility companies that applied for a permit from the Federal Power Commission (FPC) to build dams in Hells Canyon were challenged by a group of public power firms from the state of Washington. The case went to the Supreme Court, where Justice William O. Douglas in 1967 said, to the astonishment of both parties, "The Commission must hold more hearings on the subject of *whether* any dams should be built at all, not just which one [which party will build]."[5] The judgment gave preservationists new life to intervene along with a new precedent. The rest is history, with other successful battles following the same patterns as the Dinosaur and Grand Canyon struggles.

What was different in the Hells Canyon case was the strength of the political support which came so quickly. It was a testimonial to the changing environmental consciousness. Even the possibility that such a statement could be made by Justice Douglas at this period is extraordinary. First, in 1970 Cecil Andrus, then governor of Idaho (later secretary of the interior under President Carter), came out strongly in favor of keeping Hells Canyon wild. Next, freshman Republican Senator Robert Packwood of Oregon followed by introducing legislation in Congress for the same purpose; by 1973 all the senators from the concerned states and nearby western states supported the

[5] B. Evans, "Success at Hells Canyon," *Sierra Club Bulletin*, April, 1976, pp. 6–8.

bill. Finally, the powerful Congressman Al Ullmann threw his weight behind the legislation.

That the bill was debated and passed during the height of the energy fever ("Project Independence") and signed by a president not known for his support of environmentalism (Ford), who became famous for the large number of vetoes of his administration, makes the accomplishment more astounding. As advocates of the project pointed out repeatedly, the dams would be nonpolluting and save twelve million barrels of oil or four millions tons of coal annually. Two million customers in the Pacific Northwest would have been served electricity by the dams, and they eventually would probably have had to pay an additional fifty million dollars each year for alternative generating plants. The Snake River development would have been capable of almost as much power as the entire twenty-nine-dam Tennessee Valley Authority.[6]

To counter cost-benefit arguments, particularly those of the Army Corps of Engineers and the Bureau of Reclamation, wilderness advocates have been talking less about the aesthetic importance of wilderness areas—now institutionalized by law and judicial decision—and more about the alleged economic benefits the dams would bring. David Brower challenged bureau statistics as early as the Dinosaur struggles in the 1950s, but such cases were relatively rare until the 1970s. Now preservationists are ready with conflicting figures on discount rates, water flow, populations benefited, economic costs, inflation, pollutants, sedimentation, and the like. Of course these facts, born out of a different perspective and different assumptions, present a drastically different cost-benefit ratio for any given project.

That is, despite elephantine documents filled with myriads of numbers, decisions about dam building are more likely to be made because of value commitments or regional interests than because of the enlightenment generated by the massive, very expensive reports. There are dozens of examples of this process of preparing reports and camouflaging debates about costs and benefits and finally deciding on the basis of interests and/or values. The controversy over the proposed

[6] R. D. James, "Wilderness Struggle," *Wall Street Journal*, July 9, 1975, p. 30.

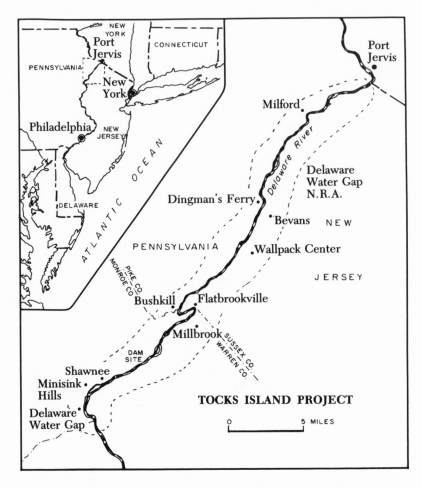

The location of the Tocks Island Project indicates why the struggle over the dam was long and complicated. People from the four states of the Delaware River Basin Commission, all with different economic, political, and social interests, fought for more than ten years over the forty-mile-long valley between the Delaware Water Gap, Pennsylvania, and Port Jervis, New York. The lower Delaware River is heavily polluted, and Philadelphians wanted some of the clean, crisp water above the Gap. Congress eventually refused to allocate funds for the project.

Tocks Island Dam on the upper Delaware River border separating New Jersey and Pennsylvania illustrates the phenomenon very well.

First, the Army Corps of Engineers presented the costs and benefits of its analysis; later, environmentalists presented an opposite conclusion drawn from their own data; finally, Congress authorized a third study—3,600 pages in six volumes, weighing sixteen pounds and costing $1.5 million—which seemed to play only a small role in the final decision.[7] During the course of the conflict between the parties most of the discussion seemed to revolve around technical matters (more than fifty studies of the dam were done between 1962 and 1975), but in fact these debates seemed only to provide more time for the opponents to do politicking and coalition building. The conservationists won the day for many reasons more political than technical; they even managed to bring the forces of the New Jersey Humane Society to the battle. The preservationists, however, provided the fundamental strength.

The purpose of the dam—flood control, increased water supply, more electrical power, a new water recreation area—seemed important enough to receive quick congressional appropriation. Floods have been a regular feature of the Delaware River basin, and federal assistance in the form of flood control has come to be expected by most regions of the country. In this instance the affected states have been working with the Army Corps of Engineers since 1939. The early sixties also brought a severe drought, another common reason for federal intervention. Electrical power has long been an activity correlated with dam construction. Water recreation is usually considered a bonus offered to urban dwellers; the National Park Service was slated to operate the Delaware Water Gap National Recreation Area.

But by 1970, when environmentalism had become a live national issue, a number of eastern conservation groups added their full support to a small group living in the valley who would be affected by the project. The emphasis of the conservationists' analysis pointed to the importance of preserving the natural setting of the area. Their tech-

---

[7] For a theoretical framework of the Tocks Island conflict, see *Boundaries of Analysis: An Inquiry into the Tocks Island Dam Controversy*, ed. H. A. Feiveson, F. W. Sinden, and R. H. Socolow (Cambridge, Mass.: Ballinger, 1975).

nical material scattered shot in all directions in opposition to facts, figures, omissions, and presumptions of the proponents. They also showed how the new recreation area would cost the affected states money because they would need to pay for new road construction, waste disposal facilities, traffic control, and the results of traffic congestion, deterioration of local services in off-season slowdowns, decline of fishing, and other effects. Preservationists, too, became vocal. They objected to man-made lakes and the features that must be created for them.

The unceasing flow of arguments and counterarguments, studies and counterstudies allowed the antagonists time to persuade undecided constituencies. By 1975 Russell Train of the Environmental Protection Agency, Russell Peterson of the Council on Environmental Quality, and seven out of the eight senators whose states were affected by the Tocks Island project all publicly opposed the dam. Each of the affected states except Pennsylvania opposed congressional allocation, signaling the death knell for the project.

A close reading of this case history, especially from articles in the papers and in the journals of environmental groups and the Save the Delaware Coalition, indicates that even unabashed preservationists have taken to the use of technical studies because they offer a wide range of establishment tools with which the preservationists can make a case and support their arguments. (The question, to repeat, is whether the studies are the best means to the end of rational discussion of values.)

(Bitter) Fruits of Victory

In 1968 when the power companies suggested that a remote glacial lake, Sunfish Pond, be converted to an upper reservoir for the proposed Tocks Island Dam, public outrage forced the utilities to find another site for the pumped-storage facility. After the Tocks Island success in 1975, the man who organized the movement to "Save Sunfish Pond" wrote a letter to a local newspaper deploring what had been happening to the pond—litter, motorcycle noise, and general carryings-on—since people had discovered it (presumably because of his effort). He said that he was almost sorry he "saved" the pond.[8]

The paradoxical message of biocentric environmentalism is that wilderness is to be both valued for its own sake and left untouched, and at the same time it is to be a source of renewal for the human spirit. Yet when too many people go to the wilderness to imbibe the spirit of life, so to speak, the wilderness loses its wildness. When wilderness is opened to uncontrolled human access, very soon it is cluttered with mobile homes and campers.

The original bylaws of John Muir's Sierra Club contained a purpose which stated that the club should attempt to make the Sierra Nevada mountains more accessible to the wider public. Thus, in the late 1940s the group did not oppose development of a ski resort at Mineral King in the Sierras and even suggested routes for roads into it. Richard Leonard and David Brower, however, not only opposed the club's decision but even deleted the phrase "to render accessible to the mountains" from the original bylaws.[9]

By 1965, after the Forest Service had solicited bids from private investors for recreational development at Mineral King, the Sierra Club went on record as opposing any recreational development in the area. In January, 1966, Walt Disney Productions was given a planning permit. Disney went far beyond the modest Forest Service proposal of a $3 million complex, submitting a proposal for a $35.3 million investment that would accommodate 3,310 visitors, thirty-six hundred vehicles, twenty-two ski lifts, and twenty thousand skiers at once (with restaurants, golf, horses, Swiss chalets, and more).

Besides early support of development at Mineral King, the Sierra Club had also at first accepted the idea of a recreational lake at Tocks

[8] I. I. Thompson, "The Tocks Island Dam Controversy," in *When Values Conflict*, ed. L. H. Tribe, C. S. Schelling, and J. Voss (Cambridge, Mass.: Ballinger, 1976), p. 50.

[9] S. R. Schrepfer, "Perspectives on Conservation: Sierra Club Strategies in Mineral King," *Journal of Forest History*, October, 1976, pp. 177–190. This article contains an excellent account of the changes in the ideology of the Sierra Club between the 1940s and the 1960s as illustrated in the history of the Mineral King controversy. According to Schrepfer, by the end of the 1960s "marginal wildernesses were now valuables, federal agencies mistrusted, and compromises with developers avoided. . . . The club set out to prove that it could stand before the courts as the guardian of nature . . . [and took on] the role of private Attorney General."

Island, but it later changed its mind. It justified its change of policies because it feared that if the club's weight were not supportive of a small Mineral King resort, other areas of greater wilderness value would be developed (for example, San Gorgonio in California) or be developed tastelessly (like the Poconos in Pennsylvania). It is more likely, as Susan Schrepfer has argued persuasively, that leadership of the group adopted the mentality of the newer, larger membership—that of biocentric preservationism.[10] Because of the club's relentless opposition in the courts since the shift in policy, the Disney development was stopped several times but started again, each time scaled down a bit more in planning. Finally, in 1978 Congress set Mineral King aside as a wilderness area.

With or without Mineral King, the National Park Service reported that there were over fifty-eight million outdoor campers in the United States in 1976, up from seventeen million in 1966, also a very high year. Even solo backpacking, which represents a "purer" form of wilderness enjoyment, had an estimated ten million participants in 1976. The Park Service predicts that two million more Americans, perhaps more, will go camping each year for an indefinite period. The wilderness industry is booming.

And so it was perhaps in desperation that in 1973 the National Park Service turned over controlling interest in Yosemite's concessions to the giant conglomerate Music Corporation of America (MCA). The job had become too big, frighteningly big, for forest or park rangers. Certainly MCA thinks big (frighteningly big for preservationists) in its plans for Yosemite—convention centers, tramways, new roads, and villages—though none of these proposals has gotten final approval. Many argue that if they are approved, more people would be able to enjoy the wonders of Yosemite Valley.

Roderick Nash calls the phenomenon "the irony of victory":

America's hunger for experiencing wilderness has come of age. The hopes of Thoreau and Marshall and Leopold seem fulfilled. Confirming Muir's forecast, "thousands of tired, nerve-shaken, over-civilized people" *had* come to the wilderness and discovered that "wildness is a necessity. . . ." But even as preservationists were celebrating their apparent victory, the more perceptive among them saw a disturbing new threat to

10 Schrepfer, "Perspectives on Conservation."

wilderness in their own enthusiasm . . . that wilderness could well be loved out of existence in the next [century].

The problem is that dams, mines, and roads are not the basic threat to the wilderness quality of an environment. People are, and whether they come with economic or recreational motives is, in a sense, beside the point. For a devotee of wilderness, in other words, a campground full of Boy Scouts, or even people like himself, is just as destructive of the essence of wilderness as a highway. Any definition of wilderness implies an absence of civilization, and wilderness values are so fragile that even appropriate kinds of recreational use detract from and, in sufficient quantity, destroy wilderness. As ecologist Stanley A. Cain has remarked, "innumerable people cannot enjoy solitude together."[11]

This short passage resounds with the message of biocentric environmentalism. While some might not agree that people are as much a threat as superhighways or dams, the graphically drawn analogy points up a real problem of public policy. Answers are not easy. The Soviet Union and other countries in eastern and western Europe have solved the problem by creating massive areas as nature preserves into which no one may enter, except with rarely given permissions. Those who would favor similar preserves in the United States no doubt would hold such a biocentric viewpoint of conservation philosophy. Two other environmental perspectives should also be presented before they are examined more critically.

[11] Nash, *Wilderness*, p. 264.

4

Enemies of Disruption

ALDO LEOPOLD enjoyed a practical turn of mind. As he discovered ecological principles or learned them from researchers like Elton, he was fond of applying them to history or to practical management. In 1933, just before he published his pioneering work of applied ecology, *Game Management*, he wrote:

A harmonious relation to the land is more intricate, and of more consequence to civilization, than the historians of progress seem to realize. Civilization is not, as they often assume, the enslavement of a stable and constant earth. It is a state of *mutual and interdependent cooperation* between human animals, other animals, plants, and soils, which may be disrupted at any moment by the failure of any of them. Land spoilation has evicted nations, and on occasion can do it again. . . .

All civilization seems to have been conditioned upon whether the plant succession, under the impact of occupancy, gave a stable and habitable assortment of vegetative types, or an unstable and uninhabitable assortment. The swampy forests of Caesar's Gaul were utterly changed by human use—for the better. Moses' land of milk and honey were utterly changed—for the worse. . . .

Unforeseen ecological reactions not only make or break history in a few exceptional enterprises—they condition, circumscribe, delimit, and warp all enterprises, both economic and cultural, that pertain to land. . . . In short, the reaction of land to occupancy determines the nature and duration of civilization. . . .

[On the other hand] within the limits of the soil and plant succession we also *rebuild* the earth—but without plan, without knowledge of its properties, and without understanding of the increasingly coarse and powerful tools which science has placed at its disposal. We are remodeling the Alhambra with a steam-shovel.[1]

George Perkins Marsh said much the same thing seventy years earlier. But Marsh did not have a generation of ecological science to support his contentions, nor did he have the audience that Leopold would command. In his writings Leopold makes two points very strongly: (1) people depend on stable ecosystems in order to survive (or, conversely, disrupted ecosystems can bring down civilizations), and (2) we must discover and follow the laws of ecology in order to preserve the land that gives us life.

The ecological perspective is fundamentally a scientific one, with assumptions dependent upon particular understandings or models that delineate what are perceived to be natural laws. Ecologists tend to follow the values they find in particular laws or ecological understandings rather than (or not only) the biocentric values that see nature as estimable in itself. (Recall the statement of Emerson.) Ecological struggles and latter-day successes have come from the public debate over the validity of each particular ecological model concerned, the supporting value structures, and consequent legal enforcement of the value structures.

Ecological Theory

Since the end of the 1960s, ecological theory has been identified in the popular mind with "ecosystem" theory, and its meaning has generally agreed with what Leopold described in 1933: humans, animals, plants, soils, microorganisms, water, and air all function together as an integrated, dynamic community in a given place. (Many pure ecologists would exclude humans from the equation.) The influential ecologist Eugene P. Odum defines two key terms: "Any unit containing all of the organisms (i.e., the 'community') in a given area interacting with the physical environment so that a flow of energy leads to a clearly defined trophic structure, biotic diversity, and material cycles (i.e., exchange of materials between living and nonliving parts) within the system is an *ecological system* or ecosystem."[2]

[1] "The Conservation Ethic," *Journal of Forestry* 31 (1933): 635–638.
[2] E. P. Odum, *Fundamentals of Ecology*, 3rd ed. (Philadelphia: W. P. Saunders, 1971), p. 14.

Thus, many ecological theorists will emphasize that ecosystems include human activity, but their studies deal with the components and activity of only natural systems, such as lakes and fields, with all of the elements that support life: inorganic substances (carbon, nitrogen, hydrogen, for example), organic compounds (proteins, carbohydrates), climatic regime (rainfall, temperature range, and the like), producers (green plants), macroconsumers (animals), and microconsumers (bacteria and fungi). The processes (functions) through which these components can be analyzed in regard to their interdependent relationships (structures) are energy flow circuits, food chains, diversity patterns in time and place, nutrient (biogeochemical) cycles, development and evolution, and control of cybernetic feedback systems—though none of these functions can be separated, in actuality, from the others.

From such fundamental concepts these ecologists have developed a comprehensive theory which applies to human ecology, or human interventions in the systems. Of course a spectrum of opinion exists in this science as in all others; some ecologists would not admit the validity of a "human" ecology. Yet a great number of ecologists would agree with Odum and others who have at different times expressed the following ecological laws which they say apply to humans:[3]

1. Humans are interrelated with and subject to all the basic processes of the ecosystem.
2. The tendency in natural ecosystems is toward stability and diversity, the preservation of which may be eventual ingredients of survival for humans.
3. Available energy declines with each step in the food chain, making it possible for more plant consumers than meat consumers to survive within the limits and possibilities of a given ecosystem.
4. It is structurally possible for unwanted and unneeded materials (for example, DDT) to become progressively concentrated on and within each step of the food chain.
5. The diversity and strength of natural ecosystems is quickly weakened by human interventions in the form of the domestication of plant life (such as monoculture in agriculture or forestry) or uncontrolled grazing by domesticated animals.

[3] E. P. Odum, *Ecosystem Structure and Function* (Eugene: Oregon State University Press, 1972), pp. 11–24.

6. Energy subsidies which are employed to increase natural, agricultural, or industrial output or yield often reduce energy in air or water for self-maintenance, thus increasing pollution of an area. This type of "ecological backlash" results from heavy use of fertilizers, pesticides, and fossil fuels because natural systems cannot dilute overload from materials of concentrated energy.

7. Human activity is tending toward accelerated decomposition of natural phenomena or materials to the detriment of the production and balance of essential substances: for example, the increase of atmospheric temperature by additional carbon dioxide from burning fossil fuels and the depletion of the ozone layer by fluorocarbons from spray cans.

8. Population growth rates have become alarmingly out of balance with resource supplies.

9. Human wastes are not being recycled back into natural systems. This fact portends long-term depletion of natural resources.

10. Pollution is likely to become a major limiting factor in the expansion of human populations.

Although human intervention into natural ecosystems has produced greater material wealth through technological development, very often second- or third-order effects have threatened environmental quality and ecological stability. As populations have grown and energy production has become more powerful, human interference has produced proportionately greater affluence along with potentially dangerous ecological consequences. Charles Cooper has noted five types of wealth-producing interferences with ecological processes: "simplification of ecosystems, intervention in natural biogeochemical cycles, concentration of dispersed energy, introduction of new species into new environments, and induced genetic and behavioral changes in organisms."[4] All of these interventions, Cooper and other ecologists maintain, contain the "seeds of trouble."

Simplification of Ecosystems

Diversity within an ecosystem simply means that a large variety and number of different species exist in it. A great number of ecolo-

[4] "Man's Impact on the Biosphere," *Journal of Soil and Water Conservation* 25 (1970): 124–127.

gists contend that the stability of the system is promoted by more diversity of species.

The development of agriculture itself has meant less and less diversity of natural ecosystems throughout the world. For example, the conversion of a rather simple ecosystem in the Russian steppes from wild plants to wheat has meant a 50 percent loss in insect species there. In the United States the complexity of the tall-grass prairies in the Midwest has given way to thousands of acres of a simple corn ecosystem. After the natural oak-hickory forests of the Southeast, which enjoyed a rich variety of undergrowth, wildlife, and insects, had been cut over, lumbermen planted uniform pine forests with virtually no undergrowth or wildlife to add diversity. The reason for such humanly induced changes (to promote simplification) lies, of course, in the resultant increase in productivity and reduced costs of cultivating and harvesting. The problem with monoculture, as the simplification of agriculture is known, is that its ease of cultivation also brings with it a much higher vulnerability to insect attack.

Diverse plant species tend to offer shelter to each other, and they minimize pest attack. However, when crops are the same and subpopulations are similar, pests and disease organisms can more easily attack the closely spaced plants without the interference of diverse species. Even as such monocultures as new wheat and rice strains are bred for increased yields, just as quickly do rusts, viruses, and herbivores seem to evolve to attack the new varieties. A new virulent strain of wheat rust evolves about every three to five years in the United States. Since the newly developed monocultures are so vulnerable to pest attack, larger and larger doses of pesticides are required.[5] Higher applications of fertilizers are also needed for the expected increase of yields.

Many ecologists-geneticists have become concerned about the loss of genetically diverse ancient plant varieties of primitive agriculture. The old types showed themselves to be variable, in equilibrium with environment and pathogens, and genetically dynamic—the result of

[5] D. L. Dahlsten, R. Garcia, and J. E. Laing, "Agricultural Chemicals—Insecticides," in *Environmental Problems in Medicine*, ed. W. E. McKee (Springfield, Ill.: C. C. Thomas, 1974), pp. 528–557. This source gives a detailed overview of the problem and an excellent bibliography.

millennia of natural and artificial selections.[6] H. V. Harlan and M. L. Martini, as early as 1936, presented the argument for the protection of ancient barleys: "In the great laboratory of Asia, Europe and Africa, unguided barley breeding has been going on for thousands of years. Types without number have arisen over an enormous area. The better ones have survived. . . . The progenies of these fields with all their surviving variations constitute the world's priceless reservoir of germ plasm. It has waited through the long centuries. Unfortunately from the breeders' standpoint, it is now being imperiled. When new barleys replace those grown by the farmers of Ethiopia or Tibet, the world will have lost something irreplaceable."[7] And many contemporary ecologists would add that the new productive rice and wheat strains taken to the world in the form of a "green revolution," with all of their fragility and need for high technologies of fertilizers and pesticides, have displaced far more valuable, more stable, irreplaceable ancient plant strains.[8]

The widely publicized case of I.R.-8, a high-yield strain of rice developed for the Philippines in the 1960s, illustrates the limitations of highly productive and marketable modern varieties of the green revolution. First the rice was decimated by tungro disease, forcing growers to change to a similar strain, I.R.-20, which was ruined by grassy stunt virus and brown hopper insects. Then they changed to I.R.-26, which was blown over by strong winds of the region. After the growers decided to go back to the original strain from Taiwan, they found that it had almost disappeared. It had been replaced by I.R.-8. In this case the variety that had been selected out by native farmers for centuries proved the best bet in the long run.

Many ancient crops have already been wiped out throughout the world: wheat from the Atlas Mountains in the Mediterranean basin,

[6] J. R. Harlan, "Our Vanishing Genetic Resources," *Science* 188 (1975): 618–621.

[7] Ibid., pp. 618–619.

[8] O. H. Frankel and J. G. Hawkes, *Plant Genetic Resources for Today and Tomorrow* (New York: Cambridge University Press, 1974). For an excellent overview article which includes arguments for the protection of threatened animal species in the world, see N. Meyers, "An Expanded Approach to the Problem of Disappearing Species," *Science* 193 (1976): 198–202. See also N. Meyers, *The Sinking Ark* (Elmsford, N.Y.: Pergamon, 1979).

the ancient rice of Southeast Asia and India, barley of the Near East all the way to Ethiopia and Nepal, and many other strains. Countless more wild plants which are plowed under and lost forever might have offered possibilities for new food species—possibilities that remain untried.

Fortunately, because of the long-time efforts of men like H. V. Harlan and others, a number of international programs for genetic resource conservation have been inaugurated. Many local and regional programs, some including United States genetic resources, have also received the support of the United Nations Environment Programme and the United Nations Food and Agriculture Organization.

The Modern Environmental Movement

Because she perceived a "menace to human health" and the "disturbances of the basic ecology of all living things,"[9] Rachel Carson wrote *Silent Spring*, a book that many consider to have given the major impetus to the modern environmental movement. Charles Elton seems to have provided Carson with links between ecological research and practical applications, as he did for Leopold earlier.[10] Although Carson's perspective was primarily ecological, her thinking was imbued as well with a biocentric transcendentalism, as the book's dedication to Albert Schweitzer suggests.

Rachel Carson was a perceptive zoologist who worked for the U.S. Bureau of Fisheries (later called Fish and Wildlife Service). She first wrote three books on the sea: *Under the Sea Wind* (1941), *The Sea Around Us* (1951), and *The Edge of the Sea* (1955). These books, lyrical rather than polemical, still prepared her for the ecological points she would later make in *Silent Spring* and further provided her with a receptive audience.

Her interest in the potential harm of the pesticide DDT began as early as 1945 but did not provoke her to action until 1958, when a friend, Olga Owens Huckins, sent her a copy of a letter she placed in

[9] R. Carson, "A Report of Progress," in P. Brooks, *The House of Life: Rachel Carson at Work* (Boston: Houghton Mifflin, 1972), p. 243.
[10] R. Carson, *Silent Spring* (Boston: Houghton Mifflin, 1962), pp. 10–11, 117, 265.

the *Boston Herald* about the lethal effect which a DDT spraying over Duxbury, Massachusetts, had on songbirds. Her concern revived, Carson tried to interest others in writing about the problem, and she began work on it herself.

She relied mainly on evidence that the deadly pesticide materials were being concentrated up the food chain: from water into which DDT washed to plankton, then to fish, and so on. Her most famous example came from Clear Lake, California, where heavy concentrations of DDT had fatal effects on the western grebe.. She repeatedly made the points that humans are often at the top of food chain processes, and they are susceptible to concentration of DDT in their fatty tissues. She appealed for limited use of DDT and for a biological control of insects. This argument implied that diversity can encourage a healthy total ecosystem—that insects can be controlled by their natural enemies.

Rachel Carson's message was immediately taken up by other ecologists, who showed how other birds—penguins, brown pelicans, ospreys—were known to be suffering from the effects of DDT. The chemical seemed to affect liver activity, where estrogen controls calcium metabolism and, therefore, eggshell development. The end result of an increase of estrogen metabolism from the influence of DDT was thin-shelled eggs which could not support new life.

The second point most often made by environmentalists of an ecological perspective was that DDT and other chlorinated hydrocarbon compounds (among them Aldrin, Dieldrin, and Endrin) do not break down rapidly but remain stored and accumulated in fatty tissues for a very long time. Environmentalists kept pressures on Congress, and later the Environmental Protection Agency as well, to ban persistent pesticides. Finally, in 1972, ten years after *Silent Spring*, Congress passed the Federal Environmental Pesticide Control Act, which empowered the EPA to cancel pesticide registration whenever, "used in accordance with widespread and commonly recognized practice, it generally causes unreasonable adverse effects on the environment."

The EPA banned DDT in the same year, 1972, though that pesticide was less and less employed for mosquito and other insect pest control because the insect was becoming resistant to it, and later several other persistent chlorinated hydrocarbon pesticides were banned. In 1974 the EPA turned up evidence that Aldrin and Dieldrin constitute a "substantial health risk" and possibly are carcinogenic. They were banned, then so were two more chlorinated hydrocarbons, heptachlor and chlordane, after heated debate and charges and countercharges during the EPA hearings and subsequent mass protests by the agrochemical industry.[11]

The Commoner Circle

A second person who figured very prominently in the early days of the modern environmental movement, and who continues to be a major force through his writings, scientific organizations, and journals, is Barry Commoner. His widely read *The Closing Circle* places him within the ecologic tradition of the environmental movement. The following passage from the book illustrates his commitment to ecological stability and diversity:

> The amount of stress which an ecosystem can absorb before it is driven to collapse is also a result of its various interconnections and their relative speeds of response. The more complex the ecosystem, the more successfully it can resist a stress. . . . Like a net, in which each knot is connected to others by several strands, such a fabric can resist collapse better than a simple, unbranched circle of threads—which if cut anywhere breaks down as a whole. Environmental pollution is often a sign that ecological links have been cut and that the ecosystem has been artificially simplified.[12]

Commoner was interested in food chains much earlier. More specifically, he studied the effects of nuclear fallout on the environment, through which radioactivity reaches humans. As organizers of the St. Louis Committee for Nuclear Information in 1958, Commoner and his colleagues decided to substitute the word "environmental" for "nuclear" in the mid-1960s when their bulletin began to be published under its new name, *Environment*. The magazine has gained in influence year by year since that time.

The Closing Circle represents a synthesis of main issues in *En-*

---

11 A. V. Krebs, *The AgBiz Tiller* 1 (1977): 3.
12 B. Commoner, *The Closing Circle* (New York: Knopf, 1972), p. 38.

vironment during its first years of publication, dealing mostly with modern threats to a stable ecosystem. Commoner discusses the impact of pollution from synthetic products like detergents, synthetic fibers, plastics, pesticides, and fertilizers and the consequent disruption of natural ecosystems such as lakes and rivers. Synthetic industries grew exponentially after World War II in proportion to increased consumption of electricity and oil and also in proportion to pollution of water and air. The book stresses two features of man-made synthetics: they require heavy dependence on artificial energy sources, as opposed to the slower, less powerful energy capacities of nature itself, and they do not easily break back down into substances that can be used in natural ecosystems. The high-temperature, pressurized, and intensified-energy processes of distillation and evaporation used in the manufacture of synthetics (detergents versus soap made from fats; synthetic fibers versus cotton and wool) lead to greatly increased air pollution. Water pollution and solid-waste problems—especially in the case of plastics—stem from heavy use of pesticides, fertilizers, and other synthetics like polychlorinated biphenyls (PCBs).

Commoner pointed out, for example, that the high concentration of nitrates in the water supply of Decatur, Illinois, from nitrogen fertilizer used in the area could be transformed by intestinal bacteria in humans to nitrates, which block oxygen transport in the blood stream. He also called popular attention to the ecological plight of the Great Lakes, particularly Lake Erie, which was "dying" because it could not handle (that is, absorb and break down) the excessive amounts of organic wastes, detergents made of phosphates and nitrates, which were being dumped into it. When water plants like algae are overfertilized, they multiply and block out the sunlight which deeper algae need. This process, called eutrophication, results in huge quantities of decomposing algae consuming the oxygen supply of the fish. This again is the disruption of a natural system by human activity.

The sponsors of *Environment*, a scientific organization now called Scientists' Institute for Public Information (SIPI), has kept up a steady stream of articles on the ecological and health effects of pollution and the political economy of ecological problems. In 1973, for example, they worked with Anthony Mazzocchi and the Oil, Chemical and Atomic Workers Union to publish background reports on health information when the union was striking Shell Oil. (The action is now termed the first "environmental strike" in the country.)

Although the large industrial unions have customarily opposed the anti-growth, anti-development stance of most environmentalists, they have become interested in environmental studies on workplace environments, many of which were first publicized by SIPI. For example, at a talk sponsored by the University of California's Institute of Industrial Relations, Commoner showed the high incidences of occupational diseases and explained how "occupational diseases often serve as a kind of an early warning system of broader environmental problems to come." He suggested a goal for workers and environmentalists alike: "Reconstruct the nation's productive system so that it conforms to the imperatives of the environment which supports it, meets the needs of the workers who operate it, and secures the future of the people who have built it."[13]

Barry Commoner later wrote *The Poverty of Power*, which attempts to integrate the connections between ecology and political economy more clearly. He distinguishes the ecosystem, the system for the physical production of commodities, and the economic system (more precisely, the financial arrangements of the economic system). Also, with a special commitment to a scientific-ecological model, Commoner directly correlates the environmental crisis with the shortage of energy and the decline of the economy. He ties the natural systems in with the socioeconomic system by explaining that the political economy of waste in capitalism necessarily forces the results of its inefficiencies onto the natural environment, which of course cannot handle the load.[14]

In the book Commoner searches for a kind of master analogy, beginning with the Second Law of Thermodynamics (phrased in terms of energy's ability to do work, to be efficient or wasteful), and applies its logic to the "production" and "economic" systems. His analysis points to the eventual necessity of a planned, rational, socialist economy because capitalism is inherently wasteful in its irrational pursuit of profit maximization instead of a rational and efficient use of energy, labor, and capital. He devotes much of his argument to the problem

[13] B. Commoner, "Workplace Burden," *Environment* 15 (1973): 20.
[14] B. Commoner, *The Poverty of Power* (New York: Knopf, 1976).

of expensive and environmentally dangerous nuclear technologies, which have been (irrationally) developed out of capitalist economies.

Commoner and his associates at SIPI have written and worked extensively for the development of alternative energy technologies such as solar power. The campaign against nuclear energy within the environmental movement has largely sprung from those with an ecologic perspective like that of Commoner.

Other Impacts on Ecological Processes

To recapitulate, Cooper noted the following types of human intervention in ecological processes:

1. Ecosystem simplification and disruption of biogeochemical cycles (such as using nitrogen fertilizers instead of manure)
2. Concentration of dispersed energy (and subsequent concentration of human wastes)
3. Chemical waste production, along with increase of wastes from combustion or cooling, all causing environmental overload
4. Introduction of new species, particularly in agriculture
5. Introduction of genetic and behavioral changes (as in monocultures with their problems)

These ecological concerns have a commonality in that they all are the results of growth and development of civilization.

A further ecological impact from population growth results in the process of clustering for settlement. Because people around the world have first settled and developed coastal regions of continents, and even today since most populations live on or near the coasts of the continents, the natural environments of coastal zones have been especially subject to deterioration.[15] The problem is not only one of growing populations concentrated in limited metropolitan areas and the toll they take on the natural environment from industrial development, waste disposal, and suburban building on choice coastal lots (the East Coast population living within fifty miles of the ocean rose from 29.8 million in 1940 to 40 million in 1970), but also more and more it involves offshore oil and gas operations, deep-water ports for supertankers, refineries, and beach activities and related needs.

[15] A. Simon, *The Thin Edge* (New York: Harper and Row, 1978).

Even the barrier islands—the long chain of relatively flat, sandy islands with a very fragile ecological quality that flank much of the U.S. coastline from Maine down and around to Texas—are being sold and developed. Massive sand-dredging operations in rivers near coastlines and where the sea is shallow have begun to alter drastically estuarine and coastal marine ecologies because the sea floor composition is being changed from sand to mud or rock. Since the climatic and geographic mix of coastal regions provides fertile and varied ecological features as well as biological productivity, ecological environmentalists have begun to intensify their scientific and political activity in behalf of the coastal environments.

Many ecologists began their campaign for coastline protection in the 1960s in state legislatures and Congress. With great effort supported by increased ecological awareness, environmentalists were able to secure passage of the federal Coastal Zone Management Act of 1972. Although its provisions are quite weak, the Republican administration and the development lobby opposed the bill. The law recognizes and provides for the ecological value and vulnerability of coastal resources, and it makes provisions to moderate the competing uses of the coastline. Federal grants are offered to states which develop coastal zone management plans for staff, public hearings, and implementation programs and establish estuarine sanctuaries.

The people of California dealt more aggressively with rapidly accelerating coastal problems. After unsuccessfully lobbying the California state legislature for several years for laws to protect the coast, several conservation groups finally forced the issue by obtaining enough signatures statewide to put the matter on the ballot in what was called Proposition 20, the Coastal Initiative. The political campaign over the issue was fierce, with ports, utilities, contractors, unions, oil companies, realtors, and local coastal communities joining forces and financial resources to oppose the initiative. Nevertheless, the environmentalists worked hard too, and the measure passed.

Regional commissions were set up to regulate development of the coast while at the same time they prepared plans for future development. The commissions held hundreds of public hearings between 1973 and 1975 and worked out regional plans to deal with preservation of marine and land environments, energy, shoreline access, recreation, transportation, development, and design. Finally, again after a complicated series of tactical maneuvers by opposing viewpoints, the legislature passed a coastal bill (based on the commission's report) that provides guidelines for local land use regulations overseen by a state coastal commission, which hears appeals from individuals who want to challenge treatment by local agencies.

Both federal and state coastal bills have established a precedent for a governmental role in land use planning, a signal achievement for those who worked for their passage. Such laws might begin to take the use of natural environment out of the adversary system of planning and encourage planning on more ecological grounds. As far back as 1968, Lynton K. Caldwell proposed "The Ecosystem as a Criterion for Public Land Policy."[16] His suggestion comes from an ecologic perspective—that the ecosystem approach to public land policy be holistic and based on scientific knowledge: "The approach begins with an assumption based on scientific inquiry. The natural world is a composite of interrelating life-systems subsisting in a highly improbable terrestial environment. . . . The ultimate necessity of an ecosystems approach to environmental policy, including land, follows from the finite amount of land, water, air and other substances upon which the human economy depends and the infinite character of human demands on the environment. . . . [What is most required by law now is] to bring man-environment relationships into ecological balance."[17]

What is most astounding about the environmental movement in the past decade is that so many people, not necessarily devotees of the wilderness, have adopted a similar ecological perspective. Some have developed considerable sophistication during this time, many with very little motivation except a sense of the deteriorating environmental quality and perhaps a sense of loss of what they once possessed. They have supported the environmental movement in steadily increasing numbers since the 1960s, and without them most of the legislation of the 1970s would have been impossible.

Perhaps their greatest victory was the National Environmental

[16] *Natural Resources Journal* 10 (1970): 203–221.
[17] Ibid., pp. 211–212.

Policy Act of 1969 (NEPA), mainly because it recognized the environmental constituency by redirecting the priorities of the federal government to:

1. Fulfill the responsibilities of each generation as a trustee of the environment for succeeding generations
2. Assure for all Americans safe, healthful, productive and aesthetically and culturally pleasing surroundings
3. Attain the widest range of beneficial uses of the environment without degradation, risk to health or safety, or other undesirable and unintended consequences
4. Preserve important historic, cultural, and natural aspects of our natural heritage and maintain, wherever possible, an environment which supports diversity and variety of individual choice
5. Achieve a balance between population and resource use which will permit high standards of living and a wide sharing of life's amenities
6. Enhance the quality of renewable resources and approach the maximum attainable recycling of depletable resources

Although they are perhaps more a symbolic gesture to a somewhat inconstant constituency than a set of hard-core objectives, the listed goals have found their way into some court cases. When a significant court victory comes out of NEPA's tenuous construction, the constituency becomes more constant, and the feelings become more optimistic that ecological science may one day win out.

5

Environmental Economists

THE name *environmental economists* seems to be a contradiction in terms. What have economists to do with environment? Marston Bates sums up the feelings of many ecological purists:

Economics and ecology, as words, have the same root; but that is about all they have in common. As fields of knowledge, they are culti-vated in remotely separated parts of our universities, through the use of quite different methods, by scholars who would hardly recognize anything in common. The world of ecologists is "unspoiled nature." They tend to avoid cities, parks, fields, orchards. The real world of the economists is like Plato's; it is a world of ideas, of abstractions—money, labor, market, goods, capital. There is no room for squirrels scolding in the oak trees, no room for robins on the lawn. There is no room for people either, for that matter—people loving and hating and dreaming. People become the labor force on the market.[1]

Bates's assessment comes down too hard on economists and perhaps not hard enough on ecologists. Both disciplines, after all, do use abstract models, with corresponding methodological values, and ecologists now are almost as familiar with statistical measures as econ-omists. Furthermore, there are more varieties of economic thought than there are schools of ecology. Surely not all should be condemned.

Like ecologists, economists use their discipline to solve prob-lems; their tools or methods change as do their perceptions of prob-

[1] M. Bates, *The Forest and the Sea* (New York: Vintage, 1960), pp. 250–251.

lems in the field. For example, during the first half of this century many economists were concerned about the economics of natural resource scarcity. The concern remains, especially in the U.S. Forest Service, over questions of sustained yield and even-flow policies, which are more complex questions than they appear to be on the surface.[2]

In the early 1960s H. J. Barnett and C. Morse attempted to prove that the early natural-resource economists in the conservation movement who worried about such things as timber or oil or phosphate "famines" need not have bothered.[3] New technologies, they said, have created enough substitutes for natural resources in the past century to satisfy steadily increasing demands. Although the study, and subsequent work confirming it, has received wide acceptance in the field of economics, a new mood of pessimism stemming from the environmental crisis has influenced a new breed of economists.[4] These have joined environmentalists in calling for a slowdown in economic growth, and they even use old arguments about rising populations; depletion of natural resources; and the disruption, pollution, and deterioration of the natural environment.

Social Costs

At the same time, another group in the field has begun to apply its understanding to more specific environmental questions. For example, the *Wall Street Journal* reported in 1975 that an economist was called in to mediate between oil developers and environmentalists at an offshore oil conference.[5] He put the question in terms he understood best: "What is the cost, in dollars and cents, of one dead sea gull?" (No more than ten dollars, he guessed.)

Environmentalists fell into a state of shock. The next day Jacques

[2] M. Clawson, *Forests: For Whom and For What?* (Baltimore: Johns Hopkins, 1975), pp. 78–107.

[3] H. J. Barnett and C. Morse, *Scarcity and Growth* (Baltimore: Johns Hopkins, 1963).

[4] "The No-Growth Society," *Daedalus* 102 (1973). See especially the work of Kenneth Boulding and E. J. Mishan, both included therein.

[5] G. C. Hill, "Off-shore Oil Stirs Heated Debate," *Wall Street Journal*, September 9, 1975, p. 1.

Cousteau attacked the economist because he failed to understand the value of each species, of life itself. In response the economist defended himself and his discipline by pointing out that these are the kinds of questions that will be raised more and more in the future—questions that deal with benefits, say, of increased offshore drilling, versus costs, risks, and disadvantages. Since environmental questions are already framed in these terms very often, he simply wanted to quantify the oil-drilling question in a way everyone would understand.

But economists have added a few terms to their vocabulary that tend to lessen the shock of dollars-and-cents prices laid on the head of a sea gull or the preservation of a Pleistocene rock formation (terms such as *social costs, option value,* and *collective* or *public goods*), and they have even sharpened their notion of concepts like discount rates, social risk, and externalities. J. V. Krutilla, for example, claims that natural environments should be examined in terms of their future value instead of their present utility for resource extraction, which may in some circumstances be considered inferior to possible future benefits.[6]

Krutilla shows (and his assumptions seem to have been confirmed) that the value of natural environments will increase yearly as more and more people experience the aesthetic pleasure of nature. At the same time, the supply of natural environments remains fairly constant and the possibility of replacing them is low. It is possible, as Barnett and Morse have argued, that replacements could be found for natural resources, but not natural environments short of something like plastic trees (which the city of Los Angeles considered for the median strip of a freeway because all the real ones were dying from auto emissions; one Los Angeles city department actually did set some up at another location). Therefore, the cost of finding a replacement for, say, the Channel Islands off the coast of Santa Barbara is extremely high compared to finding a substitute drilling site for the oil there.

---

[6] J. V. Krutilla, "Conservation Reconsidered," *American Economic Review* 57 (1967): 777–786. See also K. J. Arrow and A. C. Fisher, "Environmental Preservation, Uncertainty and Irreversibility," *Quarterly Journal of Economics* 88 (1974): 312–319.

Krutilla calls the future demand for natural environments an *option value*, referring to a term used by Burton Weisbrod to explain the "collective good" aspect of the natural environment.[7] If a great deal of a natural environment is destroyed irreversibly in the present (by a dam), for instance, it will not be possible to exercise an option for it in the future. This fact establishes the social necessity of preserving natural environments for future use.

In a later work Krutilla and Fisher further develop the notion of irreversibility.[8] They ask, "What is the appropriate social attitude toward the risk associated with the (irreversible) conversion of a natural environment to developmental purposes? What are the implications of option value?"[9] For them, the notion of option value goes beyond net social or environmental costs in conventional cost-benefit analysis. Their criterion refers to an entire process of continued development of a site over a long period of time and the consequent deterioration of the site for possible future use as untouched nature. The many examples which are offered include the geysers of Yellowstone Park, whose use for geothermal energy would cause an irreversible eyesore and reduce subsurface pressure to the extent that geyser action would eventually be eliminated.

The authors also mention sport shooting species like the passenger pigeon or the grizzly bear to the extent of extinction; clear-cutting an original climax forest and eliminating the entire ecological system along with the forest; and strip-mining areas of geologic or pedologic significance, or building dams over them (Krutilla applied the notion to Hells Canyon in another work). These areas of environmental significance, according to the account, gain in option value as time passes to a far greater extent than the extent to which mere resource extraction would provide current benefit. Thus, irreversibility adds to the option value of a natural environment.

[7] B. Weisbrod, "Collective-Consumption Services of Individual-Consumption," *Quarterly Journal of Economics* 78 (1964): 471–477.

[8] J. V. Krutilla and A. C. Fisher, *The Economics of Natural Environments* (Baltimore: Johns Hopkins, 1974), chapters 3 and 4. See also A. C. Fisher, J. V. Krutilla, and C. J. Cicchetti, "The Economics of Environment Preservation: A Theoretical and Empirical Analysis," *American Economic Review* 62 (1972): 605–619.

[9] Krutilla and Fisher, *Economics*, p. 39.

Cost-Benefit Analysis

As has already been noted, political decisions about environmental matters are rarely made because of economic analysis alone, though economic studies are usually required before a decision is made. The rationale for cost-benefit studies is not only that government projects should be justified by the most economically beneficial actions, but also that a method had to be developed to establish a price for goods that are outside the market system. Cost-benefit ratios have most often been applied to the development of large-scale water projects to determine whether the objectives of the project will be met by the proposal. If the ratio of benefits to costs is at least one to one (preferably higher), then the government investment in the project would indicate economic worth. Economic cash benefits are usually divided by investment and maintenance costs over the life of the project. The equation is usually quite complex, including such future economic benefits as crops from irrigation, electrical power, flood damage prevention, fishing, and increased property values.

Estimates of the values of projects by the Army Corps of Engineers have typically been inflated, but in recent years a number of environmental economists have begun to challenge their figures and estimates, often throwing doubt into the minds of decision makers. Even a 1974 report of the U.S. General Accounting Office, (GAO), the federal agency which oversees government expenditures, showed many irregularities in Army Corps of Engineers benefit-cost ratios in recent years—and in the ratios of the U.S. Bureau of Reclamation, the U.S. Soil Conservation Service, and the Tennessee Valley Authority.[10]

The GAO study indicated at least seven dam projects with benefits overestimated by millions of dollars. According to Julian McCaull's analysis of the report and related material from other governmental agencies, because of nineteen procedural errors and unsubstantiated claims "the total increment of benefit-to-cost ratios in the projects was $12,607,080 *per year*."[11] This analysis was done from an environmentalist perspective.

[10] J. McCaull, "Dams of Pork," *Environment* 17 (1975): 10–11.
[11] Ibid., p. 14.

Inspired by environmentalist values or not, court fights cannot be won without some hard data, and environmental economists have begun to supply the data. In a companion article to McCaull's analysis, B. T. Parry and R. B. Norgaard closely examined the benefit-cost analysis for the proposed New Melones Dam in California and found serious deficiencies on both sides of the Army Corps of Engineers equation.[12] Their analysis indicated that the corps overestimated the benefits (flood control, irrigation, power generation, general recreation, fish and wildlife, water quality, area redevelopment) by at least five million dollars yearly and perhaps by as much as nine million dollars. Conversely, the corps estimate of costs was probably half what the actual costs would be. Thus, although the corps published a benefit-to-cost ratio at 1.7:1, Parry and Norgaard placed it at from 0.3:1 to at best 0.58:1. That is, according to the revised figures, the dam would not be an economically feasible project.

Discount Rate

Another matter which environmental economists bring to discussions about the natural environment is the question of discounting or discount rate, the process by which the future value of sums of money is converted (discounted) to present value. The assumption is that a present sum of money is worth more than the same amount in the future, so a person must be rewarded for saving it at a certain rate of discount each year. If we know the rate of interest, we can calculate the future value of a sum of money. Conversely, if we know how much we will have to spend on a project in the future, we can work backwards to find out how much we will have to put away at a certain rate of interest to pay those bills in the future.

Changes in the discount rate (rate of interest) in benefit-cost studies can make a beneficial project a money loser. Government projects have traditionally been given an artificially low rate of discount because they are said to contain high social values; a low rate means that lower future sums will be needed to pay salaries and maintenance. Therefore we have been traditionally placing a higher

[12] B. T. Parry and R. B. Norgaard, "Wasting a River," *Environment* 17 (1975): 17–27.

value on available benefits for a longer period into the future. A high discount rate shortens the time value of the project because the annual rate of interest demands that more money be set aside in the present to pay future bills. Many economists, however, dispute the necessity of placing a special low discount rate on environmental projects and a high one on projects that provide goods and services.

The Krutilla alternative approach would take future options into account—the option value of unspoiled environments, which could be considered of great benefit even at a high discount rate. If a public agency knew that a natural environment would be irreversibly despoiled by a commercial activity that, according to discounted figures (even ones yielding a very high long-term return), would add a given amount of financial benefit to consumers, it is still possible that those future consumers (in the aggregate) would trade the present financial benefits in order to preserve the environment for the future. The key element in this analysis is the fact that such states of the natural environment are immemorial public goods, and as time passes new information may change the public agency's evaluation of possible benefits from the already irreversibly despoiled environment. Option value allows economic planning for possible alternative uses of the environment.

For example, to use a Krutilla-Fisher illustration, many people since John Muir's time, and probably many more in future generations, would gladly compensate water users for whatever difference in financial benefit the Hetch Hetchy Dam provided to those who preferred the dam to the Hetch Hetchy Valley left in its natural state.[13] Unfortunately they could not make the (aggregate) offer because of the irreversibility of the project. However, if those public planners who built the dam had factored in this unforeseen, unknown information—the dwindling supply of regions of great natural beauty and the public's growing preference for it—they perhaps would have been slower to build the dam, especially at that particular spot, which was a spectacularly scenic glacier-carved valley within the confines of Yosemite National Park. The valley exists no longer, nor can it be retrieved. Today's style of benefit-cost analysis was unknown then,

[13] Krutilla and Fisher, *Economics*, p. 69.

but even today the feasibility of such projects is determined without the kind of economic information that is included in the Krutilla-Fisher analysis.

For another example, clear-cutting a virgin redwood forest, which might have taken two thousand years to develop, is in practice irreversible, but the decision to refrain from clear-cutting is reversible, and as more information becomes available, the clear-cutting decision can be reaffirmed or reversed.

Option-value planning theoretically allows new kinds of economic information to be factored into discount rates in benefit-cost studies. The technique is conservative; it permits more land-use activity that allows for reversible decisions than pursuits of a destructive nature. The contribution of the environmental economists to option-value planning is not that their model can be used easily in practice. It is clearly impossible to know in the present what future generations (or people two months from now, for that matter) might be willing to pay for what they would perceive to be a significant environment. But the model underlines an important omission of benefit-cost studies: they do not factor in all relevant *economic* information that pertains to irreversible activity on public lands. It is a noteworthy contribution from the perspective of environmental economics.

Social Risk

Option-value planning requires, in policy decisions, the economic recognition of social risk taken every time a public project is approved. Environmental economists have taken the economic notion of risk (for example, as it is applied to investments, market uncertainty, innovations, and so on) and have extended its meaning to include aversion to social risk. R. B. Norgaard, for example, applies the idea to resource scarcity: "Society's major concern over resource scarcity today is not so much that there is too little but that our resources and technologies are uncertain. We do not know whether there are three or thirty years' worth of oil on the outer continental shelf, whether we can utilize oil shale with tolerable environmental side effects, or whether we can develop acceptable institutions to prevent plutonium diversion from breeder reactors. This uncertainty, in turn, can be reduced by gathering information through exploration, research and development on diverse energy sources and conservation techniques, and environmental and social assessment."[14]

Norgaard writes that social risk occurs when "a collection of interdependent public decisions has a large influence on welfare directly attributable to the public sector,"[15] as regarding exploration, leasing, taxation, import controls, power-plant siting, and pollution control. Norgaard further suggests an economic model which incorporates aversion to social risk, interdependent decisions, and the opportunity to reduce uncertainty through information collection.[16]

At the Santa Barbara conference on offshore oil and sea gulls, the participants were concerned with the social risk of offshore oil drilling and many other specifically economic questions which were tied to the decision to explore and, if exploration were to be done, at what rate. The question, as it was resolved (in favor), came down to whether the benefits for the United States incorporated in Project Independence outweighed costs and risks. Norgaard's model, if employed, would have slowed the decision until more information was gathered.

Project Independence was a political decision to move rapidly in the direction of energy development because of an embargo and escalating price increases which threatened U.S. economic interests. As the muddy waters of the decade slowly settle and federal administrations rethink many past, irreversible decisions, new questions about social and economic risk demand answers: How fast should offshore oil drilling be allowed to accelerate? Or, according to a Norgaard type of calculus, how much more of a threat to the environment would result if the thirteen thousand federal offshore oil leases granted from 1954 to 1975 were doubled in five years (the Department of the Interior's plan until it was delayed by lawsuits)? Would it be wiser, even from an economic standpoint, to emphasize option values and increase imports? How well developed are drilling technologies? (For

[14] R. B. Norgaard, "Scarcity and Growth: How Does It Look Today?" *American Journal of Agricultural Economics* 57 (1975): 811.
[15] Ibid.
[16] R. B. Norgaard and D. C. Hall, "Environment Amenity Rights, Transaction Costs and Technological Change," *Journal of Environmental Economics and Management* 1 (1974): 257–261.

instance, do they perform without threat of blowout in a world of Arctic icebergs?) Would an accelerated leasing program reduce the dollar value of bids, thus losing billions of dollars of income that could be used to develop alternatives, and how do those alternatives fit into the economic picture?

Wilderness advocates and ecologists are not usually the kinds of people who are equipped to answer such questions. Economists are, and many have shown that their discipline has developed an effective package of concepts which has aided the environmental struggle.

Economic Concepts

At the very foundation of neoclassical economic theory is the doctrine of the "sovereign consumer," who allegedly shows preferences in the marketplace by the prices he or she will pay. The marketplace is regarded as functioning properly when the preferences of consumers are filled and as failing when they are not. Such a theory of consumer sovereignty, whether or not the idea squares with reality, is not necessarily conducive to a theory of social or environmental good.

Yet early in the century A. C. Pigou, and later Vilfredo Pareto, did pioneering work from which a "welfare" theory of economics was constructed. Welfare theory adds the notion that an economic ideal is achieved when no one's welfare is worsened while someone else's welfare is bettered, as by competition or technology. When one applies the "compensation test," another economic concept from the late 1930s which prescribed that in the same ideal economy those who gain from a change must compensate those who have lost, the application to environmental economics becomes clear. The compensation test underlies the concept of option value as well as the notion of externalities. A Pareto-optimal state is undermined by pollution, the elimination of which should be paid for by polluters.

The idea of external effects caused by the market system is most familiar to environmental economists.[17] An external effect is one that

___

[17] See E. S. Mills, *The Economics of Environmental Quality* (New York: Norton, 1978); A. V. Kneese, *Economics and the Environment* (New York: Penguin, 1977); S. L. McDonald, *Petroleum Conservation in the United States:*

is uncompensated because it is not included in the market transaction. In some cases, third parties receive benefits or suffer damages because, say, a steel mill dumps arsenic and cyanide in the Mahoning River so that automobile prices are lower (for other third parties), but the people in the Mahoning Valley can no longer use the water for recreation. The same problem occurs with air pollution (from the same mill) and has been expanded to include noise, unsightly wires and buildings, fumes, congestion, destruction of natural beauty or historic places, and so on.[18]

Environmental economists devise models to internalize these externalities by showing how social costs should be taken into the costs of production through more efficient organization of the production processes. Since business managers tend to ignore costs borne by society while lowering their production costs, most economists recommend pollution taxes or incentives to encourage the application of anti-pollution devices.[19] They assume that the free market is an efficient mechanism both to allocate resources and to achieve social goals.

The theoretical task of pollution economists lies in the design of social institutions which would guide economic activities in accordance with the public goals of pollution abatement. They have taken as their practical task the determination of which structural rules will most completely internalize the externalities generated by production.

The effect of pollution taxes, light for light polluters and heavy for heavy polluters, would tend to raise prices for goods which bring with them socially adverse effects and thus would lower production along with pollution in some cases; pollution taxes should also induce businesses to clean up their production processes, or at least the taxes should bring in revenues to the government to clean up pollution at

---

An Economic Analysis (Baltimore: Johns Hopkins, 1971); and A. C. Fisher and F. M. Peterson, "The Environment in Economics: A Survey," *Journal of Economic Literature* 14 (1976): 1–33.

[18] E. J. Mishan, *The Costs of Economic Growth* (New York: Praeger, 1967), pp. 67–79. See also E. J. Mishan, *Welfare Economics* (New York: Random House, 1964).

[19] A mathematical formula is presented in W. H. Baumol, "On Taxation and the Control of Externalities," *American Economic Review* 62 (1972): 307–321.

its sources or reimburse those who have been otherwise uncompensated.

Economists have tended to approach pollution or environmental degradation in three ways. All three methods entail putting a price on pollution at some state of the pollution-reparation transaction, thereby internalizing an externality. As such, pollution economists are not usually concerned about such matters as option value, social risk, and irreversibility. One approach would require a property owner to quantify the damage done to him or her; a second would require that some management agency be informed of the optimum level of taxes of subsidies to account for pollution; the third would look to the replacement of damaged goods or land. Each approach attempts to estimate the external cost of pollution.

This threefold scheme can be applied to the problem of the Santa Barbara sea gulls, as it was stated by the typical pollution economist at work. He was simply trying to determine the economic market value of an external effect (pollution affecting sea gulls), that is, to approximate the value of the gull in quantifiable terms. He first tried to ask representative landowners or visitors at the conference what the value of one gull would be. Then the economist went one step further. He tried to find a piece of inland property comparable to the despoiled beach in both size and development possibilities. The difference in marketplace value could be said to be derived from the existence of sea gulls on the beach. When the economist adjusted for an average number of sea gulls, he found his own answer to the question, What is society's assessment of a sea gull? The question of who would receive compensation for the death of the gull would fall to the courts.

The economist could have approached the problem with one of two other methods. He might have tried to quantify damage costs by measuring the costs to clean up the sea gulls if an oil spill took place. Much data was already put together after the 1969 Santa Barbara oil spill. The cost of cleaning up one sea gull might be considered as the hours per gull required by the 1969 volunteers times the minimum wage. If this cost, added to the cost of production, did not generate an unfavorable benefit-cost ratio, the project's value to society might be assumed to be positive (according to this way of thinking).

Or last, the economist could have simply attempted to compensate the injured parties with fresh replacements for the damaged gulls. This approach differs in that it does not recommend a financial compensation but instead attempts to replace a public good, as by bringing in new gulls from other locations or from pet shops (where sellers or property owners could be compensated). The value of the gull might be the pet shop owner's determination or only the transportation costs of moving a load of gulls.

The approach of pollution economists can thus be understood as not attractive to many environmentalists. Yet when these methods are used to solve problems of air and water pollution, or even land despoilment, their application has proved to be a powerful institutional tool—not only for temporary problems, but also for long-term economic behavior and social habits. It is obvious, however, that the values of economics remain on a level which is limited to a material understanding of the natural environment. At worst these values give people license to tinker with serious environmental problems with inadequate tools. Furthermore, the three approaches described above do not solve the problem of irreversibility. That is, they cannot deal with the social cost of damage to natural environments like Hetch Hetchy, which may be lost forever, in which case replacement costs are meaningless. This much of the work of Krutilla and Fisher and others seems still to be confined to the academic journals.

Values of Environmental Economics

A single thread links the values of the early conservation economists with the concerns of more recent economists: purposeful, efficient use of natural resources over a long period of time (optimal use and allocation of resource reserves over time) defined in economic terms. The Forest Service itself was established in 1905 to see that the national forests were conserved for the long-term use of the American people. First under Gifford Pinchot, then under more and more professionally trained forest managers, the Forest Service formulated policies to "develop, manage and protect the National Forest System." One of these policies is a method of multiple-use management for sustained yields of wood, water, forage, wildlife, and recreation.

Forest Service economists have developed economic models which appear realistic enough to their supervisors. Yet other environmental economists have pointed out that their decisions carry with them preferences for one form of activity over another. The activities of sheep grazing or surface mining reduce total benefits of the forest by lowering overall quality. Lumbering curtails other activities and excludes protective responsibilities of the Forest Service. The ideal of multiple-use management (grazing, mining, recreation, and so on) is difficult to implement in practice, and it also tends to use dollar values exclusively in decision making.

Thus, among environmental or conservation economists as well as among economists concerned with pollution, a great number of approaches appear, manifesting a variety of values. Most of them, however, define their fields in terms of economic efficiency and avoidance of waste. As recently as the congressional hearings before passage of the National Forest Management Act of 1976, economists from the Forest Service, the forest industry, and environmental groups debated the "sustained yield, even-flow" provisions of the bill, all indicating that their respective different models would achieve the least waste of the resource.

Clawson and many others claim, for example, that Forest Service policies are so economically conservative with regard to cutting practices that they are wasteful.[20] Other forest economists have suggested that the Forest Service imitate the cutting schedules of large timber companies like Weyerhauser and Crown Zellerbach in the West because they have been forced by market exigencies to adopt the most efficient long-term practices.[21] Other environmental economists would factor preservationist values into their models.

Yet the concept of future use of natural resources as the paramount conservation value has been stressed in most definitions of conservation; for example, S. V. Ciriacy-Wantrup's classic treatment describes it as a shift "in the inter-temporal use (of a resource) in the direction of the future."[22]

[20]Clawson, *Forests*, pp. 78ff.
[21] H. E. Clepper, *Professional Forestry in the United States* (Baltimore: Johns Hopkins, 1971), pp. 276–283.
[22] S. V. Ciriacy-Wantrup, *Resource Conservation: Economics and Policies* (Berkeley: University of California Press, 1952), p. 52.

These concerns are related to the central values of economics itself, even given the various emphases and conflicting values.[23] The economic process uses the most efficient mix of labor, capital, and natural resources to produce and distribute goods to users. "Most efficient" means that sacrifices by producers and users should be minimized among the many possibilities of resource allocation (this last is sometimes called Pareto optimality).

Resource allocation can be designed to yield current satisfaction or future satisfactions. Economic activity is projected for future satisfactions either to produce durable goods (such as machines and factories) through capital formation, that is, through "real investment," whereby present consumer satisfactions are delayed, or to provide for future satisfaction by slowing down the rate of consumption of natural resources, that is, by "conservation of natural resources." This is to say that conservation is preeminently an economic activity, an integral part of the economic process.

McDonald shows that both real investment and conservation require sacrifices of present consumption for possible future satisfaction.[24] Therefore, some economic indicator is required to justify such a transfer of present satisfactions to future consumption, as is the case with the discount rate. If conservation is so intertwined with economics, then such models as have been discussed in this chapter—Krutilla, Norgaard, and so on—intersect all environmental values when these touch the real world of social and political life. In the economic account, conservation is considered to be an investment which constitutes a provision to increase future satisfaction. It also promotes the intentional value judgment that the future is at least as important as the present.

The economic value which complements waste avoidance, one indeed which is the other side of the economic coin, is that of economic efficiency. It is achieved when an optimal allocation of resources obtains most net satisfactions among many possible uses. Thus, waste or economic inefficiency occur when resources are underemployed or used when alternative products would be more efficient

[23] McDonald, *Petroleum Conservation*, pp. 59–74.
[24] Ibid., pp. 61–62.

and would yield more satisfaction for less sacrifices, all considered in terms of current or future uses. McDonald emphasizes that

the optimum allocation of resources is not some fixed pattern of resource use which can be specified and achieved once and for all. Its specifications change with every advance in technology, every alteration of consumer preferences or expectations, and every change in the quantity or quality of productive resources. In short, its specifications change continuously in a growing, dynamically developing economy. It must be continuously sought. Consequently, the efficient economy is one which has built into its structure a flexible, positive mechanism for continuously seeking the optimum allocation of resources. . . . *Conservation is action designed to achieve or maintain, from the point of view of society as a whole, the optimum distribution of natural resource use over time.*[25]

McDonald was primarily concerned with the problem of the optimum use and allocation of the known and unknown stocks of petroleum over time. His analysis of market prices, use and postponement of various stocks, and investment in exploration and development covers what he considers to be the optimum time distribution of the total natural stock of petroleum.

McDonald's insistence that "specifications change continuously in a growing, dynamically developing economy" and the consequent necessity for adaptation have rung true in many areas of environmental concern in recent years. For example, the nuclear energy which only a decade ago was hailed, and mostly accepted, as the road to cheap energy and a more abundant economy has become economically questionable, probably as much because of the "alterations of consumer preferences and expectations" (read "environmental pressures") as for any other reason. Delays in construction of facilities, soaring costs of uranium, political responsiveness, and a governmental reluctance to underwrite all the development costs of the nuclear industry, as well as the uncertainty and risk of investment, have made nuclear power much less economically feasible than it once appeared to be. Delays in the construction of the state of Washington Public Power Supply System's five nuclear projects will cost the state agency an additional $1.05 billion, bringing the cost to more than $8.5 billion. More and more studies factoring in natural-resource and en-

[25] Ibid., pp. 64, 70.

vironmental concerns are changing the complexion of the nuclear industry in the United States.[26]

When the economist who was assailed by environmentalists for trying to put a price on a sea gull came to his own defense at the Santa Barbara conference, he claimed he was only trying to inject a semblance of rationality into the debate. Of course it was his own brand of economic rationality which interested him, but though the thought might have been distasteful to environmentalists, as this entire chapter might be, a similar kind of economic rationality has helped the environmental movement, past and present, much more than it has hurt it.

The reason is simple. American society was conceived, born, and bred on the principles of economic rationality. The principal tenets of the American system have been challenged significantly only in recent years, and even if some changes were made in its societal structure, it is doubtful that the doctrine of economic efficiency would be displaced. Thus, those conservationists who have gained access to key political and economic positions have often attempted to institutionalize conservationism (impose efficient taxes, improve energy-conversion efficiencies, and so on) as part of the process of government.[27]

Economics embodies values of efficiency applied to the natural environment. Then deeper questions of the suitability of the market system to deal with unquantifiable values, as well as questions of growth and the inequities associated with increasing production, consumption, and waste, remain. Efficiency solves many of the lesser human problems and enables quicker accumulation of wealth, but it hardly represents the full measure of environmental or social values.

[26] J. McCaull, "The Cost of Nuclear Power," *Environment* 18 (1976): 10, 11–16.

[27] Of course legislators have not often applied economic concepts like effluent fees so much as specific pollution standards which industry has been required to meet. Nonetheless, many economic data have been used by government to determine the level of the standards. For a superb treatment of the relationship between pollution taxes and air pollution standards (the Clean Air Act), see A. F. Friedlander, ed., *Approaches to Controlling Air Pollution* (Cambridge, Mass.: MIT Press, 1978).

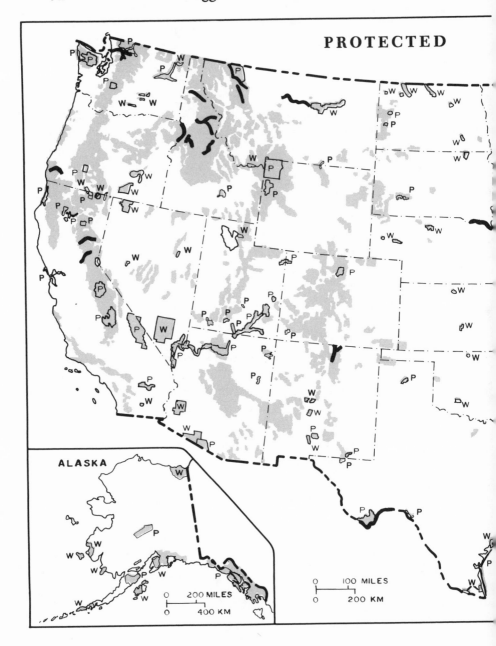

PROTECTED

ENVIRONMENTS

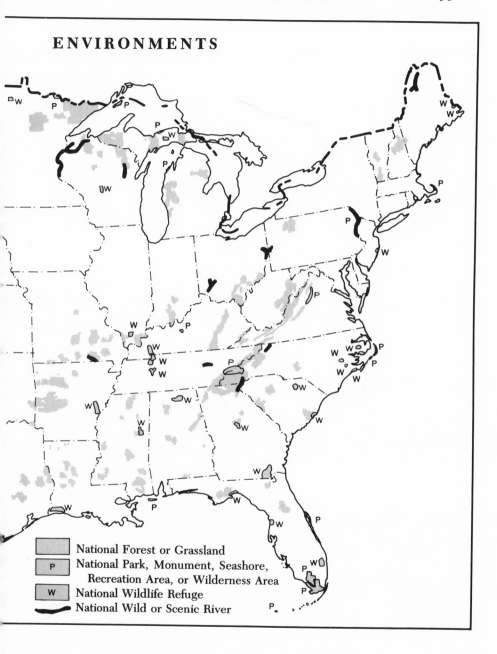

National Forest or Grassland

P National Park, Monument, Seashore,
   Recreation Area, or Wilderness Area

W National Wildlife Refuge

National Wild or Scenic River

PART III

CRITICAL ISSUES

6

Varieties of
Environmental Argument

BECAUSE of the cross-currents of traditions, purposes, and values in the environmental movement, it is not surprising that the movement should contain arguments, dogma, insights, and perhaps even outrageous conclusions. Any large social movement will have dozens of possible interpretations. This is even more true of environmentalism, the interests of which are derived from many diverse assumptions. It is enough to note first of all that each tradition holds strong values which tend to influence the definition of environmental problems which they present to the outside world in a manner similar to the way the values of social class affect the perception of social problems. Second, these assumptions and values often work against the very objectives and concerns of the groups which hold them, both because they tend to circumscribe the understanding of environmental issues and because they polarize groups around ideologies instead of rational discussion.

Moreover, a few environmental dogmas have dominated the ecological discussion in recent years. They call for closer examination; they may be termed dogmas because of their adherents' almost blind obedience to certain principles and reliance on certain shibboleths (that is, passwords or pet phrases distinguishing the good guys from the bad guys).[1] Closed societies—groups that separate themselves

[1] Ancient Israelites were able to capture spies who infiltrated their camps because the spies could not pronounce the word *shibboleth* the way the Israelites did.

from the outside world in some way and develop an in-group consciousness—use a lot of shibboleths because in the language of subcultures they are code words which become reference points to signal mutual support in a social system.[2] Of course it also happens that these groups are forced into a closed defensive posture because of attack from the outside, as has occurred in the contemporary environmental movement and other movements as well.

The more individuals are able to find others with similar attitudes, values, and assumptions, the more they tend to associate with them and the more they are able to reinforce their common values: hawks or doves, feminists or male chauvinists, wilderness advocates, ecologists, and economists alike. Polarization has resulted even among groups within the environmental movement itself, but they usually will close ranks in the face of a common enemy.

Henri Bergson explained the phenomenon by distinguishing between "open" and "closed" societies.[3] There is a tendency, he noted, for groups or "societies" to become closed through the subtle demands they put on members for conformity to dogmas, principles (shibboleths), even beyond (more than) the group loyalties to which most people are accustomed. Soon members of a closed society identify those dogmas with personal commitments, cherished beliefs, and the "truth." Embattled truth is easily transformed into a righteous cause.

Rhetoric and Distortion

Environmental groups and their critics have tended to cluster in closed societies and build walls around themselves through the language of their arguments and the tactics of their struggles. Perhaps this is inevitable, since the struggle itself seems inevitable. The ideas of the groups are the weapons used in the public forum and are simultaneously the means used to rally supporters or convince prospective converts.

[2] D. G. Meyers and H. Lamm, "The Polarizing Effect of Group Discussion," *American Scientist* 63 (1975): 299–300.
[3] H. Bergson, *The Two Sources of Morality* (New York: Henry Holt, 1935).

Consider, for example, the titles of a few of the early books of the modern environmentalists: *Silent Spring, The Closing Circle, The Population Bomb.* These books appeared along with those which use terms like *ecosuicide, crisis, exploding populations,* and *survival.* Spring will be silent because no wildlife will be left in the wake of increased use of insecticides, the world itself is beginning to suffocate as the circle of modern technology closes in around us, or it will be wiped away by a time bomb ticking under us all—and so on.

At the same time, opponents of the environmentalists have more than outdone their adversaries in the use of emotive language, which perhaps in turn pushes environmentalists into higher levels of stridency, which affects opponents, and on and on. For example, some of the opponents' titles include: *Ecological Fantasies*; *Ecological Sanity: A Critical Examination of the Bad Science, Good Intentions, and Premature Doomsday Announcements of the Ecology Lobby*; *Models of Doom*; *The Disaster Lobby: Prophets of Ecological Doom and Other Absurdities*; *The Doomsday Syndrome*; and *In Defense of People.*

These and other extravagant and emotive titles on both sides are used to persuade readers to accept the viewpoints of the authors. That is, terms like *fantasies, sanity,* and *doomsday* establish the context into which critics would like to place environmentalism; words like *survival* and *ecosuicide* play the same role for the environmentalists. The words and arguments serve to convert or reinforce incipient attitudes of readers and listeners. For example, the "in defense of people" argument picks up on the widespread notion that most environmentalists care more about wildlife than about people. Here, an antienvironmentalist conflict group would seek the support of a wider quasi-group to discredit environmentalist opponents.

The problem is not only one of closed versus open groups but also one of differing assumptions, methodologies, values, and class interests—often in different ideological mixes. A fundamentally religious argument made in behalf of (or against) nature can be cloaked in a thousand guises. And a patently class-oriented position can be justified by an appeal to the most pious-sounding phrases. All sides can have appeal to science, to natural law, and to the interests of the poor.

The traditions which have been examined here indicate that the basis and assumptions of the biocentric argument are quasi-religious; the methodological assumptions of the ecologic argument are scientific and based on a natural-law notion of truth; and the assumptions and methodologies of the economic argument are founded on middle-class, capitalist notions of efficiency and the optimistic belief that environmental problems can be quantified and solved.

Then there are more obvious factors which are important for an understanding of environmental-antienvironmental conflicts. It would be naive to assume (based on at least a century of experience) that corporations like the oil companies do not want to keep the automobile culture strong, to sell as much oil as possible at the highest possible profit, and to explore for new sources of their commodities with as little government interference as possible (except for large tax writeoffs). The same kinds of assumptions can be made about the steel industry, the chemical industry, the power companies, the automobile industry. If they are closed societies, it is because they are bent on capital expansion and profit maximization over the longest period of time for the security of their investors and their social class. At the same time, it is precisely because capital has taken its toll on the natural environment that opposition environmental groups have been formed.

What complicates any analysis is that thousands of those allied in some way with corporate goals simultaneously belong to opposition environmental groups. To use our earlier terminology, the conflict groups are formed from some of the same constituents in quasi-groups of the larger populations. That is, people are predisposed to or see something of value in both capital expansion and environmentalism; thus, they support only those environmental issues which are compatible with the interests of their social class. Therefore, a person could confine his or her environmental interests to particular wildlife issues in remote areas of the world or refuse to recognize certain health issues as environmental problems—in other words, selectively sort out what issues fit into his or her own interests and challenge fellow environmentalists on others. The process tends to isolate environmental groups into different camps based on assumptions and interests.

Nature Preservationists

Whatever their religious assumption or social class, open or closed, those committed to nature or wilderness preservation have made inestimable contributions to the political and cultural development of American institutions. The religious quality or at least the philosophical commitment of their effort seems transparent.

Yet because of the aesthetic or quasi-religious commitment to nature itself, or an exclusivism which seeks to keep nature for itself, advocates of the biocentric viewpoint who close themselves to other viewpoints find it impossible to accept opposing value statements. It is quite possible to value nature and not seek to protect each and every species. In the case of a discussion of endangered species, some appreciation of the multitude of all species and their evolving character must be kept in mind.[4] There are well over one million species of animals (not including insects), over two hundred thousand plant species (a much larger number of lower plants such as fungi and bacteria are counted), and perhaps two to three million insect species either known and cataloged or estimated conservatively. These species have survived thousands of years of struggle for survival, including natural catastrophes and the effects of human economic developments.

The very least that can be said about the quantity and multifarious variety of nature is that it seems to be very difficult to stamp it out. Nor is it likely that very many wonderful and admirable species can be saved from extinction, if for no other reason than that they always have been accustomed to doing each other in. Consider the ice age, which wiped out entire continents of species.

The question of nature's right to life has to be considered in the context of biological competition and an evolving universe,[5] even if one grants what David Brower calls "the rights of creatures other than man" or if one feels the scientific and aesthetic need to preserve as many endangered species as possible. Predator-prey relationships were known aeons before ecological literature popularized them. For

---

[4] D. Goodman, "Ecological Expertise," in *Boundaries of Analysis*, ed. H. A. Feiveson, F. W. Sinden, and R. H. Socolow (Cambridge, Mass.: Ballinger, 1975), pp. 317–360.

[5] L. B. Slobodkin, "The Strategy of Evolution," *American Scientist* 52 (1964): 342–357.

that matter, it has long been known that there may be several predators after the same prey, fighting for food and space. The evolutionary
result provides at least a temporary advantage to the victor, while
other species evolve to challenge the winners. In the meantime, there
may be not the slightest trace of the myriads that lost.

Since the assumptions of the biocentric argument are quasi-
religious, undoubtedly bolstered by Albert Schweitzer's principle of
"reverence for life" (each creature intrinsically valuable), the emphasis of biocentric advocates has tended to be concern with the loss of
individual species or objects of nature in themselves rather than the
rate at which species are being lost. The extremely important question
here revolves around the acceleration of the rate of extinction of
(known) species in the present century (as objects of commercial
exploitation for furs, shoes, and handbags, for example) and the
pragmatic consequences of the acceleration—the important implications of a genetic reservoir for science, for agriculture, and even for
domesticated animal species, and new possibilities for medicinal use
and less toxic industrial or energy uses. As more land is plowed up,
continued overgrazing is permitted, and pesticides and sprays are used
to kill ever-growing numbers of wild flowers (weeds) along with insects. Entire habitats are being wiped out, and their variety diminishes year by year.

In testimony before a 1978 congressional subcommittee which
was reviewing a revision of the Endangered Species Act, Michael
Bean of the Environmental Defense Fund pointed out that many
species once appeared worthless, and later important uses were found
for them. One plant provided the chemical (later derived synthetically) which was found to work in birth control; the blood of the
horseshoe crab can detect toxins in the intravenous fluids used in
medicines; and since the armadillo is the only species besides man
which contracts leprosy, it no doubt will "furnish the vehicle for the
development of a leprosy vaccine," Mr. Bean argued.

The biocentric argument can go in many directions, since it begins as a generalized statement of value. The strength of the position
in the "marketplace of ideas" depends on its openness to more pragmatic lines of thought, since the value statements of the opposition

can rely on "hard" economic facts against its "soft" values. Yet those who value life and nature highly have been able to precipitate a questioning of the fundamental structure of a society based on purely economic values. Buoyed by their successes, they have often placed undue emphasis on objects of nature rather than the dangerous effects of an accelerated rate of extinction. If preservationists demand that others accept their values instead of reasoned arguments, the response is bound to come in the form of another demanding value statement.

The Ecological Model

Ecologists start their investigations with a model of something like a stable system—a certain mix of species of plants and animals along with particular natural conditions like temperature, humidity, and soil structure which is in or near a state of equilibrium. After reaching a certain level—sometimes called a climax or mature state—the system maintains itself by homeostatic regulatory mechanisms. The model indicates how the system establishes itself in static or dynamic equilibrium: energy received and flowing through the system, wastes recycled, and other elements in balance. Such a system is perceived by the ecologists to be diverse and stable until some outside force disrupts its capacity to regenerate itself.

What often happens in the books of environmental ecologists who pick up the ecological method and perspective, and even in those of ecologists themselves, is a reification (made static and rigid) of the model. Sooner or later it is made into solid dogma, and exceptions are rarely admitted. Disruption of these stable systems is presented as foreboding dire consequences in many ecologic-environmentalist accounts.

Since scientific language, laws, paradigms, or examples tend to change from generation to generation, an outsider has the right to question the validity of the ecological model. How exact is the ecological expression of what is supposed to be happening in nature? The presumption implicit in most environmental writings is that they are presenting the scientific truth of nature; yet other scientists admit that scientific expression provides only a flimsy analogy of the complexities of nature. Many philosophers, following Hume and Kant, hold that it is either impossible or extremely difficult to interpret the reality of nature with any exactness.

Even on the surface of the ecological argument it is apparent that a great many changes of ecological systems have occurred over the centuries as regional ecologies moved from one state of evolutionary imbalance to another. For example, in the pre-Cambrian period the oxygen cycle itself went through drastic changes as green plants proliferated and opened up possibilities for new ecological systems which led to human development and domination. Later, floods, hurricanes, earthquakes, volcanic eruptions, and glaciers drastically altered ecological systems; fires many times changed them for the better and allowed more diversity. Since a completely balanced ecological state seems to be antievolutionary, such a state does not appear to be even a possibility in reality, models to the contrary notwithstanding.[6]

Rene Dubos takes the argument against naturally stable systems a step further, claiming that "in a given area, there is more than one possible equilibrium state, and there is no evidence that the natural solution is necessarily the best or the most interesting solution. . . . In fact, the symbiotic interplay between man and nature can generate ecosystems more diversified and more interesting than those occurring in the state of wilderness."[7] Dubos rates the beauty and benefits of agricultural lands on the plus side for mankind and points out that natural catastrophes and the inability of nature to recycle fossil fuels prove that "nature doesn't always know best." He could also have said that the people of some places in northern Europe, India, and China have recycled manure wastes for such long periods of time that they have developed their own very rich, man-made soil, in some cases over rock or worthless clay.

These considerations raise questions about the axiom that humans should fit into a predetermined natural ecological cycle or law. That is, how much room do ecological principles allow people to transform their environment? What are the rules for changing the

6 See, for example, C. S. Holling, "Resilience and Stability of Ecosystems," in *Evolution and Consciousness: Human Systems in Transition*, ed. E. Jantsch and C. H. Waddington (Reading: Addison Wesley, 1976), pp. 73–92.

7 R. Dubos, "Humanizing the Earth," *Science* 179 (1973): 770.

environment if one wants to adhere to the ecological model? How much technology, or even agriculture, would be permitted? May humans rebuild any natural ecosystem? What precisely is the man-environment relationship?

Diversity-Stability

What about the diversity-stability hypothesis—the claim (of Commoner and many others) that the more links there are in a system, the more stability there will be? The assertion goes back at least as far as Charles Elton's *The Ecology of Invasions by Plants and Animals*, published in 1958 but based on research which began a generation earlier. Marston Bates came to similar conclusions at the end of *The Forest and the Sea*.[8] Then in 1963 Ramon Margalef stressed the theory that "mature" ecosystems are more stable and diverse than they were in their earlier stages. Since the early 1960s many environmentalists have used these and similar studies to support the stability argument. Although the principles may be true in many cases and circumstances, they are far from absolute. Other studies have shown the following:[9]

1. Diversity does not always increase with succession.
2. Interdependence and interactions of many plant associations within mature communities are far less significant than is usually claimed.
3. Mathematical models have proved a relationship opposite that of Commoner's web; that is, the more factors, the greater the fluctuations in the face of interference, making the system the most vulnerable to failure.
4. Direct ecological evidence has also shown that stable, diverse systems are more vulnerable under stress than simpler ones.

[8] *The Ecology of Invasions by Plants and Animals* (New York: Wiley, 1958), pp. 143–153, 155; *The Forest and the Sea* (New York: Vintage, 1960), p. 261.

[9] D. W. Ehrenfeld, "The Conservation of Non-Resources," *American Scientist* 64 (1976): 651–652. See also *Diversity and Stability in Ecological Systems: Report of Symposium Held May 26–28, 1969*, Brookhaven Symposia in Biology, no. 22 (Upton, N.Y.: Brookhaven National Laboratory, 1969); and R. H. May, *Stability and Complexity of Model Ecosystems* (Princeton: Princeton University Press, 1974).

The reason for emphasis on the importance of diverse ecosystems has been the ability of the idea of diversity to demonstrate the ecological model, particularly with regard to human intervention into natural ecosystems. But the extension of the insight into diversity to the point of universally provoked scientific challenges. (The fact that the ecological model does not provide a ready answer for every environmental issue does not detract from its general validity, however.)

For example, there is no doubt that people are at the top of the food chain. They are the final recipients of unwelcome persistent chemicals stored in fatty tissues. Neither is there any doubt that some chemicals cause serious disease and death. These facts should not lead to an overstatement of the case. One legacy of *Silent Spring* has been the fear that DDT or other persistent chemicals will be ingested by humans, whose bodies will store such chemicals until they sicken and die or pass on mutations. However, foreign substances are discharged as quickly as the bloodstream can carry them away.

There is no need to make the environmental argument artificially stronger than it stands on its own merit. Since *Silent Spring*, a few of Rachel Carson's alarms, such as the dangers of the carcinogenic effects of certain pesticides or the hazard of hepatitis and cirrhosis caused by them, have been strongly questioned. Even Lake Erie seems to be holding its own at the moment instead of lying dead. Yet individual cases do not detract from many valuable notions of the ecological perspective. Human intervention into ecological systems is in fact the basis of the contemporary environmental crisis. If those who hold this viewpoint close themselves off from other possible modes of understanding—if they make their norms into universal laws—their model, exposed to critical challenge, loses the effectiveness it might otherwise have.

Human Ecology

Some ecologists, notably Howard Odum, have carried the ecological model to an extreme. For example, Odum integrates physical, biological, and social systems—microorganisms, plants, animals, humans—through chemical energies which are cycled and recycled through various natural components. In human society language and economic exchanges are measured in terms of physical energy.[10] Such an analysis reduces the human world to the physical-material and raises more problems than it solves.

In *Poverty of Power* Barry Commoner does not descend so far toward the concrete in his methodology, but he does suggest that there must be actual links among what he calls the ecological, the production, and the economic systems. Starting with the second law of thermodynamics, he constructs an analogy between energy and the production and exchange of goods. However, the human institutions of producing and exchanging goods follow patterns which cannot be forced to fit the human-devised constructs of ecology and energy. Carnot's laws of thermodynamics themselves were developed within the confines of a closed steam-power system. Human systems are not closed. In fact, it is difficult to imagine that humans could contrive institutions as efficient as those which Carnot's experiments suggested. Commoner's questionable model integrates physical and human systems; his commitment to this model weakens the formulation of the argument.

Even ecological writings which make looser connections between physical and social systems contain difficulties. S. Z. Klausner has noted that social and natural scientific languages are neither commensurate nor logically compatible because they have different frames of reference.[11] It is one thing to do ecological experiments, with or without the effects of human interference, and to suggest that they reflect the human environment. If so, perhaps they also signal the need to make drastic changes in social life. It is quite another thing to insist that people relate within an ecological system in actual correspondence with the ways the physical and biological components relate.

Population growth analysts like Garrett Hardin also tend to ap-

[10] H. Odum, *Environment, Power and Society* (New York: Wiley, 1971). See also H. Odum and E. C. Odum, *Energy Bases for Man and Nature* (New York: McGraw-Hill, 1976).

[11] S. Z. Klausner, "Some Problems in the Logic of Current Man-Environment Studies," in *Social Behavior, Natural Resources and the Environment*, ed. W. Burch, N. Cheek, and L. Taylor (New York: Harper & Row, 1972), pp. 334–363.

ply mechanical models to explain human interaction.[12] They use images like the following:

1. The commons. Limited space and resources, together with the freedom to breed, lead to the destruction of the commons when overpopulation occurs.
2. The spaceship. Earth has limited resources in an enclosed space.
3. The lifeboat. Only a few who are responsible can fit into the lifeboat.

By using such images, the population growth analysts can show that humans propagate simply because they are capable of doing so, in other words, under the same ecological laws as plants and animals.

Ecologists should not assume that the same pattern of breeding exists for pandas and people alike. A great number of studies correlate high population rates with poverty and reductions of population rates with increases of wealth.[13] Where the death rates and poverty levels are high, parents (rationally) choose to have a large number of children so that the surviving few might be able to care for each other in times of exceptional crisis and in their old age. When parents are able to increase their material security in other ways, they are less inclined to have large families. Therefore, United Nations studies indicate an overpopulation trend at the time of colonization and falling death rates, followed by sometimes dramatically decreasing population rates as material wealth increases among the lower social classes.[14] An "increase of wealth," of course, is simply a shorthand way of indicating that population rise or decline is directly correlated with many other economic, political, and social factors. Population is not an independent variable that determines institutions. Instead, population is itself influenced by economic, political, and social institutions.

A major problem caused by rigid ecological models is that they do not allow for human creativity and response. People can change and have changed social and economic institutions to enhance their survival and life chances. One can certainly sympathize with the de-

[12] G. Hardin, *Exploring New Ethics for Survival* (New York: Viking, 1972).
[13] M. Mamdani, *The Myth of Population Control* (New York: Monthly Review, 1972).
[14] B. Commoner, "How Poverty Breeds Overpopulation," *Ramparts* 13 (1975): 21 ff.

sire to limit dangerously high population rates, but an alarmist ecological reductionism overlooks the unique and unpredictable ability of human beings to adjust—to cope with and respond to serious problems when they are perceived.

The famous "Blueprint for Survival," published by *The Ecologist* in 1972, also discussed problems of planetary survival under the ecological requirements of a stable ecosystem: "The principal conditions of a stable society—one that to all intents and purposes can be sustained indefinitely while giving optimum satisfaction to its members— are: 1) minimum disruption of ecological processes; 2) maximum conservation of materials and energy—or an economy of stock rather than flow; 3) a population in which recruitment equals loss; and 4) a social system in which the individual can enjoy, rather than feel constrained by, the first three conditions."[15]

"Blueprint" places humans under the constraints of an ecological system with little possibility for creative adaptation. Population growth is seen as capable of being contained only by "famine, epidemic, war," and the like; carrying capacity of the land is inherently limited by natural constraints (not broadened by human contrivances); and social ills like crime, delinquency, vandalism, alcoholism, and drug addiction are accelerated by demographic and economic growth.

The report applies ecological assumptions to industrial growth, which "necessarily" demands more natural resources and energy and produces more waste. Then it connects growth with "the industrial way of life" and a "Gross Domestic Product (GDP)—population multiplied by material standard of living." Thus, people are called "homo sapiens industrialis," which pretends to be a biological term that encompasses all social classes: rich and poor, ethnic groups, producers, consumers, and so on. Everyone is expected to consume and waste because everyone is "industrial," and population rates necessarily increase in an industrial way of life. In this scheme of thinking, the crisis point is imminent. That is not an irrational conclusion if one defines social units in ecological terms and substitutes physical for social meanings.

There are other future-oriented projections based on ecosystem

[15] "Blueprint for Survival," *Ecologist* 2 (1972): 8.

models. *Limits to Growth* was a pioneer study that led the way for dozens which have come out since its publication.[16] It links world population, industrialization, pollution, food production, and resource depletion systemically. The study takes a historical data series between 1900 and 1970, and through the application of mathematical systems analysis and the use of a computer it offers a scenario of the future. The report concludes that exponential growth is a systemic property of population and capital increases despite the fact that there are physical limits to both. No data were included in the program for a variety of social responses. In subsequent studies some of the contributors have tried to correct their aggregated figures, which represent large-scale systems.[17] But the fact that little significance was attached to social, political, or other cultural factors indicates the kind of mechanistic reductionism that is difficult to avoid in computer models, ecological or otherwise. Such reductionism calls the models and their forecasts into question.

Nevertheless, it is true that humans are involved inextricably with natural processes, which in turn are dangerously affected by the activities of humans, individually and through their economic and technological institutions—especially those institutions that are expanded for profit. For instance, cancer increases rapidly with industrial pollution, and global weather disturbances may come from increased waste carbon dioxide. It is not so easy to determine, however, to what extent or degree an ecological problem exists and whether nonactivity is a better solution than alternative kinds of action. If ecologists give an exaggerated or inaccurate diagnosis, they will not be given full credence any more than the economist will. In many cases, it would be preferable to eliminate the use of *ecology* as a catchword.

Utilitarian Conservationists

From the days of John Muir himself, conservationists have tended to distrust anyone, including other conservationists, who have

16 D. H. Meadows, D. L. Meadows, J. Randers, and W. W. Behrens (New York: Universe, 1972).

17 M. Mesarovic and E. Pestal, *Mankind at the Turning Point* (New York: Signet, 1976).

tended to think economically about the natural environment in terms of resources or commodities. The old Progressivist conservation principles espoused by Pinchot and his successors had a deadly economic ring to them. They spoke for "use of natural resources for the benefit of all the people now, not just the few, or for future generations; for the preservation of waste; for the greatest good of the greatest number for the longest time."

Preservationists, it turned out, had reason to distrust the utilitarians, for the only way that the early conservationists felt they could balance the conflicting multiple claims on the natural environment was through the application of an economic calculus.[18] During the history of the Forest Service the "highest" use of a natural environment generally took the course of the highest dollar value put on the environment in question, usually because corporate interests were standing just behind the executive branch and its agencies and even closer to the new states of the West, where so much wealth in natural resources existed. In the past few decades benefit-cost ratios have been developed and weighted on the side of development for a variety of reasons: pork-barreling, increasing dollar income, making and keeping connections with development interests, and even promoting high-minded motives.

Of course conservationists of all sorts, including preservationists, have also used economic tactics to accomplish their purpose.[19] If they want to preserve a particular area, as has the Sierra Club during much of its history, they make certain that aesthetic (scenic) and recreational (hiking, camping, hunting) *values* (even values to preserve mental health) are factored into the ratio. Other potential economic values have been found for theretofore commonplace activities or items such as natural history study, undeveloped resource value (for example, potential oil from desert shrubs or the jojoba bean), ecosystem stabilizing values (versus monoculture forestry practices), and habitat reconstruction. In all such cases an economic value is sought in order to preserve pieces of the natural environment. Perhaps be-

[18] G. McConnell, "The Conservation Movement—Past and Present," *Western Political Quarterly* 7 (1954): 463–478. See also S. P. Hayes, *Conservation and the Gospel of Efficiency* (Cambridge, Mass.: Harvard University Press, 1959).

[19] Ehrenfeld, "Conservation of Non-Resources," p. 652.

cause of historical precedent or the adversary system, or insecurity with other types of argument, environmentalists have felt constrained to stretch a point—putting dollar values on unquantifiable values—almost beyond belief. The question of who is convinced by these quantified schemes remains moot.

Environmental Economists

Environmental economists are much more serious about the economic model, perhaps too serious if they would consider the results it brings. For the tax, enforcement, or technological environmental fixes all have serious limitations as solutions to pollution problems. Most of the time it is impossible to determine the total damage done by pollution. The more data is collected, the less is the certainty. By the time any kind of certitude is reached, the damage could be so widespread or irreversible that no assessment would be possible. The problem applies to all forms of pollution—including noise. The marketing of thousands of new synthetic substances each year increases pollution still more. Taxes, enforcement laws, and technologies do not touch problems like bronchial diseases, coronary diseases, nervous diseases, and the many types of cancer (all of which no doubt are also caused by other factors besides environmental pollution). Furthermore, the incidental costs which pay for the administration of taxes and controls often exceed the very considerable costs of controls themselves. Should all taxpayers be forced to pay for administration, or only the consumers of the products of polluting industries? The fundamental question deals with the definition of damage. Is damage the sum of money victims are willing to pay to reduce pollution, or is it the sum of money victims would demand for pollution abatement?[20] The economists of environmental pollution have some distance to go before they achieve an adequate economic calculus.

Even the economic argument of Krutilla and Fisher is not so powerful as it first appears. Although the approach places a high value on many natural environments in themselves, others have ques-

---

[20] R. B. Norgaard and D. C. Hall, "Environmental Amenity Rights, Transaction Cost and Technological Change," *Journal of Environmental Economics and Management* 1 (1974): 257–261.

tioned the value as amenities of these special environments, since such experiences of nature seem to be reproducible.[21] It might be better for environmentalists to admit frankly that in some cases great economic loss will result if certain areas are taken out of natural resource production. For instance, consider the Santa Barbara Channel. And it is also conceivable that other areas are not worth (collective) preservation because they are relatively inaccessible.

Krutilla's point about irreversibility depends on the possibility of substitutes whose future availability is as difficult to know in the present as are the proclivities of future citizens. They someday might want to preserve some natural environments which we have already despoiled. Krutilla and others of like mind are telling the policy planners that they or their descendants might regret it if they let development occur. (But then they might not. It is impossible to know what any of us will want in the future.) Even though the practical implementation of the Krutilla-Fisher suggestion does not seem to be possible, and although some debate would undoubtedly occur over special applications, it at least forces the consideration of possible future consequences of an ecological action.

Environmental problems are simply not always quantifiable. The economic model might be considered in the same way as wilderness appreciation and the ecologic approach have been described, as a "state of mind." The economic state of mind wants to find completely rational solutions in a less than rational world and economic precision where values are imprecise. The preferences or choices (values) of consumers (say, for preservation) or even their "welfare" (environmental compensation) can only be wildly guessed at even in a science that tries to be exact. The efforts of environmental economists have helped improve many environments. But it is small wonder that they have a difficult time reaching agreement over a suitable approach.

So long as conventional economics is concerned only with individual choices that can be quantified into monetary values, it will have limited usefulness in the solutions of environmental questions, particularly where values (quasi-religious, natural-law, aesthetic, or contemplative) cannot be assigned monetary weightings. Moreover, individ-

[21] M. J. Krieger, "What's Wrong with Plastic Trees?" *Science* 179 (1973): 448.

ual considerations (or the sum of individual economic preferences) with which economics is most comfortable cannot be logically ordered into rational social policies, as Kenneth Arrow states in his "general impossibility theorem."[22] The numerical neatness of economics with "objective" costs and benefits simply cannot be forced into the political arena where public decisions, social costs or benefits, and values are fought out in democratic societies.

Furthermore, pollution taxes or subsidies simply cannot account for undetected impacts of many pollutants. As we shall discuss in a later chapter, some long-term efforts of exposure to a pollutant can cause disease and death. Would increased wages to a coke worker compensate for lung cancer? How much is land worth after it has been subjected to radiation and removed from accessibility for twenty thousand or more years?

Another difficulty comes from the origins of economics itself in the development of capitalist societies. If undifferentiated capital expansion necessarily takes its toll on the environment, and economics cannot distinguish between types of capital (a value question) and the types of commodities that capital produces, then economics is less than suited as a scientific discipline. Economics cannot then point the way to states of environmental quality and social equality. Yet the economic viewpoint seems to be needed both by advocates of continued capital expansion and by those who would oppose the effects of such expansion.

The purpose of the discussion above has been to illustrate how assumptions, methodologies, and ideologies can influence one's argument. Such influence is usually obvious in the case of class interests for or against environmentalism. It is less so in the case of the quasi-religious commitments of biocentrism. Ecological arguments tend to get stuck in the logic of closed natural-law systems, and proposals for economic efficiency do not necessarily work for environmentalist goals.

Nevertheless, the environmental movement has been strong because people with different values and perspectives have been able to join forces for environmental protection of land and other causes.

[22] K. J. Arrow, *Social Choice and Individual Values* (New York: Wiley, 1963).

It has been of tactical importance that environmentalists have been able to identify those biocentric (contemplative, aesthetic), ecological, and economic (utilitarian, functional, recreational) values of open space in order to gain public support. Hundreds of surveys throughout the country have confirmed that such values and culturally shaped attitudes are widespread and have been instrumental particularly in the preservation of open space.[23]

Significant Environments

Unfortunately, environmentalists cannot always illustrate contemplative, ecological, or utilitarian values, and they have been forced to admit that some areas of the natural environment deserve preservation for no other reason than that they are in some way "significant." The argument is related to those used to defend the Grand Canyon, Hells Canyon, and Dinosaur National Monument. But in many other cases environmentalists cannot point to anything spectacular at all about the land they are defending.

For example, the western deserts traditionally have been, like the early American forests, considered more of an obstacle to be crossed quickly than anything of worth. The unstable desert ecologies have recently begun to crumble under the relentless and ever-broadening attack of motorcycles, dune buggies, Jeeps, and other off-road vehicles which, according to a 1968 Bureau of Land Management report, "rip out [rare] vegetation and tear up soil. . . . Quail, chukar partridge, and deer live in the hills. Their forage is damaged. During the nesting season, birds are flushed from their nests. Young birds are scattered, increasing their chance of natural mortality." Natural scientists find fewer and fewer examples of rare desert biota—birds, mammals, reptiles, amphibians, plants, cacti—and more and more sheet and gully erosion resulting from tire tracks. Does the desert contain enough environmental significance to be protected from those who exercise their recreational rights by racing motorcycles after a week of hard work?

Under multiple-use policies, the Bureau of Land Management,

[23] D. Perry, "Preservation of Open Space and the Concept of Value," *American Journal of Economics and Sociology* 35 (1976): 113–124.

which has control over 452 million acres of western lands, has tried to reconcile the concerns of bikers and environmentalists. The Environmental Defense Fund and the Sierra Club have gained much support for their viewpoint by showing that many sections of the desert environment are significant because they are rare, not necessarily because they are economically valuable. Some areas with fossil beds of camels, saber-toothed cats, three-toed horses, and mastodons and with prehistoric Native American rock art, pottery, stone tools and weapons, hearth sites, sleeping circles, trails, and other desert archeological sites have already been destroyed by off-road vehicles. Environmentalists who want to stop such destruction refer to the unique nature of each element, not to the value of the land in the usual sense.

Another lesser-known effort along the same lines dealt with a rare ecological environment on the California coast—Jug Handle Creek staircase and pygmy forest in Mendocino County. Terraces have been formed out of the seas over a period of hundreds of thousands of years in five long steps, each about one hundred feet higher and one hundred thousand years older than the one below it and each nurturing a unique and significant ecological environment. The phenomenon provides a striking demonstration of glacial activity during the Pleistocene ice age, and it also displays processes of ecological succession, the highest level of which contain a unique pygmy forest formed slowly out of the sea one-half million years ago.

In a 1960 *Sierra Club Bulletin* Professor Hans Jenny pointed out that some ecosystems need protection, not because of aesthetic, recreational, wilderness, or economic qualities but because they are significant unique environments. He showed that the Mendocino staircase was a good example of such an ecosystem, and with his wife and a group of others he worked for many years to save the area from a million-dollar motel complex. After the successful completion of that struggle, Hans and Jean Jenny organized the Significant Natural Areas Involvement League (SNAIL), made up largely of California Native Plant Society members and other preservationists. The acronym describes, they say, the pace at which environmentalism progresses. In one project they worked with Mendocino County residents to stop nickel mining from remote Red Mountain. Dr. Jenny has shown that the reddish soils (and the vegetation on them) are unique, rich in kaolinite and iron oxides that give rise to unusual absorptive properties for water and nutrients, such as fixation of phosphates. His point is that nickel may be obtained at dozens of locations, but the particular mix of climate, soils, and plant and animal life on Red Mountain is extremely rare. Both of the Mendocino environments have obvious scientific value, but the argument which has gained legal and public support is a value judgment that the areas are unique and significant in themselves.

Many other natural environments could be classified as significant and rare: salt marshes, barrier islands, other wetlands, places with unusual soils which support rare plants. The type of value statements based on uniqueness either gains or loses public support in itself. It is clear and it does not depend on peripheral economic or ecologic data (though the latter are obviously connected to the argument).

The point of view that considers the intrinsic values of the environment has much to recommend it, because it takes each situation case by case without prejudgment from a predetermined environmental position. The value statement is clear and open. It tends not to be dogmatic or exclusive, and its sources are biocentric, ecologic, and aesthetic. Even an economic argument like Krutilla's could support it.

Of course the class of significant environments is much broader than the few cases cited above. For example, every soil type can theoretically be considered significant because there is no other group of soils like it. More important, soil types have undergone more rapid rates of depletion or extinction than plants and animals, most especially during the past century when agriculture has become widely mechanized.

It is not necessary for an environment to be small to be considered significant, nor must it be confined to a single species. Conservationists throughout the world (as illustrated by an international program directed by UNESCO) are more and more indicating how entire ecosystems, huge tracts with all their plant and animal species, should be isolated from all human activity so that wildlife can evolve as though humans never appeared. This policy is quite different from species preservation or wildlife and land management common in the United States. Such huge reserves have already been established in

Australia as well as the Soviet Union (over 4.3 million hectares in sixty-eight reserves). Setting up such reserves seems to be a sensible policy response to the problem of exponential species depletion.

Historically in the United States, large tracts of land have been set aside more because they were unwanted by timber and mining interests than because of a national policy of ecological preservation. In early 1979 the U.S. Forest Service recommended that 5.5 million acres of land in Alaska be placed in the country's wilderness system; at the same time, President Carter designated 56 million acres as national monuments. Although the land was unclaimed wilderness in inaccessible regions, a "monumental" furor was created by interest groups in both the private and the public sectors. In any case ecological considerations played little or no role in the choice of designated areas.

The question of significant environments is raised because environmentalists have begun to sort out issues based on priorities beyond simple biocentric, ecologic, and economic assumptions and to employ arguments encompassing data from wider criteria. These priorities include two other broad classes of environmental problems in which environmentalists of all perspectives have shared concern and struggles—those involving growth and risk. Furthermore, conceptual movement toward a broader critical understanding has penetrated the domain of "environmental ethics" discussed in the final chapter of this book.

7

Growth and Decay

ANOTHER slice of environmental consciousness cuts across all three positions—biocentric, ecologic, and economic. It eschews materialist commercial values. It also fears and warns against unstable, uncontrolled, irrational growth of ecosystems. This conjunction of environmental thinking perhaps can be termed antigrowth, but a wide range of perceptions of the problem (which go beyond the population question or economic growth) and many varieties of active participation in the movement preclude easy generalization about its name, precursors, successes, limitations, and values.

Antigrowth environmental philosophy is more of a reaction to developments in western culture than a positive philosophy. By the turn of the century in the United States nearly every voice was raised against the ugly faces of the mills and the grime of the cities, but no universal scapegoat could be agreed upon. Progressives, anarchists, socialists, reformers, churchmen, and other commentators prescribed short- and long-term remedies. Some blamed the capitalist economy; very few pointed the finger at economic growth in itself. Whatever solution anybody proposed, it nearly always included or assumed more material development, which was identified with progress. It took a century, a few persevering prophets, and the blending of other environmental ideas into its message for the antigrowth sensitivity to precipitate in environmentalism.

One of its first modern spokesmen was Lewis Mumford. His ideas have found their way directly or indirectly into a score of environmentalist writings. One of his most common themes is the tyranny of technology. In the 1920s and 1930s Mumford wrote about nine-teenth-century America, when a simple life and rich culture were not overwhelmed by what he later termed the *Megamachine*.[1] During that period, Patrick Geddes, a Scotsman who wrote on the development of cities, was an important influence on Mumford, who began to see cities as barometers of the quality of life. (The impact of the "garden city" concept of Englishman Ebenezer Howard was beginning to be felt in the United States. Mumford agreed with garden cities.)

Geddes used the term *megalopolis* in the pejorative sense. Mumford picked up this usage. Geddes first emphasized the impact of technology, a referent also developed by Mumford in *Technics and Civilization*. Combining the ideas of Geddes and Howard, Mumford proposed an antidote to the evil megalopolis. It would be a planned garden city, surrounded by a greenbelt, where necessary work could be isolated but still within reach of the workers.[2] Mumford even did a series of films on the history of the city, with the garden city idea as his conclusion.

In *Technics* Mumford invented new terms to illustrate the impact of technologies and their energy sources on the natural environment and civilization in general: *ecotechnic* for the ages of wind and water, *paleotechnic* for the age of coal, and *neotechnic* for the emerging technologies of the twentieth century. In each case he attempted to prove how energy and technology shape or change social and cultural relationships.

In most of his writings Mumford interprets history to show how the world got into its present situation. *The Pentagon of Power* represents a lifetime of reflection on the problem of growth and its technological progeny. He castigates the early exponents of the scientific world view for conceptually subjugating culture with their rationalizations and reductionism. He points out the fallacies of progress and its technological apparatus, and he laments the homogenization of a

---

[1] D. H. Fleming, "Roots of the New Conservation Movement," in *The House of Life*, ed. P. Brooks (Boston: Houghlin Mifflin, 1972), pp. 74–91. See also W. Kuhns, *The Post-Industrial Prophets: Interpretations of Technology* (New York: Weybright and Talley, 1971), pp. 32–64.

[2] L. Mumford, *Technics and Civilization* (New York: Harcourt, Brace and Co., 1934). See also L. Mumford, *The Pentagon of Power* (New York: Harcourt Brace Jovanovich, 1970).

culture based on economic rationality and standardization. Mumford concludes that western civilization has married, for better but especially for worse, the Megamachine.

By the 1950s the effects of the automobile, economic growth, and the consumerist society gained Mumford, who regularly excoriated the automobile for what it brought to western culture, a number of converts. The same was true of Paul Goodman, who had begun to write on questions of quality of life and technology. A widely recognized thinker, John Kenneth Galbraith, wrote in 1958:

> The family which takes its mauve and cerise, air-conditioned, power-steered, and power-braked automobile out for a tour passes through cities that are badly paved, made hideous by litter, blighted buildings, billboards, and posts for wires that should long since have been put underground. They pass on into a countryside that has been rendered largely invisible by commercial art. (The goods which the latter advertise have an absolute priority in our value system. On such matters we are consistent.) They picnic on exquisitely packaged food from a portable ice box by a polluted stream and go on to spend the night at a park which is a menace to public health and morals. Just before dozing off on an air mattress, beneath a nylon tent, amid the stench of decaying refuse, they may reflect on the curious unevenness of their blessings. Is this, indeed, the American genius?[3]

Galbraith goes on to illustrate that these "benefits" came in the wake of a steadily rising gross national product and a steadily heating American economy. In the 1960s other economists, notably Kenneth Boulding and Ezra J. Mishan, continued the discussion on the effects of growth. Boulding mainly has emphasized the exponential depletion of natural resources in the world, characterizing capitalist economies as "mines to dumps" or "cowboy" economies and popularizing with Barbara Ward the concept of Spaceship Earth.[4]

Mishan's *The Costs of Economic Growth* brought the full force of the antigrowth argument to readers who were not as yet completely prepared for it. He placed the full blame for the deterioration of the environment on economic growth, and with great intensity he blamed the rich for creating an unlivable environment in the cities and then

[3] J. K. Galbraith, *The Affluent Society* (New York: New American Library, 1958), pp. 199–200.

[4] K. Boulding, "Fun and Games with the Gross National Product," in *The Environmental Crisis*, ed. H. W. Helfrich (New Haven: Yale University Press, 1970). See also K. Boulding, "The Economics of the Coming Spaceship Earth,"

leaving them for greener places. Mishan especially blamed automobiles and airplanes for noise pollution, congestion, fumes, destruction of the landscape, and even mass tourism.[5] Another theme repeated by Mishan in other writings is that there is need in modern capitalism to create dissatisfactions and new needs through the advertising industry to maintain the pace of economic growth.[6] The results are waste, pollution, destruction of natural beauty, noise, and enslavement to commodities. Thus, Mishan was tabbed the "father of modern antigrowthmen" in the epilogue of the 1973 *Daedalus* issue on "The No-Growth Society."

The most popular of the antigrowthmen of the 1970s was the late E. F. Schumacher, who published a collection of loosely connected essays in 1973 under the title of *Small is Beautiful*, subtitled *Economics As If People Mattered*. The thrust of his argument was that society's heavy commitment to economic growth, high technology, pompous scientism, and materialistic consumerism has brought social and environmental catastrophe. The drift of the book follows much in the Mumford tradition, especially repeating a number of Mumford's ideas regarding technology. Schumacher, however, was mostly concerned about the loss of "intermediate technology."[7] Economic growth has forced society to choose either primitive tools or exorbitant capital-intensive technology. Therefore, to create meaningful, small-scale employment and to control environmental impact, he created the Intermediate Technology Development Group. This organization still exists. It designs and develops technologies for small-scale, face-to-face economic and social systems. (Energy efficiency in the work units has also represented an important goal of intermediate technology advocates.)

---

in *Environmental Quality in a Growing Economy*, ed. H. Jarrett (Baltimore: Johns Hopkins, 1966); and K. Boulding, "The Shadow of the Stationary State," *Daedalus*, Fall, 1973.

[5] E. J. Mishan, *The Costs of Economic Growth* (New York: Praeger, 1967).

[6] E. J. Mishan, "Ills, Bads, and Disamenities," in *Daedalus*, Fall, 1973. See also E. J. Mishan, *The Economic Growth Debate* (London: George Allen and Unwin, 1977).

[7] E. F. Schumacher, *Small is Beautiful: Economics As If People Mattered* (New York: Harper & Row, 1973).

Energy Development

Central to the problem of growth has been that of energy production, which doubled every ten years from 1850 to 1910 in the United States. It fluctuated until the 1940s. Since then, electrical production, the more recently used energy indicator, has continued doubling every decade. The pattern of doubling has been referred to as exponential growth. Exponential growth is a term environmentalists have used to emphasize both rapidly depleting natural resources and accelerating environmental degradation.

In the United States in 1975 an enormous amount of energy was used—68.8 units measured in 10^{15} British thermal units (BTUs)—over half of which was unusable, rejected, or lost through inefficiency or waste. Despite oil and natural gas shortages, an explicit "go-slow" federal policy, and a slackened period of energy use in 1973, energy consumption began to climb again from 1974 to 1977. In order to meet the demand, government, utilities, and industry planners have developed blueprints for "energy parks" with clusters of five to forty nuclear and coal-fired plants constructed in each giant complex. About two dozen of these "parks" are projected to be built by the end of the 1980s. The reason for the energy clusters is economic. It is easier to raise capital for them, more efficient to hire labor, and simpler to coordinate energy production. The environmental effects, of course, are compounded in proportion to the size of each cluster, in terms of heat waste, air pollution, and the consumption of hundreds of millions of gallons of water every day. The cost of the parks would run well over one hundred billion dollars, but the plan has been waiting for congressional approval of loan guarantees for several years since the beginning of Project Independence. The plan already has much support because of its alleged efficiency, yet its future remains in doubt because local organizations work against its implementation. Also, national politics have changed somewhat.

What is significant about the energy park proposal, which is still a real possibility, is that it pinpoints the issue of growth and concentrates the forces of those opposed to it. For example, the energy parks would use up large tracts of land and water—thousands of rural acres. They would create new cities of workers to construct and maintain the facilities. This kind of development is repugnant to environmentalists of all stripes, both for what it represents ideologically and for its concrete impacts on land and water resources.

The Four Corners area in northwestern New Mexico is a mini-example of what one of these parks would look like. It was a prototype for six other generating complexes to be built in the Southwest.[8] Coal strip-mined at nearby Black Mesa on the Hopi Indian Reservation in northeastern Arizona is ground to a powder and mixed with well water at the rate of 2,700 gallons a minute. It is then fed to the Mojave power plant 275 miles away at the tip of Nevada. Other coal from Black Mesa is carried by rail 80 miles to the Navajo power plant in northern Arizona near Lake Powell.

Four Corners started operations in 1963. It has its own supply of coal and is now the largest coal-burning facility in the United States. Technological advances in both extra-high-voltage transmission lines and strip mining equipment were influential in the decision to build plants at Four Corners.

The rationale for building power plants in the Southwest in the 1950s was booming economic growth. This growth included industrial development in the desert and more tract houses for the expanding Los Angeles and Phoenix regions. Even Las Vegas put in a claim for more electricity to brighten the desert night sky with more neon lights.

The new power plants have accomplished their purposes. Four Corners alone generates more than 2.25 million kilowatt hours. Los Angeles, Phoenix, and Las Vegas have expanded. Industry has doubled in the desert. The costs in terms of environmental pollution have been the several tons of coal wastes—sulfur, nitrogen oxides, and ash—that are thrown into the air every day: more ash and soot than all New York and Los Angeles sources combined can generate. Visibility is severely limited. Clear air is gone. Vegetation is attacked or changed by sulfur emissions which are often combined with water vapor into sulfuric acid. Human health problems occur among Indians on reservations and others in a one-hundred-mile radius who are seriously affected by higher incidences of acute and respiratory ailments.

[8] L. A. McHugh, "The Four Corners Power Complex: Pollution on the Reservations," *Indiana Law Review* 47 (1972): 704–724.

The plume of pollutants from the Four Corners generating plant can be seen from orbiting space vehicles.

Four Corners has become a celebrated case and a symbol of the worst aspects of American growth. Environmental groups of the Southwest—the Sierra Club, Friends of the Earth, and others—closed ranks. David Brower came out with one of his group's eye-opening ads, quoting the words of a young Hopi, who said building Four Corners was "like ripping apart St. Peter's in order to sell the marble."

Of course the environmentalists did not stop economic growth or power-plant production. Seven power facilities are still operating in Nevada, Arizona, and New Mexico. Coal is still being stripped from Black Mesa and other locations in the Southwest, but environmentalists (with energetic support from actor Robert Redford) stopped the construction of the billion-dollar Kaiparowits coal-fired plant in southern Utah near dozens of national parks, monuments, and recreational areas. But despite strong environmentalist opposition, this region of the Colorado Plateau—southern Colorado and Utah and northern Arizona and New Mexico—remains a prime site for development. Cheap, strippable coal is abundant. Enough water is present for cooling and for transporting coal through slurry lines as long as this use for it takes precedence over others. Land is cheap to lease or buy from federal or state governments. Land use and plant-siting state laws favor industrial development. Pollution is spread over a wide area by means of tall smokestacks, thus diluting the ash and emissions enough to conform to requirements at the site itself. Both energy parks and coal gasification plants would have been constructed in this region in 1975 if Congress had approved loan guarantees.

The Coal Rush

Federal energy advisors have agreed with utilities and industry that development of coal is a key element in a future energy program. Although the history of underground coal mines is grim—accidents, black lung, pollution of the water table, long-lived fires, land subsidence—and although strip mining leaves water supplies or rivers charged with acidity and silt, even where land is reclaimed, and although coal burning takes a heavy toll on the U.S. natural environ-

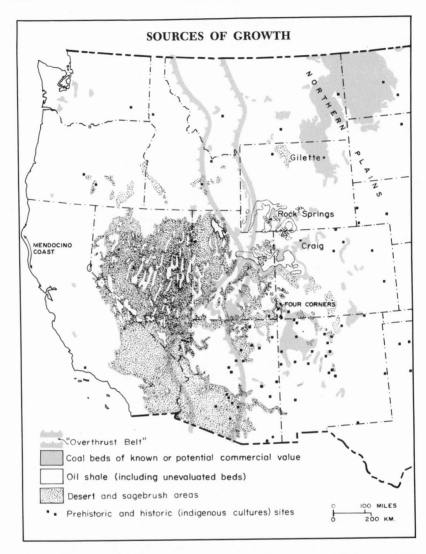

SOURCES OF GROWTH

"Overthrust Belt"

Coal beds of known or potential commercial value

Oil shale (including unevaluated beds)

Desert and sagebrush areas

Prehistoric and historic (indigenous cultures) sites

Since Project Independence was articulated in 1973, national efforts have been directed toward making the United States self-sufficient in terms of energy sources. The quickest route toward the accomplishment of that goal is the exploitation of the thick, shallow deposits of coal and oil shale from the western states. Natural gas and oil are believed to be trapped among the faults and folds of the Overthrust Belt, which spans the continent from Alaska through Arizona. The loss of tranquility in small towns and of the fragile eco-systems of significant natural environments might be part of the price the nation must pay for high energy use.

ment with millions of tons of ash and sulfur dioxide sent into the sky each year, coal remains the country's most economical energy resource.

National reserves of clean natural gas will begin to decline by the 1980s, current U.S. oil reserves will not last more than a few generations, and nuclear energy has become problematic. Thus, there is a rush to exploit the 3.2 trillion tons of coal under the lower continental United States. About 70 billion tons of it can be found in the four states of the Colorado Plateau, along with the Dakotas, Wyoming, and Montana, lying in thick seams near the surface soil, which is easily scraped off by mammoth earth-moving equipment to expose the coal. Coal is so abundant that because of the oil crisis in the early 1970s the head of the Federal Energy Administration ordered 155 major oil- and gas-burning units to switch to coal, and the dozens of new facilities will also burn coal in the future. Energy planners also expect that about half the 300 million tons mined each year will be transformed into quadrillions of cubic feet of gas.

Coal gasification is an old idea going back to nineteenth-century coke making, when the gas by-product was sold for home heating and steel furnaces. The process now—changing coal to gas by adding hydrogen in the form of steam—is still in development stages, but all such techniques require immense amounts of energy in the form of intense heat and pressure and vast amounts of water. Various production steps create hydrogen-rich gas and then purify the mixture (by methanation) to enhance its heating capacity.

The federal Department of Energy is supporting research in coal gasification as a high-priority investigation. The largest coal deposits for energy development lie in Montana, Wyoming, and the western Dakotas, according to the Bureau of Reclamation's North Central Power Study. The thickness of the seams (seventy to two hundred feet) makes the region's deposits especially desirable. (In eastern mines, five feet is considered exceptionally thick.)

The study recommended the construction of forty-two power plants in eastern Montana, to burn forty-two million tons of coal from the area a year, and a complex of dams, reservoirs, and aqueducts for storing and delivering water for boilers at the power plants and for coal gasification plants. Most of the entire water supply from the Yellowstone River in Montana, and much of the water from the Missouri River in North Dakota, has long since been requested by large private firms, water companies, and utilities for the plants.

In 1974 a team from the National Academy of Science reported that electrification and gasification in the northern plains pose "staggering" water problems which effectively eliminate or preclude agricultural development. A plant producing 250 million cubic feet of gas a day would need about 30 million gallons of water for the day, about half the amount required for a conventional steam power plant. The Department of the Interior is leasing hundreds of thousands of acres to those large firms which can afford the enormous capital costs for strip mining equipment. The smaller ranches are offered lucrative leasing agreements as well. The country has already begun to exploit these regions for coal. The question is, which local areas will be developed first (to provide energy for other areas)? Also, how and when will the accompanying social and environmental costs be dealt with? Massive energy development will not be an abstract issue to you (as it seems to be in Washington), if yours is the region where coal, oil, nuclear, or energy park development is planned. Few areas of the country will be untouched, from port cities to grazing lands.

Local Skirmishes

The sudden demand for energy from the East, South, and Far West has threatened to tear apart the previously tranquil, sometimes sleepy, economy of the northern Great Plains. Most of the towns in the vicinity of the new black treasure are small, so the financial impact of coal and industrial development can double or triple their populations. A rapid shift from an agricultural-grazing structure to an industrial structure can also crush the social viability of the traditional towns.[9]

Colstrip, Montana, was one of the first new coal boomtowns.[10]

[9] K. R. Toole, *The Rape of the Great Plains: Northwest American Cattle and Coal* (Boston: Little, Brown, 1976). See also G. Atwood, "The Strip Mining of Western Coal" *Scientific American* 233 (1975): 23–29.

[10] L. Gapay, "Western States Begin to Worry over Push for Sources for Power," *Wall Street Journal*, January 4, 1975.

There was an influx of workers and subsidiary suppliers. The mining companies brought huge stripping equipment, and the operators brought hundreds of trailer homes, new drive-in liquor stores, and, ultimately, the newly constructed power plants with smokestacks almost as tall as the Empire State Building. All these things were soon surrounding a tiny town with a few stores, houses, and a school house. Ranchers and farmers near Colstrip were confronted by "No Trespassing" signs around their homes, while immigrant teenagers on motorcycles chased their calves, cars sped by their houses and through their meadows, and strangers wandered past their barns, as K. R. Toole reports from Montana. Land speculators bid up the price of land, played neighboring ranchers against one another, and pitted long-time friends against each other over the advantages and disadvantages of coal development. Whatever sense of community was present in the past in many of these towns was lost soon after the arrival of the coal promoters.

Not only do the new coal towns bring a massive influx of new people—Colstrip went from a few hundred to nearly four thousand in a few years and reached seven thousand by the end of the 1970s— but also consequent health, housing, education, and crime problems. At Colstrip, trailers are crammed into a small area without pavement or landscaping. Only a few medical or professional people want to live there; one nurse does most of the medical work; schools are overcrowded. The crime rate doubled in one year. Inevitable air pollution came with the power plants. Long-time residents and newcomers alike must support the new economic vitality in the form of school bonds and rapid rises in property taxes.

Gillette, Wyoming, represents another case study just across the border from Montana in the northern part of the state.[11] By 1980 Gillette and its surrounding county are expected to produce almost 109 million tons of coal a year from their hundred-foot seams of coal. The area is also a ranching community which doubled in population between 1960 and 1970 to seven thousand people; then increased another 55 percent between 1970 and 1975, up to eleven thousand, three times the 1960 figure; and was continuing its rapid

[11] D. S. Whipple, "The Social Costs of Coal," *Environmental Action,* September 11, 1976, pp. 3–8.

growth rate in 1977 when the population was over twelve thousand people.

Trailers also surround and penetrate Gillette; its schools and hospitals are overflowing; few doctors are interested in moving there. The county had a seven-million-dollar school bond debt by 1977; it had none in 1968. Rock Springs, Wyoming, is experiencing similar growth pains. Craig, Colorado, had advance warning about the effects of new development, but it could not adequately prepare for the impact, either. Its population doubled in two years.

The *Wall Street Journal* summarized the history of the 1970s in northwest Wyoming as follows: "Formerly debt-free little ranch towns now face complex municipal financing needs. Suburban sprawl now invades the open range. Costs escalate: In Gillette, a water and sewer hookup costs over $2,000 today instead of the $75 it cost in 1970. And the taming of Wyoming, considered by many to be 'the last frontier' of the continental U.S., is producing classic cultural confrontations: man against wildlife; strangers against old-timers; cattlemen against mine companies."[12]

The experience of the northern plains states follows that of other regions where new resource exploitation or construction projects have brought in a large outside labor force. Expanded services are demanded; the social and economic structure adapts in the best way it can, but very often the "boom" is short-lived and the initial boom phase passes. Social well-being and the natural environment suffer most.[13]

Concerned about the sudden surge of economic interest in their states, ten western governors have set up an office in Denver to study the effects of rapid energy development. Some of them have expressed fears that the phenomenon may destroy the traditional character or social fabric of the states. Environmental effects of strip mining have

[12] K. G. Slocum, "Wyoming Boom Spurs a Range of Problems and Confrontations," *Wall Street Journal*, September 28, 1977.

[13] *Environment and Behavior* 7 (1975), especially M. A. Shields, "Social Impact Studies: An Expository Analysis," and G. Krebs, "Technological and Social Impact Assessment of Resource Extraction: The Case of Coal." See also J. S. Gilmore, "Boom Towns May Hinder Energy Resource Development," *Science* 191 (1976): 535–540.

created doubts in the minds of a few ranchers who fear that their land will not support vegetation after the fertilizer used in reclamation has leached out. Others are worried that the topsoil will be washed away and that their groundwater and streams will become polluted. (Streams and rivers near stripped areas in Appalachia suffered serious pollution problems for generations in the past century.) Western soils that have been compacted for thousands of years will be broken open to yield iron, copper, manganese, zinc, and other minerals when they are dissolved and leached by rainfall. Therefore, some ranchers have joined local environmentalists in calling for more research and slower development.

On the other hand, Utah officials were incensed when two California utilities dropped their proposal to construct a $3.5 billion power plant complex at Kaiparowits. They counted on the capital that would have been generated and accompanying industrial development to pull them out of a century of relative depression. Many supporters of the facility welcomed the idea of boomtowns in southern Utah to wipe out the poverty of the area. Nonetheless, a National Parks Service study pointed out that pollution and decreased visibility would cause a $24 million drop in the region's recreation income over a period of thirty-five years. The controversy is likely to continue.

Alaskan Oil

The boomtown syndrome has also penetrated the communities along the Alaskan pipeline. Environmentalists fought the pipeline from 1968 to 1973, when, under pressure to become "independent" of Arab oil, Congress passed the Trans-Alaska Pipeline Authorization Act to get quick access to the ten billion barrels of crude oil under the tundra at the northern end of the pipeline. At the same time, the conservation effort focused on wilderness preservation and other problems of the natural environment. Few argued that the social and cultural environment of the pipeline route could be seriously disrupted. But according to a correspondent who observed the building of the line for a year and a half, the project killed dozens (some say

hundreds) of people, turned many native Eskimo women into prosti-
tutes, and "shattered the quiet life-style of the communities along its
798-mile route."[14]

About twenty thousand people poured into the area to work with
Alyeska Pipeline Service Co., many of them from Oklahoma, Texas
and other parts of the Southwest. These newcomers, referred to by
the native sourdoughs as "pointy-toed" invaders, were paid well. They
spent much of their money, created long lines and shortages at local
stores, and pushed up prices for everything at an incredible rate.
The situation created an impossible problem for those living on a
fixed income.

Other social impacts followed the pattern of the coal rushes in
the lower forty-eight states and of Alaska's earlier gold rush. Among
them were lack of housing, health care, and educational facilities;
traffic and population congestion; sharp increases in the crime rates;
and an extraordinary number of worker casualties. The major question of 1977 dealt with what to do with the boomtowns after the
twenty thousand workers left, or with the thousands of additional
arrivals and workers who might stay. Not even the high royalties paid
to the state for oil are expected to cover the costs for social services
and education brought on by the construction of the pipeline. Keeping the state's economy on an even keel will remain a problem for
many years, though some workers will be employed for other energy
projects, such as the construction of a natural gas pipeline. Energy
planners are also trying to find a way to develop some trillion tons
of coal (a two-thousand-year supply) that lies buried under the snow,
mostly on the bleak North Slope where the oil is, but as yet there is
no economical way to dig and ship it out.

The ironic side of the Alaskan oil story is that the Pipeline
Act of 1973 was passed to fill future oil needs of the Pacific states.
By the end of 1976 the federal energy administrator reported that
the Pacific states could refine and transport only 50 percent of the
Alaskan oil. Then followed a great debate about what to do with the
other half of the oil, given the high costs of transporting it east.

[14] G. Griffith, "Blood, Toil, Tears and Oil," *New York Times Magazine,*
July 27, 1975, p. 8.

The oil companies still want to ship the oil to Japan (despite difficulties in getting an "in kind" oil trade from Mideast suppliers). They want to ship it to Japan because oil tankers are mobile; pipelines are not. Government officials agree that it would be more efficient to ship oil to Japan, but politicians remember that Alaskan oil was supposed to have been developed for domestic needs. Shortsighted energy planning did not anticipate an obvious bottleneck in the shortage of port and other facilities on the Pacific coast. (Tanker safety is another environmental problem.)

Here again, the question of growth for the country (or world) at large must be examined against the certainty of local environmental and social disruption. Environmental consciousness must surely begin with considering the effects of industrial expansion on the personal lives and the regional geographies of the exploited natural resources.

The Dow Project

The purpose of mining western coal and Alaskan oil ultimately lies in obtaining increased energy and industrial growth. Alaskan oil was slated to meet greater residential energy demands (to feed the new power plants) and the further development of heavy industry along the Pacific coast. One such industrial complex which was slated to use the fresh supply of Alaskan oil was planned by Dow Chemical and Atlantic Richfield. It was to be built near the mouth of the Sacramento River at San Francisco Bay. The multibillion-dollar petrochemical complex would have taken advantage of the cheaper transportation costs for West Coast markets for chemical and plastic products, receiving petroleum by tanker from Alaska and naphtha from refineries nearby. About six thousand acres were initially purchased or optioned. Pipelines and a new power plant were planned, and other subsidiary industries took options for land in the county.

The traditional use of the land was agricultural—grazing or barley crops—with marshland, recreational, and game management areas on the river. Nearby communities are small and rural in character; roads few and narrow; housing limited. Arrangements were made to dredge the river bottom to provide for an enlarged shipping channel and deep-water port, and new dock facilities were to be constructed. Other heavy industry and refineries already cluster along the banks of the river near the proposed complex, and they all take tens of thousands of gallons of water per minute for industrial cooling purposes. The new facilities would add substantially to that amount. Of course the proposed facilities would add greatly to local populations; new roads and schools would have to be constructed and other services provided.

Environmentalists attacked the project in and out of court on many grounds: acceleration of already deteriorating air quality and consequent health problems; questions of health hazards from vinyl chloride exposure; the possibility of increased oil and chemical spills on San Francisco Bay; increased urban pressures; degradation of agricultural and open-space land; destruction of the scenic value of the river region; and adverse effects on wildlife and fish (from dredging). The Sierra Club and the Environmental Defense Fund challenged Dow's environmental impact report on these and other technical grounds.

After two years of planning, filing environmental impact reports, or getting other permits, and after spending ten million dollars, Dow dropped the Bay Area project, complaining that "environmental red tape" forced the decision. The main stumbling block for Dow was the denial of a construction permit by the Bay Area Air Pollution Control District because the region already failed to meet overall air quality standards established by the state and federal governments. Apparently the Dow project would compound an existing health problem for area inhabitants. Beneath the surface of this situation was the potential that dozens of other firms would want permits to provide industrial services for Dow.

While environmentalists rejoiced over the decision, many local businessmen, residents, labor unions, and chamber of commerce people were chagrined and alarmed over the loss of potential jobs and economic activity. Ultimate blame was laid on the complicated procedures of the permit process—and, of course, the troublesome environmentalists.

Growth: For Whom and For What

Most environmentalists admit the importance of moderate economic growth. They feel that more important considerations involve the kind and quality of growth, the locations of the growth and environmental quality management. Although a steady-state economy might be considered an ultimate objective by most environmental groups, and their writings warn of impending ecological disaster without a steady state, they will, when pressed, admit that growth presents very complex problems. For example, some recognize that environmental problems do not necessarily occupy a one-to-one relationship with population or with economic growth. Very old, highly polluting steel-making plants or power plants can be replaced with plants using more efficient combustion processes and pollution control equipment. Simpler technologies could be used in countless industrial developments for regional rather than national markets. This is a message which Schumacher stressed and attempted to demonstrate with his institute's projects.

The Dow plant was set up to be highly capital-intensive (and polluting). It would have created one thousand jobs at most, compared to forty-seven thousand jobs which were created by the federal government in their water cleanup and waste treatment program. Other jobs with the power plant, the oil unloading terminal, and heavy industry are also capital-intensive, whereas those in light industry and service industries tend to emphasize labor and technological creativity.

Regardless of the benefits that can be gained from changes such as those mentioned, residents of any area will want, and need, to know the *nature* of technological ventures near them. In the Dow case, for example, the residents were seriously worried about the plastics proposed to be made.

At the bottom of development questions lies the problem of the quality of economic growth itself. A 1977 article in the *Wall Street Journal* presented the energy and growth problem with striking clarity. The story recounted several close calls (brownouts) experienced by utilities because electrical demand is rising to the limits of present capacity. The Federal Energy Administration stated that according to present projections the nation's utilities will have to expand their generating capacity by more than 57 percent by 1985, at the cost of billions, if the country's energy needs are to be met. Therefore, rates will have to be increased to pay for the new nuclear or coal-fired plants, and coal production (along with regenerated rail and pipeline networks) will have to be stepped up quickly. These are problems stressed by President Carter in his 1977 energy message with his proposals to Congress, along with an increased emphasis on energy conservation.

Midway through the article, the *Wall Street Journal* writer dropped in the following seemingly innocuous information: "Yet the greatest growth in the use of the electric power comes not so much from homes and industry switching from oil and gas, as from the rising demand by existing customers. The increase in electrical gadgetry, from self-cleaning ovens to air conditioners, caused the average number of kilowatt hours for each residential customer in the U.S. to rise by more than 60% between 1965 and 1975. And in manufacturing, the continuing trend to automation caused the use of electricity for each manhour to rise by 51% between 1964 and 1974."[15]

The writer could have added that during the same period a spate of new devices, from electrical knives to hair driers, also appeared on the market. Although no one of these appliances uses much electricity, when the number is multiplied by fifty or one hundred million, the total electrical demand is increased considerably. The admirable and deceptive side of electrical consumption is that the process is so rationalized—supplying power for gigantic machines and tiny shavers alike—that it is difficult to differentiate among its various uses and waste. The value assessment of gadgets compounds the problem.

Thus, when an internal General Electric Company study estimates that the coal-mining industry will have to expand its production from 665 million tons in 1976 to 1.1 billion tons a year by 1985 ("Any hope of getting out of our short-term energy dilemma mandates the use and rapid development of our vast coal reserves"), one

[15] T. Metz, "An Electricity Crisis Looms If Atom Plants and Coal Output Lag," *Wall Street Journal*, February 24, 1977.

might justifiably inquire—despite government promises for direct and indirect aid: What is that expansion for? Gadgets and automation?

The "natural monopoly" status of private utilities and their consequent public economic advantage add structural impetus to "growth-mania." In all of capitalist enterprise except in the natural monopolies the amount of investment in an industry depends on the expected profitability in the future. The entrepreneur risks his capital in the enterprise in the hope that the investment will earn more in the marketplace than in the bank. Thus, investments are not made carelessly. Growth is not courted for its own sake.

Private utilities normally do not have to worry about plant investment capital. They are guaranteed a fixed return on their capital investment. Moreover, when they build more plants (add to their capital stock), they make more money for their investors. That is, even if the rate of return on investment is fixed at 10 percent, the company will make twice as much on a two-hundred-million-dollar capital outlay as on one hundred million dollars' worth of power plants. It is even more profitable to build new plants than to make an electrical distribution system more efficient; thus, utilities' resistance to improving facility distribution systems is responsible for most power failures.

Furthermore, the electrical companies' customers are largely paying for expansion costs. Therefore, it is in the utilities' economic interest to expand (without financial risk), regardless of how their electrical power is used or what kind of fuel (polluting, nuclear, or whatever) is employed. All the while, private utilities like to speak in advertisements of their public-spirited desire to serve the demands and needs of the people.

Ideally, the citizens of this country should deal with structural distortion of growth. After they deal with it on a policy level, they can better focus on the problem of quality—that is, what is being produced and how much its environmental cost is, along with its purposes and distribution. Highly polluting power plants, electrical gadgets, and even automobiles and roads should not receive higher priorities than houses, child care, bicycles, education, and a far-reaching public employment program.

John Kenneth Galbraith, quoted earlier, was not disturbed by growth so much in itself as by the inequality of its distribution. In *The Affluent Society*, Galbraith advocated an expansion of the public sector in "education, health, housing and other services" so that the poor would benefit instead of those already affluent. Along with many other economists, he has been convinced that the affluence which economic growth creates does not "trickle down" to the less affluent. Instead, society spawns more luxuries, entertainment of dubious quality, and commodities which have to be forced into the consciousness of the people by massive blanket advertising. Galbraith and others have called for a different kind of growth—one which would be directed to the social and environmental betterment of society.

Theoretically, at least, it is possible to accept a kind of growth which is compatible with quality of life and social values. In practice the goal is difficult to realize. Whether or not it is possible to convince people, à la Mishan or Schumacher, that less is more and small is beautiful remains an open question. What is more certain is that economic growth as a positive value in itself can no longer be taken for granted and that conservation has established itself on the natural agenda as an important key to the solution of many growth problems.

The president has stressed the importance of conservation and more efficient use of electricity. A California study indicated that no new power plants would be needed in that state through 1995 if certain energy-efficient designs were mandated. Another study showed that six hundred million dollars' worth of U.S. natural gas a year is burned up in pilot lights alone. Still more studies indicate that the nation could enjoy the same mix of goods and services with available technology and at the present prices with 40 percent less energy if the energy-conserving technologies were used.[16]

It is obvious that economic growth could continue theoretically without increased energy output as long as energy efficiency is the fundamental premise of conservation. In the past, energy was used

---

[16] L. Schipper, "Raising the Productivity of Energy Utilization," in *Annual Review of Energy 1976*, ed. J. M. Hollander and M. K. Simmons (Palo Alto, Calif.: Annual Reviews, 1976), pp. 455–519. See also the well-documented chapter on conservation in R. Stobaugh and D. Yergin, eds., *Energy Future* (New York: Random House, 1979).

more efficiently by the switch from steam power to electricity and from steam locomotives to diesels. In the future the same kind of efficiency can be realized by more efficient power plants and factories, a shift away from huge, low-mileage cars toward autos with economy, more efficient appliances, better-designed homes and offices, and more efficient industrial processes. In a 1978 study sponsored by the National Academy of Sciences and the National Academy of Engineers, the National Research Council concluded that in the long run the United States could sustain moderate economic growth and still cut its energy growth in half. The Ford Foundation's Energy Policy Project "A Time to Choose" drew the same conclusion in 1975.[17]

Yet many industry and utility spokesmen still claim that conservation measures will fall far short of demands in the 1980s. It is certain that brownouts will occur if:

1. Utility companies continue to offer lower rates for greater consumption of electricity instead of the opposite
2. Las Vegas and its imitators multiply neon lights
3. The uninterrupted flow of electrical novelties continues
4. Gargantuan capital-intensive, automated industry is encouraged by local governments and their electric companies in place of smaller firms
5. The entire process of energy development is not subjected to long-range scrutiny and planning

The coal and oil boomtowns are only symbolic representations for environmentalists of their deeper concerns about the irrationality of the basic processes of growth in the country. The suburbs provided the first clue about how random development would occur. Then came highways and the automobile culture. Now the many sides of the energy question are signaling contradictions in our culture. It is not even certain that final depletion of fossil fuels would solve the problem of growth, since as the price of energy goes up, new technologies continue to be developed—steamflooding of old oil fields to gain billions of extra barrels, new mining techniques for coal, and nuclear and

[17] A. B. Lovins, *Soft Energy Paths* (Cambridge, Mass.: Ballinger, 1977). This book gives a cogent analysis of alternative sources of energy, including examination of their respective futures.

sophisticated fusion or laser technologies. More energy means more growth and usually more pollution or risk.

Environmentalists would probably prefer not to be considered obstructionists, but in the absence of rational planning, some form of obstructionism may be the only democratic way one can let an alternative approach be known. All segments and traditions of environmentalism have indicated their stake in this latest critical struggle.

8

Risk and Conservation

A COMMON characteristic can be uncovered among many of the environmentalist precepts—a hesitancy to take undue risks. This hesitancy can be found in both conservatives and conservationists. It attracts like-minded groups who are otherwise quite unwilling to support environmentalist causes. Thus when environmentalists are successful in showing serious risks or dangers of ecosystem disruption, drastic changes in natural environments, or potential danger to human health or the nation's future, many persons from other movements support the environmental effort. The solidarity stems from unwillingness to accept personal, physical, or collective risks for the potential economic advantage of someone else or another social group.

Risk Taking

In studies of risk taking in recent years,[1] an individual's willingness to take risks is seen as linked either to measurable benefits ("voluntary" risk taking) or to a perceived ability to handle the risk involved. Such is the case when people do not believe they are in

[1] C. Starr, "Social Benefit versus Technological Risk," *Science* 165 (1969): 232; C. Starr, R. Rudman, and C. Whipple, "Philosophical Basis for Risk Analysis," in *Annual Review of Energy 1976*, ed. J. M. Hollander and M. K. Simmons (Palo Alto, Calif.: Annual Reviews, 1976). See also H. J. Otway, P. D. Palmer, and F. Niehaus, "Risk Assessment," in *Second Status Report of the IIASA Project on Energy Systems 1975* (Luxembourg: International Institute for Applied Systems Analysis, 1975), pp. 149–171; and W. W. Lowrance, *Of Acceptable Risk* (Los Altos, Calif.: William Kaufman, 1976), pp. 13–70.

control of a situation. Here, factors are controlled by another person, social group, or faraway technological system (for example, transportation in an airplane, energy dependence on a utility, or food supply from a distant farmer). In such situations, beyond our control, we take involuntary risks. Lack of control comes from a separation of technologies and managers geographically, and sometimes politically and temporally, too. In such a situation some people feel that they are taking a great risk; the benefits they might derive simply do not outweigh what they perceive as possible dangers. According to Chauncey Starr, under certain conditions a person would be a thousand times less willing to take involuntary risks than voluntary ones.

Environmentalist warnings about future risks have given rise to derogatory epithets like "the Doomsday Syndrome." Because of repeated dangers, the warnings have lost a degree of credibility, yet in many cases they have been successful because they have been able to convince others of the seriousness of the dangers. When involuntary risk is perceived as "excessive" or "high" as compared to possible benefits of the risk situation, the public has supported some environmentalist concerns.

In evaluating possible risks in the future, Starr, Rudman, and Whipple distinguish among

1. Real risk, as will be determined eventually by future circumstances when they develop fully
2. Statistical risk, as determined by currently available data, typically as measured by actuaries for purposes of establishing insurance premiums
3. Predicted risk, as derived analytically from system models structured from historical studies
4. Perceived risk, as seen intuitively by individuals[2]

The following example illustrates the differences among real, statistical, and perceived risk. Because individuals feel a lack of control over the possibilities of accidents or because a particular type of accident might prove fatal or excessively severe, they would prefer driving to flying, or skiing to taking a ski lift, despite the fact that ac-

[2] Starr, Rudman, and Whipple, "Risk Analysis," p. 631.

tual accidents (from statistical data) occur far less frequently from airplanes and from lifts than from autos or from skiing. People perceive danger in terms of lack of control and severity (death as opposed to a broken leg, though of course auto accidents also very often result in death) instead of the probability of an accident. Environmentalists predict ecological risk from their own models or from time studies that very often are based on personal assumptions or perceptions or on limited scientific models instead of the actual probabilities, which are either very difficult or impossible to factor into their equations.

Many environmental conflicts center on challenges to a historically justified way of life: incentives to growth, the automobile culture, incursions into the natural environment, air and water pollution. When risk is predicted as connected to certain activities, questions of value arise, since Western society has customarily accepted the risk involved in growth and pollution and often has justified the risk taking on statistical grounds. Environmentalist challenges indicate that their own perceptions and predictions conflict with those of groups that represent the mainstream of culture. Much in previous chapters has dealt with such value conflicts over social and environmental costs and their (at least temporary) resolution in the public arena.

The idea of risk is connected to the side effects of new technologies or economic activity which affect the environment and human health. Because of new perceptions of risk brought on by technological change, environmentalists have forced governmental response to deal with problems of risk. The pattern can be clearly observed by the brief history of the pesticide controversy. In a society which must grow enormous quantities of food to support large populations, quick solutions have been found to control pests by applying pesticides to a large amount of land. A large ecosystem is affected because it is not possible to eliminate individual harmful pests one by one. The entire ecosystem, including soil and organisms beyond the target pest, is subject to the toxicity.

Environmentalists began to publicize the hazards of pesticides not only to wildlife, crop plants, domestic animals, and farm workers but also especially to people who consume the food from crops, fish, and animals. People began to realize that they were risking their health by ingesting increasing amounts of toxic substances being passed up the food chain to their own bodies. Environmental activity upset a previously entrenched agrochemical industry by pointing to the potential carcinogenicity and possible genetic disturbance brought about by the chemicals. The widespread publicity of these studies had influenced the eventual passage of the federal Toxic Substances Control Act of 1976 (TOSCA) but much earlier had exercised a great effect on a number of federal agencies concerned with environmental health, including the Environmental Protection Agency (EPA), the Occupational Safety and Health Administration (OSHA), the Food and Drug Administration (FDA), and the Consumer Product Safety Commission (CPSC).

Federal Legislation Regulating Toxic Substances since 1970

Clean Air Act, 1970
Occupational Safety and Health Act (OSHA), 1970
Federal Environmental Pesticide Control Act, 1972
Federal Insecticide, Fungicide, and Rodenticide Act, 1972
Federal Water Pollution Control Act, 1972
Safe Drinking Water Act, 1974
Resource Conservation and Recovery Act, 1976
Toxic Substances Control Act (TOSCA), 1976

The EPA has been charged with administering TOSCA and generally controlling health hazards in the U.S. environment. The agency is to review the safety of existing chemicals, to stop the manufacture of those that are found to create the "risk of injury to health or the environment," and to require corporations to show that new chemicals do not constitute a danger to health or environment. The critical issue has been the linking of substances in the environment, especially those of the workplace, with cancer victims.

The number of synthetic organic chemicals developed each year is extremely difficult to estimate. One congressional committee guessed that their production expanded 233 percent in the decade preceding 1976, that almost ten thousand different chemicals are in widespread use, and that about one thousand new chemicals are tried each year.

At the end of 1977 the EPA ordered major U.S. chemical producers and importers and petroleum refiners for the first time to tell the government what substances they produce, the first step required under TOSCA. The EPA also regulates about thirty-five thousand pesticides made up of about fifteen hundred different chemical preparations. In general the EPA is charged with guarding the environment (water and air) from pollutants like auto emissions and chemical wastes.

The other agencies also hold jurisdiction over a number of activities. OSHA, for example, created in 1971 as a branch of the Department of Labor, is supposed to regulate about twenty thousand chemical compounds in workplace environments, whether factories, offices, stores, or mines. The FDA, along with the Department of Agriculture, watches over food, particularly meat, and also regulates about twenty-five hundred food additives. In addition, the FDA has authority over twenty thousand prescription drugs, two hundred thousand over-the-counter drugs, and four thousand chemicals in cosmetics.

The agencies listed above and others, such as the Nuclear Regulatory Commission, which monitors radiation, have come into existence as each new health or environmental regulation has been passed by Congress, mainly in the past decade. The proliferation of agencies and commissions has not solved environmental or health problems. Increasingly the agencies have been criticized for fragmental responsibility, passivity, indecision, unaccountability, administrative inefficiency, inflexibility, foot dragging, and undue respect for the chemical industry, which they are supposed to be regulating.

Environmental Health

Pollution was not perceived as representing a major problem or risk to health until the industrial revolution and rapid growth of cities. Awareness that pollution might cause death and major diseases came even later, and a widespread concern has been a result of the modern environmental movement. The coincidence of the technical ability to measure microscopic amounts of pollutants in the atmosphere, water and vegetative or animal life and the publication of Rachel Carson's

Silent Spring at a time of high industrial expansion and capital investment provided the springboard for contemporary environmental
health concerns.

Environmentalists in many cases only have had to point out what
people had personally experienced in central-city districts where automobiles were emitting large quantities of carbon monoxide, oxides of
nitrogen, lead, and a variety of hydrocarbons. Residents have often
become dizzy and nauseated; they have gotten headaches; they have
had difficulty breathing and hearing because carbon monoxide inter-
feres with the oxygen-carrying capacity of the bloodstream. Others
have developed lung difficulties (emphysema, bronchitis, pulmonary
fibrosis) from exposure to large doses of nitrogen dioxide. Most people have noticed and smelled photochemical smog. Lead poisoning
has also been a long-range health problem. Thus, until gasoline prices
began to skyrocket, air-quality standards and emission requirements
seemed less important as people realized they had to pay personally
for the benefit of clean air.

At the same time, the nation's collective environmental perception has become sensitive to industrial pollution: particulate matter
(carbon and other substances from incomplete burning or heating of
metals) from smoke or from the grinding and pulverizing of materials
to produce cement, chemicals, and fertilizers, and gases of sulfur
oxides, hydrogen oxides, and fluorides (from the burning of coal and
oil or from steel or metal mills). All of these pollutants react in the
atmosphere or dissolve in water vapor and affect human health and
vegetation.

Since the passage of the Clean Air and Water Acts and the establishment of the EPA, hundreds of government and private studies
have been made to attempt to establish the risk of environmental
pollution. J. P. Holdren and R. J. Budnitz divided the studies me-
thodologically as follows:[3]

1. Direct observation of specific individuals
2. Epidemiological studies of suspect population samples
3. Controlled dose/effect studies with animals or occasionally with
   humans

[3] "Social and Environmental Costs of Energy Systems," in *Annual Review
of Energy 1976*, p. 555. See also Lowrance, *Of Acceptable Risk*, pp. 75–85.

4. Biological-biomedical studies of physiological indices or system functions

The same authors distinguish among health impacts studies and the effects of chronic exposure to a pollutant or resultant genetic damage. The studies propose to ascertain the real risk involved in the continued exposure of large numbers of people to environmental pollution. That is, of the thousands of agents already blowing in the wind and flushed into the water supply, which are most hazardous to human health? Of the thousands of new substances about to be let into the environment, which should be stopped?

The reason no easy solution is in sight is the fact that simple agents do not act upon people alone but only in relation to other agents in a myriad of possibilities. It is difficult to study these interactions under laboratory conditions and make definitive pronouncements. Death and disease are effects which can come from long-term activity in many situations: a particular diet together with physical inactivity and cigarette smoking in a factory, for example, or just a very heavy amount of cigarette smoking. Substances breathed or ingested can undergo many different sets of transformations: different people have different disease thresholds; climate and humidity affect gases like sulfur dioxide in different ways. It is even possible for some people in certain geographic areas to develop a resistance to pollution which would severely handicap people in other areas.[4]

In terms of factors which cause cancer, for example, the most certain statement that can be made is that a number of items contribute to its development and usually more than one carcinogen can be identified. Some of them are

1. *Enzymes.* Susceptibility to certain kinds of cancer may depend on the activities of various enzymes, which are proteins that influence chemical reactions in the body.
2. *Hormones.*
3. *Smoking.* Smoking is known to cause lung, mouth, and other cancers.
4. *Air pollution.*

[4] The *Los Angeles Times*, May 19, 1975, reported that, according to a scientific study, Los Angeles residents adapt to ozone doses faster and easier than do Canadians living in communities with cleaner air.

5. *Exposure to industrial chemicals.*
6. *Use of medications.* In our drug-oriented society, scientists suspect this could sometimes be a factor.
7. *Infection with viruses or bacteria.*
8. *Age.* The risk of cancer is greatest at two periods during our life-spans—childhood and old age. Of growing concern is the possibility that an infant in the womb may develop cancer as the result of its mother's on-the-job exposure to cancer-causing substances which are then passed from bloodstream to bloodstream.[5]

Furthermore, a particular combination of chemicals at the same time can affect the possibility of cancer development. Budnitz and Holdren summarize a number of studies on this subject regarding the chronic effects of gaseous and particulate sulfur compounds:

. . . the response of humans to air pollutants is a very complicated, possibly synergistic response whose etiology is only beginning to be understood. . . . There has never been any definitive work to demonstrate how the various compounds, separately or together, produce the effects observed. . . . Definitive dose-response relationships still elude the investigators, partly because of the difficulties in generating realistic polluted air in a controlled laboratory. Epidemiological studies have produced associations with various respiratory diseases and impairment of pulmonary function, but no completely satisfactory studies have been performed; there are always intervening variables in air pollution parameters, socioeconomic effects and/or other disease symptomology.[6]

All this is to say that scientists have not always achieved reasonable certainty about the complete risks of air and other kinds of pollution. In most cases only very general guidelines can be applied. Therefore, conflicts arise over how much risk people should have to accept from society in particular situations, not only from known pollutants but also from the more than 170 substances associated with cancer.

One conflict became stormy after OSHA proposed a crash program to identify and control carcinogens in 1978.[7] The government

[5] New York Academy of Sciences, *Cancer and the Worker* (New York: The Academy, 1977), p. 7.

[6] Holdren and Budnitz, "Social and Environmental Costs," p. 558.

[7] D. Burnham, "Dispute Arises over Agencies' Plan to Identify and Curb Carcinogens," *New York Times*, March 3, 1978.

proposal pointed out that over a thousand Americans die of cancer every day and that from 60 to 90 percent of deaths are caused by toxic substances in the environment. Chemical and related industries responded by funding a new American Industrial Health Council, which published contrary studies and evidence. They argue, for example, that cancer has not been increasing rapidly since 1900 because of industrial chemicals but instead because of cigarette smoking and longevity, since cancer is more apt to attack older people. Such conflicts loom large in the public arena because they determine the way the EPA regulates air and water pollution, the way the FDA regulates food and drink, and the way the Nuclear Regulatory Agency controls atomic radiation.

Cancer and the Environment

In recent years environmentalists have found cancer research scientists to be among their most potent allies, for they have linked the disease with environmental factors. In 1975, for example, the National Cancer Institute published a cancer map of the United States which registered the cancer deaths of 3,056 counties of the contiguous forty-eight states between 1950 and 1969. Environmentalists were quick to note that high rates of bladder cancer occur in the industrialized Northeast, particularly in counties with high employment in petroleum manufacturing. In rural areas of the West, where the smelting industry is located, lung and liver cancer rates are high. Bladder cancer is highest among chemical workers or regions where the chemical industry is located, and overall cancer rates are much higher in urban than in rural areas. Lung cancer is high in rural areas where it should not be expected except that the same regions also contain government chemical testing and chemical warfare facilities. The National Cancer Institute places about 80 percent of all cancer diseases into the "environmentally caused" category. These correlations do not offer absolute proof of the linkages (most probably they have long latency periods and interlocking relationships), but they do point up the risks involved in a highly industrialized region.

Many scientists are fairly certain about the relationships between

Chemicals Known to Be Carcinogens in Humans

Aflatoxins	Hematite
4-aminobiphenyl	Isopropyl oil
Arsenic compounds	Melphalan
Asbestos	Mustard gas
Auramine	2-naphthylamine
Benzene	Nickel compounds
Benzidene	*N,N*-bis(2-chloroethyl)-2-naphthylamine
Bis(chloromethyl) ether	Oxymetholone
Cadmium oxide	Phenacetin
Chloramphenicol	Phenytoin
Chromates	Soot, tars, and oils
Cyclophosphamide	Vinyl chloride
Diethylstilbestrol	

cancer and pollutants from petrochemical, asphalt, steel, and coal tar production. Arsenic used in mining and smelting seems to cause lung, skin, and liver cancers. Asbestos from insulation and brake linings is another known carcinogen (as is tobacco). Benzene and benzidine, products of oil refineries used by rubber factories and pesticide producers, are related to cancer of the bone marrow. Fly ash from coal-fired plants may cause cancer, as do wood dust in wood products plants and dusts in the textile industry. Even nickel compounds in such products as baby powders can cause cancer. The synthetic hormone diethylstilbestrol (DES), fed to sheep and cattle to hasten the fattening process, is also thought to be carcinogenic. Then there are the artificial sweeteners—cyclamates and saccharin—which have received notoriety as disputed carcinogens.

Although there is some disagreement about the carcinogenic effects of industrial pollutants dispersed over a wide area, few would dispute the effects on industrial workers. Several studies in the Los Angeles region and corroborating data by the Oil, Chemical and Atomic Workers Union and OSHA have illustrated a clear relationship between common industrial pollutants in the family of chemicals called polycyclic aromatic hydrocarbons (PAH) and a high incidence of lung cancer among industrial workers exposed to them. The California Air Resources Board has gone further in asserting that the rising death rate from lung cancer in the Los Angeles and San Francisco Bay areas indicates that heavy industry is affecting the general population as well as the workers.[8]

Synthetically derived organic compounds which are contaminating drinking water supplies of several major cities, apparently through runoff from industrial wastes and applications of farm fertilizer, have also been suspected of causing cancer in those who drink the water. Even chlorine, which is supposed to purify drinking water, interacts with organic materials like dead leaves to form possible carcinogenic substances. The EPA has proposed a new standard of limitations of the adulterants and has mandated that contaminated water systems have granulated carbon processers installed to filter out potentially carcinogenic substances from the drinking water supply of at least one hundred million Americans. The rules are to be adopted over a number of years.

Environmentalists and some unions have played a significant role in pushing the EPA to require that air emission controls be placed on factories that produce vinyl chloride and the related compounds ethylene dichloride and polyvinyl chloride, plastics used in making packaging and water pipes. The gas was linked to a rare liver cancer found in employees of the plants; then it was discovered that the vinyl chloride migrates to foods and liquids from some forms of polyvinyl chloride semirigid packages and bottles. Consumer and environmental groups also pressured the FDA to halt the marketing of these products.

Environmentalists were very suspicious of polychlorinated biphenyl (PCBs) even before a related chemical, PBB, was accidentally mixed with animal feed prepared by the Michigan Farm Bureau in mid-1973. The PBB caused the death of an estimated two million farm animals and sickness in an uncounted number of humans. (Investigators determined in 1978 that 8 million of Michigan's 9.1 million residents were carrying PBBs in their bodies because of the accidental mispackaging.)

---

[8] D. Y. Sauter, "Synthetic Fuel Hazard," *The Elements*, April, 1977, pp. 3–4. This article includes Sauter's study and review of literature, "Synthetic Fuels and Cancer," *The Elements*, November, 1975. See also R. Gillette, "Study Linking Smog to Cancer Erred," *Los Angeles Times*, November 6, 1977.

One reason for environmentalist wariness is that PBB is a highly toxic and persistent type of chemical similar in structure to DDT. PBBs and PCBs are fire retardants used in plasticizers, coatings, paints, transformers, and power capacitors. They are known to cause liver and thyroid abnormalities, bronchitis, nerve damage, skin lesions, pregnancy problems, and, in animals, growth retardation and cancer. They remain in the environment many years; PBBs and PCBs already exceed DDT levels in wildlife and other environmental accumulation.

In the mid-1970s environmentalists complained to the EPA about widespread effects of PCBs, which decimated a striped-bass fishery on the Hudson River, contaminated salmon in Lake Michigan, and were found in fish in other areas around the country, especially near electrical manufacturing plants.[9] Simultaneously, they were reported in countries of Western Europe, at the North Pole, and in urban areas elsewhere in the world.

Although the general alarm was not sounded until 1974–1975 (PCBs have been in use since 1929), evidence that PCBs accumulate in animals was recognized as early as 1966 by Swedish scientist S. Jensen in the tissues of fish and wildlife. In 1968 more than one thousand people in Japan suffered from a disfiguring skin disease called *yusho* as well as from liver and abdominal problems later traced to a rice oil contaminated by PCBs. Then in 1972 a federal government report strongly recommended that PCBs be restricted to essential or nonreplaceable uses which "involve minimum direct human exposure, since they can have adverse effects on human health." Monsanto Chemical, the sole U.S. producer, claimed at the time that they stopped selling the chemical "voluntarily" to "several thousand" customers except those who had "closed-system" electrical applications, thus minimizing harm to humans. But as scientists from around the world found out, the systems were not as closed as Monsanto claimed. For example, at the Velsicol plant which made the PBBs that were mixed with the cattle feed, it was discovered that the entire

---

[9] A. K. Ahmed, "PCBs in the Environment," *Environment* 18 (1976): 2. See also J. S. Tannenbaum, "Industrial Pollutants May Be Worse Threat than DDT to Ecology," *Wall Street Journal*, October 16, 1975; and D. Jordan, "The Town Dilemma," *Environment* 19 (1977): 2.

complex of buildings—including a food-making section—was contaminated by PBB residues, probably spread around by airborne dust, by use of common equipment, or by river water circulating through the plant.

The chemicals were finally subjected to controls under TOSCA and were completely banned by 1979, when a workable substitute was supposed to be available. General Electric claims, however, that nothing will truly replace PCBs, and banning them will accelerate the risk of transformer fires and explosions. In the meantime, scientists are wondering how long it will take before those exposed to high levels of PBBs and PCBs will develop cancer, if at all. These are risks which many warned about at least five years before the ban.

Skin cancer and the risk of potential climate changes led to a campaign to ban spray cans that use fluorocarbon gases. The controversy began in the mid 1970s; it revolves around a series of complex chemical reactions which occur when the fluorocarbon aerosol propellants (also used as refrigerants) are released into the atmosphere. Many scientists, among them environmentalists who are especially concerned with such matters as ecological balance, contend that the inert fluorocarbon gases dissociate under intense radiation, leaving free chlorine atoms which, over a period of time, will react with and deplete the protective ozone shield high in the atmosphere of the earth. Ultraviolet radiation reaching the earth's surface will then increase, since it will not be blocked by the ozone layer. Melanoma, a skin cancer that is fatal for one-third of its victims, will increase by 0.5 million to 1.5 million additional cases in the world each year. In addition, fluorocarbons will trap heat radiation from the earth, and the lower layers of the atmosphere will then be heated, creating a greenhouse effect—a general rise in temperature worldwide.[10]

In 1976 a blue-ribbon panel of the National Academy of Science recommended that fluorocarbon gases should be restricted, but industry had already begun to scale down production under the threat of actual prohibition of sale of the aerosol cans in several states and by the federal government. The nation was already acquainted with the ozone argument, since it was propounded by environmentalists

[10] A. K. Ahmed, "Unshielding the Sun . . . Human Effects," *Environment* 17 (1975): 3.

and others against the government sponsorship of the supersonic transport (SST), which emits large quantities of nitrogen oxides and poses a similar threat to the ozone layer. Increased use of nitrogen fertilizers may also imperil the earth's ozone shield.[11]

The amount of risk involved in these several cases is controverted; environmentalists say it is great, and industry spokesmen claim it is quite small. The National Academy of Science recommended a two-year period to gather more information, though several roomfuls of research data already existed at the time of their report. The academy seemed to reflect conflicts of value, and it made its recommendation in the hope that one side or the other could present a more convincing case to the general public about potential risks. If the public is convinced, it is likely that other products which contain fluorocarbons, such as the chemicals in air conditioning and refrigeration units and those used as blowing agents to make plastic foam, will be banned. If new refrigerants are developed, they are likely to be more expensive than fluorocarbons.

Renewed publicity about the danger of cancer arising from environmental causes followed widespread accounts of ground pollution at Love Canal near Niagara Falls, New York, in 1978.[12] The problem at Love Canal came from the 1940s when the Hooker Chemicals and Plastics Corporation began to dump hundreds to thousands of fifty-five-gallon drums filled with waste chemicals in the abandoned canal. In 1953 the canal was filled in and sold to the city for an elementary school and playground for a token price of one dollar. Single-family homes were constructed nearby.

After a variety of illnesses were reported over a period of time, earth above the rotting drums began to collapse, and many homes began to deteriorate quickly. When these homes were found to contain highly toxic chemicals in their basements, the New York State Health Department began an investigation in the spring of 1978. They discovered a long history of health problems in the area: birth defects, mental retardation, miscarriages, epilepsy, liver abnormalities,

[11] *Wall Street Journal*, November 13, 1975, and September 14, 1975.
[12] See M. H. Brown, "Love Canal, U.S.A.," *New York Times Magazine*, January 21, 1979, pp. 23–44.

sores, rectal bleeding, headaches, and an incidence of cancer more than twice the national average.

Since that time the disposal of toxic wastes has been recognized by the EPA as one of the nation's most urgent environmental problems. At and near Love Canal, Hooker disposed of over 80,000 tons of such toxic substances as mirex, C-56, and lindane pesticides and chemicals used to manufacture plastics—as well as 3,700 tons of trichlorophenol waste, which contains the deadly chemical dioxin. Small quantities of dioxin were discovered to have leached out of the periphery of Love Canal and above the city's public water supply intake on the Niagara River. As little as three ounces of dioxin properly distributed could kill over one million people. It was dioxin which was dispersed in Sevesa, Italy, after an explosion at a trichlorophenol plant, and one thousand acres had to be evacuated.

About 92 billion pounds of wastes from the production of seventy thousand chemical compounds have to be disposed of every year. Over 800 of the known U.S. disposal sites have the potential of ground pollution worse than that of Love Canal (out of at least 32,254 storage, treatment, and disposal sites in the country). The EPA estimates that only about 7 percent of the 92 billion pounds of wastes receive proper disposal. The risk of chemical wastes thus takes its place among the other varied environmental risks of the twentieth century.

Nuclear Energy

The dual problems of growth and risk coincide in the U.S. nuclear power program. About 56 nuclear reactors are already operating in the country; at least another 160 are under construction or planned despite nationwide opponents that number in the millions. Whether or not all of these people completely understand how great the real or statistical risks are, it is clear that they perceive the danger as one which they are not willing to accept. Environmentalists have joined forces with dozens of local groups to stop construction of the new plants in their areas. In urban locations, mainly with public interest groups like those led by Ralph Nader, they have initiated or supported legislation to stop the reactors until safety and waste-disposal problems have been solved.[13]

Although it is difficult to summarize the nuclear safety question in a few paragraphs, it is important at least to present some idea of the complexity of the problem. There are several types of nuclear reactors and many stages of the nuclear-fuel cycle, each of which poses some technological risk or possibility of human error. At present in the United States the nuclear industry uses light-water reactors (LWRs), which are reactors cooled and regulated by ordinary water in a boiling-water reactor (BWR) or in a cooling circuit pressurized so that the water in the reactor does not boil (PWR). Nuclear researchers are also working on a fast breeder reactor (LMFBR), that is, a reactor that can produce more fuel than it consumes.

The nuclear fuel cycle is made up of a number of steps. Before nuclear fuel gets to the reactor it is mined, milled to extract uranium oxide from the raw ore, converted into uranium hexafluoride gas, enriched by separation of the fissionable uranium 235 from the heavier uranium 238 and concentration of the isotope 235, and then converted back to solid pellets and used in the reactor. After use, the spent fuel is cooled for a short time before being shipped in heavily shielded containers to a reprocessing plant, which separates the reusable uranium and the man-made plutonium from radioactive waste products, mostly uranium 238.

The risks about which most people are concerned deal with routine radiation but especially with potential accidents or other threats. The International Commission on Radiation Protection has recommended maximum permissible concentrations (MPCs) of radioactive

[13] Literature on nuclear reactors and nuclear safety has proliferated at an amazing rate in the 1970s in both the popular and the scientific press. *The Bulletin of Atomic Scientists* 30 (1974) gives an excellent overview of the problems, written in untechnical language. In that volume, see especially J. P. Holdren, "Hazards of the Nuclear Fuel Cycle," p. 18. See also U.S. Atomic Energy Commission, *The Safety of Nuclear Power Reactors and Related Facilities*, Reprint No. WASH 1250 (Washington, D.C.: Government Printing Office); U.S. Congress, Joint Committee on Atomic Energy, *Hearings on Reactor Safety*, 93rd Cong., 2d sess., 1974; and U.S. Nuclear Regulatory Commission, *Reactor Safety—An Assessment of Accident Risks in U.S. Commercial Nuclear Power Plants*, Repr. No. WASH 1400 (NUREG–75/614) (Washington, D.C.: Government Printing Office, 1975). This last document is referred to as the Rasmussen Report. Finally, see also J. H. Hendrie, "Safety of Nucelar Power," in *Annual Review of Energy 1976*, pp. 662–683.

isotopes in air and water so that individuals do not exceed permissible dosages of radiation—5 rems a year for nuclear workers and one-tenth of that amount, 500 millirems a year, for individuals in the general population. An even smaller amount, 170 millirems a year, is allowed as an average dose for large segments of the population—in addition to natural radiation from cosmic rays or radiation from medical X-rays and treatments.

Since a 1972 National Academy of Science study was published there has been mounting pressure on nuclear regulatory agencies to lower the average allowable dosage.[14] The report stated that if all Americans were subjected to the full 170 millirems per year, the nation could expect eleven thousand to twenty-seven thousand serious cases of genetically induced diseases each year, along with a 5 percent increase of "ill health" and about three thousand to fifteen thousand additional cancer deaths each year. In response, the Atomic Energy Agency reduced the permissible amount of emissions at reactor sites, but regulatory agencies have not yet extended the tightened regulations to reactors other than light-water reactors or to earlier and later stages of the nuclear fuel cycle. Reprocessing plants have been notorious for exceeding the maximum emission limits, and their failings have caused severe radiation problems.

In 1977 the General Accounting Office (GAO) criticized the EPA for "not effectively accomplishing its goals of preventing radiation contamination to the environment and protecting the public." The GAO cited the twenty-two thousand Americans who develop leukemia, other forms of cancer, and genetic disorders each year because of radiation exposure and claimed that new sources of radiation continue to grow.

Although many environmentalists and others are willing to admit in principle that routine emissions of the nuclear cycle could be controlled, they contend that the possibilities of human error, accidents, and sabotage are so great that they preclude any advantage nuclear power might bring. If, for example, a single reactor melt-down occurred near a metropolitan area, the enormous amount of radiation dispersed from that reactor could contaminate or eventually kill hundreds of thousands of people and ruin property for generations.

[14] Holdren, "Hazards of the Nuclear Fuel Cycle," p. 16.

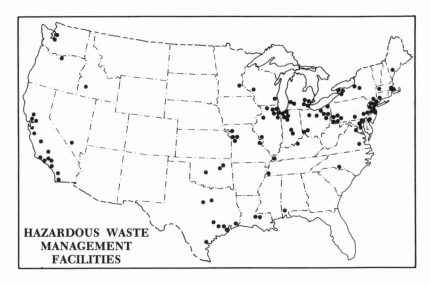

HAZARDOUS WASTE
MANAGEMENT
FACILITIES

Two major sources of risk in highly industrialized societies come from nuclear power plants, which multiply as energy demand increases, and from the toxic wastes of virtually every major industry. The danger is present not only from reactor accidents (as at Three Mile Island) or from dump sites (as at Love Canal), but also from groundwater contamination near waste sites. The U.S. Environmental Protection Agency has identified more than fifty waste sites which represent a danger to surrounding communities because of contaminated groundwater supplies, and dozens more are suspected of polluting the water. The contamination results from toxic industrial wastes, from leaching of mu-

Transportation is a very weak line in the nuclear cycle, with each shipping cask containing millions of curies of radioactive waste. Fuel reprocessing plants will be handling great quantities of radioactive materials, and someone will have to watch the radioactive waste for tens of thousands of years; experts are still uncertain how radioactive wastes can be disposed of or stored safely. Furthermore, nuclear reactors themselves last for only about thirty years and remain highly radioactive for thousands of years. Some way has to be found to cut them up and transport them to a burial site.[15]

In all stages there are possibilities for human error, mechanical failure, natural catastrophes such as earthquakes and tornadoes,

[15] K. E. House, "U.S. Is Facing Problem of How to Dismantle Used Nuclear Reactors," *Wall Street Journal*, October 12, 1977.

[16] B. L. Cohen, "Perspectives on the Nuclear Debate," *Bulletin of Atomic Scientists* 30 (1974): 18, 35–39.

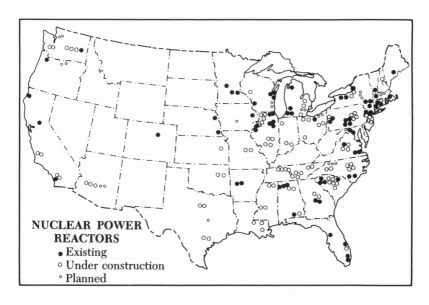

NUCLEAR POWER
  REACTORS
  • Existing
  ○ Under construction
  ° Planned

nicipal and industrial wastes, from waste runoff through oil and gas fields and other excavations, from leaching of wastes from landfills, from salt and other chemical contamination of aquifers by irrigation and other agricultural activities, and from inadvertent contamination caused by well drilling, harbor dredging, and excavation for drainage systems. These activities have an impact on the entire country, but their main effects are felt in the northeastern urban corridor where high rainfall causes faster rusting of steel containers and leaching of contaminants. The Resource Recovery Act of 1976 has mandated the EPA to develop standards for the present and future management of hazardous wastes.

sabotage, and terrorism. Although engineering failsafe systems have been installed to prevent such disasters, and statistical probabilities are high that they can be averted, experience with nuclear power has been too short, and the number of reactors is too small worldwide to make certain predictions, according to critics of nuclear power development. Yet only one knowledgeable terrorist need get his or her hands on fissionable materials for the benefits of the system to be nullified. These possibilities could excuse governments for violating civil rights for the purpose of "providing adequate protection" of the general population.

Fast breeder reactors only intensify the problems of the lightwater reactors, because a correspondingly greater number of shipments will be necessary in their plutonium cycle, increasing the possibility of malicious diversion of the materials. Also, the man-made plutonium 239 is deadly even in the most minute quantities. One ounce of plutonium produces ten trillion particles of plutonium dioxide, which could inflict tens of millions of people with lung cancer and poison the atmosphere for thousands of years.

On the other hand, proponents of nuclear power point out that the air pollution from a typical coal-fired plant probably kills about 50 people a year as compared to the average of 0.01 killed from a nuclear reactor with the same capacity.[16] The coal-fired plants also destroy the earth's vegetation with their pollution, devastate soil because of strip mining, consume two hundred pounds of a valuable resource every second, and may be causing long-term climatic change. Recent research has turned up evidence that the fly ash from coal-fired plants contains substances capable of causing mutations in bacteria, and many mutagenic substances are known to cause cancer in animals and presumably in humans as well.

In fact, because of backup systems the probability that a major accident would occur in a light-water reactor is about one in one million operating years, and it would cause about 500 deaths, averaging to about 0.0005 deaths a year. Even if a nuclear accident came suddenly or shockingly, so do airplane accidents, bombing during wars, and terrorist activities. Furthermore, smoking a pack of cigarettes a day is a quarter-million times as dangerous as nuclear power in terms of national deaths, according to nuclear power advocates.

Proponents also claim that future generations should not mind taking care of radioactive wastes, since they would be getting an important energy resource in return, and fossil fuels would be better used in medicines, textiles, steel production, gas fuels, and even plastics (though it is difficult to understand how already created radioactive wastes can provide energy). There are many counter-arguments against the plutonium peril (for example, over five tons of plutonium have already been emitted to the atmosphere as the result of past nuclear weapons tests, and their ill effects are difficult to establish). Plutonium's toxicity is questioned (other substances like potassium cyanide are much more lethal, and weight for weight caffeine is almost as deadly). Some question the capabilities of homemade bombs, and others claim exaggerations by antinuclear critics. The controversy is overloaded with probability statistics. Like ecology, economics, and other middle-class morals discussed in this book, risk-taking, one might conclude, is a state of mind.

The theoretical arguments for and against nuclear power, along with the statistical odds for or against a serious accident happening at a nuclear plant, took on a new level of historical intensity in March, 1979, when the million-to-one possibility actually occurred. The accident took place at the Three Mile Island nuclear power plant about eleven miles south of Harrisburg, Pennsylvania. Mechanical failures compounded by human errors led to the formation of a bubble of radioactive gasses in the reactor dome which threatened to explode. At the same time, radioactive contaminants were released into the air and water collected around the reactor as experts worked to stop a possible melt-down. The ultimate disaster never occurred, but many experts testified at later congressional hearings that it was dangerously close for several days.

The year 1979 was a bad one for proponents of nuclear power. Two weeks before the accident, the Nuclear Regulatory Commission closed down five East Coast plants because of design deficiencies in the capacity of the plants to withstand earthquakes. On the same day a prestigious committee established by President Carter announced after a year of study that the storage of radioactive nuclear wastes for tens of thousands of years was a problem that seemed to defy solutions both technically and politically. Also at the same time, the Nuclear Regulatory Commission concluded that not enough evidence existed to support the claim that a serious accident at a nuclear reactor was a once-in-a-million-years possibility.

In the wake of the Three Mile Island disaster, new scientific estimates of the worst possible reactor accident in an urban area were calculated at 3,300 immediate deaths, 45,000 immediate injuries, 45,000 latent cancer deaths, and 248,000 other injuries, including genetic defects.[17] Despite the controverted mathematical odds against the possibility of such a catastrophe, the experience of Three Mile Island proved to be a turning point in the rapid development of nuclear power in the United States. Historical consciousness merged with the

---

[17] D. Burnham, "Large Question Marks Hang over the Future of Nuclear Power," *New York Times*, April 1, 1979, sect. 4.

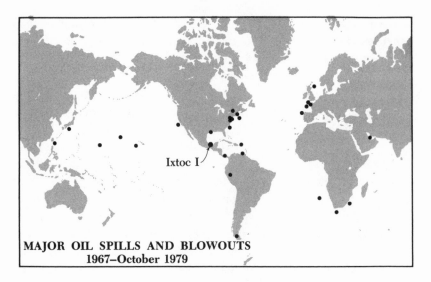

MAJOR OIL SPILLS AND BLOWOUTS
1967–October 1979

One reason for the rising number of major oil spills in the world is the grow-ing fleet of supertankers plying the world's waterways. These giant ships are as long as a half-dozen football fields and take about ten miles of water in which to come to a dead stop. Although they are extremely difficult to maneu-ver, international regulations for their manning and navigation do not exist, nor do inspection standards for them. More than twenty tankers of all sizes were lost in 1977. Nonetheless, the distinction for the largest oil spill to date goes to Ixtoc I, the runaway oil well off the coast of Yucatán, Mexico, which blew out more than a million gallons of oil during the summer and fall of 1979 and threatened the rich breeding grounds for marine life in the marsh-lands, lagoons, and inland bays around the barrier islands of Texas and as far north as Louisiana.

accelerating economic costs of building reactors at that moment in the nation's history to conspire against the nuclear power industry.

Risks of Environmental Damage

Besides the possibility of physical injury, members of society are often asked to risk damage to personal property or public property.[18] For example, an accident at a nuclear reactor could contaminate—de-pending on meteorological conditions—an area up to two miles wide and two hundred miles long, and if the contaminant is plutonium 239 (half-life 24,500 years) the contamination will for all practical pur-poses be permanent. Radioactive waste which might leak into ground-

[18] Budnitz and Holdren, "Social and Environmental Costs," p. 559.

water from a storage site is another risk; for example, by 1975, out of the 149 tanks stored underground in Hanford, Washington, 11 had sprung leaks, with about fifty thousand gallons of radioactive wastes escaping from one of the tanks. Radioactivity in groundwater contaminates the nearby soil, but groundwater also moves downhill and ultimately leads back to rivers and the seas. Nobody knows where the Washington radioactivity will end or emerge. Over a billion gallons of the wastes have already been stored throughout the country; more continue to pile up until adequate sites are found.

Greater demand for energy multiplies risks, over and above those of strip mining, coal gasification, and others. For example, natural gas from Alaska and Algeria is liquefied at minus 162.2 degrees Centigrade and shipped to U.S. ports in ultrarefrigerated tankers. The technology is extremely dangerous, with risks of vapor clouds, fire, and flameless explosions.

As the country increases energy facilities, those who live near such installations incur the risks of accidents. Depending on the accident—major dam failure, port explosion, a runaway nuclear reactor, or whatever—the property damage could reach millions to billions of dollars beyond loss of life and health.

The potential environmental risk of oil spills constitutes another hazard which seems to be tied inevitably to contemporary life. The pace of outer-continental-shelf drilling, as well as increased tanker traffic, especially from Alaska to California but also from foreign oil-exporting nations, has been accelerated for reasons cited throughout this book. The outer continental shelf is submerged coastline ocean floor which averages about two hundred meters in depth. About 875,-000 square miles of outer-continental-shelf land in the United States extend to five miles off the shoreline of some places in California and up to three hundred miles from parts of the New England and Alaskan coasts.

The risks of oil spills stem from the currents and tidal flow, which take nutrients to the shoreline, where the most productive life of the oceans lives in the estuaries, tidal flats, and wetlands. Oil spills foul shorelines, aquatic animals, and sea birds. State impact reports written to assess potential damage from oil spills off the Eastern seaboard usually state that environmental risks (for fishing industries and recreation) greatly outweigh economic and energy benefits from offshore oil drilling. In the case of "one of the most productive fishing grounds in the world," the Georges Bank off the Massachusetts coast, the million acres leased for oil drilling would produce between eight and twenty-eight days' supply of oil for the nation yet endanger a half-billion-dollar fishing industry.

Crude oil is mainly a mixture of hydrocarbons in countless combinations of atoms. It can be refined into a variety of products, and it can also be separated out to some degree by discharge into the ocean. Some parts of the crude oil of low molecular weight quickly dissolve, but they can kill many organisms before they do. Other, heavier fractions can oxidize, sink to the ocean floor with sediments, or be broken down by bacteria. Toxic chemical compounds can be ingested by plankton and find their way into food chains. Oil spills in the Arctic regions present special problems because it is almost impossible to recover petroleum once it goes under the ice; oil can move in large congealed masses hundreds of miles away from the original spill following a "giant clockwise current that operates at the top of the world, forming layers, or lenses, inside the ice that probably would work their way to the surface as ice melted above and froze beneath."[19]

Risk from drilling and transport increases as new sources of oil are found. How great is the risk? The *New York Times* (February 17, 1975) reports: "The Pacific and Gulf coasts both bear witness to the damage that may be done by offshore drilling. According to the Council on Environmental Quality, a medium-sized field may be expected to produce in its lifetime one large platform spill (over 1,000 barrels) and either one large pipeline spill or two tanker spills, depending on which form of transport is used."

Increasing oil-tanker traffic is an even greater cause of spills than blowouts or pipelines. During 1975, according to a consultant's analysis of the files of the Coast Guard and the EPA, there were twelve thousand reported spills, dumping twenty-two million gallons into U.S. waters. This was a fraction of the amount spilled in other parts of the world.[20] In 1977 the Coast Guard implemented stringent regu-

[19] R. O. Samseier, "Oil on Ice," *Environment* 16 (1974): 4.
[20] W. Chapman and T. O'Toole, "Oil Spill Controversy Grows," *Los Angeles Times*, November 25, 1976. See also E. R. Gundlach, "Oil Tanker Disasters," *Environment* 19 (1977): 9, 16–20.

lations for oil tankers that were intended to reduce spills, but most tanker oil pollution comes from illegal oil flushing, prohibited by federal and state laws but still common on older vessels. It happens at least once or twice a week; in brief, both U.S. waters and international waters are filled with oil pollution from a variety of sources.

Each year, biologists produce additional evidence of the toxicity of oil to marine life in coastal ecosystems. They further indicate connections with food chains in the global ecology. The risk surely extends beyond the cost (in the dollars and cents of the Santa Barbara economist) of one dead sea gull. One must also question what benefits would specifically accrue from offshore oil, since it would provide the smallest fraction of U.S. needs at a time when oil is available from many other world sources. Its unavailability could have the positive effect of accelerating the search for substitute, environmentally sound energy sources.

Social and Real Perceptions

At the end of the above-quoted article "Philosophical Basis for Risk Analysis," in which models of mathematical probabilities are presented in risk-benefit analysis, the authors conclude: "Risk-benefit analysis is an increasingly important part of technology assessment. As the capability to estimate the external effects of technical systems develops, a methodology to deal with questions such as "How safe is safe enough?" is needed to efficiently allocate social resources."[21]

As important as mathematical models of probability might be to scientists and policy makers, it is difficult to find cases in which they have played a role for decision makers in a risk situation or to foresee a time when they will. Values—conservationist, conservative, entrepreneurial, from ideals, academic training, or economic interests or necessity—seem to determine which numbers the evaluator chooses, which choice the citizen makes, which decision the policy maker implements. One hopes the values will be informed with solid information, but it will have to be information all can understand.

For example, in a choice between risks of coal-fired plants or nuclear reactors, the first step to a decision is not mathematical/quan-

[21] Starr, Rudman, and Whipple, "Risk Analysis," p. 659.

titative but value-oriented/qualitative. As Budnitz and Holdren point out: "The problem seems to boil down to the proverbial one of comparing entities that are fundamentally incommensurable—apples and oranges. How does one weigh a small chance of a big disaster against a persistent routine impact that is significant but not overwhelming? How much social disruption should be tolerated to implement an energy technology that diminishes air pollution?"[22] Some people do not like the thought of the possibility of a big disaster and are quite willing to tolerate a small amount of air pollution in order to avoid the bigger risk, however small the actual possibilities are.

Environmental values manifest a concern for real problems but in some measure lie in the perceptions of the groups they represent. The nuclear energy versus coal debate presents a telling case study in that environmental groups have not mounted the same kinds of massive national campaigns against pollution from fossil fuels, despite grave health risks from their combustion, as they have against nuclear power.[23] Some reasons may be that radiation is an invisible risk—as opposed to visible pollution—and therefore possibly a very grave one, that most Americans have more or less accepted fossil-fuel power plants as inevitable without realizing the enormous health risks which result from them, or that they believe the problem will be taken care of through enforcement of emission standards. With or without environmental opposition, very little has been done to reduce health risks from fossil-fuel power plants, whereas millions of dollars—up to a billion—have been spent to reduce potential hazards of nuclear plants.

The difficulty with financially procured technological "fixes" for potential nuclear disasters is that no amount of money can completely cover human error, fanaticism, guile, deception, or even misguided values, quite apart from the safety backup systems in reactors. For example, about two hundred pounds of enriched uranium turned up missing from a Pennsylvania factory in 1965. (A nuclear bomb can be made from about ten pounds of enriched uranium.) A ten-year investigation by the FBI, the Justice Department, and the Atomic Energy Commission led many (though without positive proof) to

[22] Budnitz and Holdren, "Social and Environmental Costs," p. 576.
[23] D. J. Rose, P. W. Walsh, and L. L. Leskovjan, "Nuclear Power—Compared to What?" *American Scientist* 64 (1976): 291–299.

conclude that the uranium was diverted to Israel to build up its nuclear arsenal.[24] Unidentified government investigators and a former CIA official claimed that during the same period the Israeli government was able to hijack uranium from European sources.

It is conceivable that technological problems associated with nuclear processing can be solved, but uncertainties stemming from human factors are not so easily resolved. This could be the primary reason why the nuclear industry has lobbied heavily for government-backed insurance and a limit on the liability of nuclear plants in the event of a breakdown or a catastrophe. On the one hand, power companies claim that nuclear plants are safe from technological risk; on the other hand, they are not willing to assume liability in the case of accident (presumably because of the human element). It is noteworthy that the famous Rasmussen report on nuclear safety gave the industry high marks on safety but would not factor in any possibility which was not quantifiable. (Neither hijacking nor terrorism can be quantified, for example.)

Yet willingness to accept risks—human or technological—seems to be quite relative. Sometimes it has to do with age, cultural group, necessity, or many other factors. Dam failures have occurred fairly often historically, yet people continue to live below dams. The Federal Bureau of Reclamation study in 1977 concluded that seventeen western dams do not meet safety requirements, and tens of thousands of people could be killed in the event of dam disasters. Yet there seems to be no mass movement organized around this issue. It has been estimated that failure of Folsom Dam above Sacramento, California (not judged to be unsafe by the bureau, however), would cause 260,000 deaths, yet the subject is hardly discussed in the region.[25] In Iran and other countries in the Near East, most families return to their homes after earthquakes and realistically expect them to occur again, perhaps several times in their lives. But even though experts continue to insist that probabilities of nuclear disasters are much, much lower than are those of such natural catastrophes, dam failures,

[24] D. Burnham, "U.S. Agencies Suspected Missing Uranium Went to Israel for Arms," *New York Times*, November 6, 1977, p. 3.
[25] A. M. Weinberg, "The Maturity and Future of Nuclear Energy," *American Scientist* 64 (1976): 19.

or other technologies, a large portion of the American population is not convinced that the risks are low.

These people have good reasons for their opinions, but those opinions should not be considered as necessarily applying to all people in all places. During the First World Conference on the Human Environment in Stockholm in 1972, a significant contrast distinguished rich and poor countries. Third world countries were not concerned about pollution, because smoke plumes from smokestacks meant (and still mean) industrial production to them. And production means better living conditions. Poverty, disease, and hunger constitute *their* definition of a bad environment. Most of these countries are willing to accept huge risks from any kind of energy system, especially including nuclear reactors. Even in the United States, polls taken in some steel-producing areas have indicated that a majority of the population would rather work in an environment with high risks of disease than not work at all. Obviously their options are quite limited.

The same attitude is fostered by highly industrialized nations which do not have large supplies of coal and those which cannot afford the high costs of oil and need continued energy systems to support a high standard of living. They believe they have no option other than nuclear energy, short of dismantling their societies. In any country, energy is needed to reduce unemployment, clean up cities, and reduce pollution, but these are fairly simple goals. The forces that dictate use of dangerous fuels include the cultural values of each society, which govern what it produces beyond a comfortable life for all its citizens; how much it attempts to conserve; and the problems of world politics that might increase the risk of terrorist hijacking of nuclear fuels. That is, the problem of risk is only one factor among the many factors that influence decisions of a society.

An Array of Considerations

William Lowrance summarizes the "array of considerations" with the following outline regarding the range of opposing types of risk:[26]

---

[26] Lowrance, *Of Acceptable Risk*, p. 87.

1. Risk assumed voluntarily ....Risk borne involuntarily
2. Effect immediate ....Effect delayed
3. No alternatives available ....Many alternatives available
4. Risk known with certainty ....Risk not known
5. Exposure is an essential ....Exposure is a luxury
6. Encountered occupationally ....Encountered nonoccupationally
7. Common hazard ....Dread hazard
8. Affects average people ....Affects especially sensitive people
9. Will be used as intended ....Likely to be misused
10. Consequences reversible ....Consequences irreversible

Most of these possibilities apply to environmental risk.

1. It *does* make a difference whether a person bears a risk voluntarily, say, in a factory, but it still may be unethical to assume that a person assumes all risks when he or she accepts a job. It is worse when a person is forced to accept a dangerous position because of financial duress.
2. Immediate safety from risk does not necessarily mean long-term safety. This is the case with many carcinogenic agents such as asbestos, which cause long-range effects or possible genetic disturbances.
3. Some nations feel that few or no alternatives exist besides those that involve risk. In 1974, U.S. EPA Administrator Russell Train permitted the use of DDT on the tussock moth in the Northwest because, he claimed, the infestation by the insect was an emergency situation, and, according to him, "no alternative" was available.
4. Scientific certainty is lacking in a number of areas; values play an important role in determining personal certainty.
5. It is no doubt more essential to face the risks involved from industries which support a regional economy than the risks from cigarette smoking.
6. Occupational risks have been demonstrably more dangerous than nonoccupational risks.
7. Some "dread" risks like those linked to cancer tend to sway opinion more than common hazards like those from the automobile or from fossil fuel plants.
8. People who are especially sensitive to particular risks are likely to be ignored or cared for last.

9. Some products, like pesticides and artificial fertilizers, tend to be overused (thereby creating greater risks) because of manufacturers' specifications and a fear of losing crops from underuse.

10. In many environmental questions, the reversibility or irreversibility of an action, that is, whether it can be "undone," is paramount in risk assessment.

"Rationality" and Risk-taking

Finally, the problem of risk can be reduced to society's "prudent" judgment, that is, how much society is willing to pay to save x number of lives, even though almost every human action contains some built-in risk. Richard Wilson of the Energy and Environmental Center at Harvard University contends that establishing a public policy goal of zero risk, or of eliminating any possible risk of cancer at any cost, is an irrational goal. He cites the OSHA proposal for benzene regulation as a typical example:

I have calculated, using OSHA's own numbers for the cost of regulation, that the proposal would require the expenditure of $300 million to save one hypothetical life. (On this basis, the whole gross national product of $2 trillion would be expended in saving about 6,000 lives.) But the situation carries with it a deeper paradox: Lives will be lost in the process of manufacturing the control equipment—my estimate being on the average, one life is lost for $75 million of such expenditure. Thus, enormously expensive steps are proposed that will possibly take four lives in order to save possibly one life. Although it is probable that benzene exposure should be controlled further, the level and detail of control proposed is clearly not appropriate.[27]

Wilson suggests that if data are not available, policy makers should assume that cancer incidence is proportional to exposure levels. They should not attempt to root out all possibility of human susceptibility to cancer. Presently, the 1959 Federal Code's Delaney Clause for the Food and Drug Administration demands that no detectable carcinogen may be used in food, no matter how minute the amount. Yet, to be consistent, if policy makers wanted to ban all known carcinogens, they would have to stop all cigarette smoking,

[27] R. Wilson, "A Rational Approach to Reducing Cancer Risk," *New York Times*, July 9, 1978, p. E 17.

fossil fuel burning, and wood or charcoal broiling of steaks. The list could be made much longer if they were to include many more carcinogens which are suspect but not fully proved.

Lowrance's schema is helpful to clarify the debate about risk and conservation attitudes. Some further conclusions can be made about risk and the drift of American society.

First, it appears that avoidance of risk itself has a value that teaches that a culture need not throw itself headlong into more energy development which leads to problems of health and nuclear energy. There are many kinds of energy consumption, some ludicrous and wasteful, some important and essential. Risk avoidance pushes us to find a way to establish priorities, needs, and lifeline energy systems; to mandate conservation measures; and to rethink societal goals and objectives.

Second, statistical information is often guesswork. The carcinogenic effects of chemicals usually are known only after feeding doses to laboratory animals and then extrapolating the results to humans. Measuring radiation effects on humans is more precise but difficult to pinpoint. We know that exposure to chemicals and to radiation is harmful; the question is, How important is it that we are exposed to either?

Dr. Arthur C. Upton, director of the National Cancer Institute and an internationally recognized expert on the biological effects of radiation, summed up the problem: "Virtually every responsible radiation body has accepted the hypothesis that there is no dose of radiation so small as to do no harm. No one can say categorically that a threshold does not exist, but on theoretical grounds it seems unreasonable to support the existence of one. We need to balance radiation risks versus other risks. The question is not whether radiation is harmful, but whether other risks—from cutting back on electric power or foregoing a dental or medical x-ray—are greater."[28]

The list of priorities seems especially important in the exploration and exploitation of oil reserves. Some sites on the outer continental shelf, such as the Channel Island Outer Continental Shelf near Santa Barbara, the Georges Bank off the coast of Massachusetts, and the Alaskan shelf, should be exploited last because of excessive vul-

[28] R. T. Lyons, "Radiation Studies Are Stumbling at the Threshold," *New York Times*, February 11, 1979.

nerability to spills and blowouts (caused or exacerbated by earthquakes and icebergs) or because of extraordinary beauty and productivity of marine life.

Third, the citizens of the local area which is to be developed
should be given the option of accepting or rejecting a project involving risk after all other permits have been approved and a full discussion aired. If the public has the right to build schools or roads, it
surely has a right to determine whether a nuclear reactor or industrial
complex is built.

What Can Be Done

From Part II, where the recent history of environmentalism is
discussed, one might draw the conclusion that the environmental
movement has been gaining strength in recent years and that it can
hardly fail to continue its momentum in the future. The scientific-
ecologic tradition has bloomed into clearly defined environmental
health concerns. If one looks closely at the types of environmental
gains that have been made, it appears that likelihood of success increases only when biocentric, ecologic, or economic traditions can
support an issue, along with a strong political and economic base, of
course. Yet it has been very difficult for environmentalists to win
support for issues connected with risk or national development and
growth.

The reason can be found in the dynamics of institutional change.
Traditionally it has not been difficult to change aspects of the system
which have not threatened society's basic economic structure and distribution of privileges. Large tracts of nature can be preserved for
aesthetic appreciation or conserved for wise use, and a certain sensitivity to the necessity of ecological balance can be incorporated within larger societal goals. When and if environmentalists step beyond
those traditional goals to the extent of challenging the assumptions
of material progress, or of criticizing the effects of economic development and advocating alternatives or changes in the structure of the
political economy, the power of the vested interest swings against
them.

It is foolish to try to predict the long-range resolution of the struggle over environmentalist goals, because a number of short-range legal and legislative victories have tended to consolidate environmentalist support (and opposition) and have made more sweeping later changes possible.

The quality of environmental politics in the past has depended on the quality of both environmental analysis and support. It will be much more difficult to establish environmental priorities in the future because more sweeping societal questions are at stake. Conflicts of values, politics, and ethics are woven into these questions.

PART IV
EMERGING PRIORITIES

9

The Public Good

IN early 1977 the following editorial appeared in the *Wall Street Journal*:

Heroes of the Movement

Jack B. Weinstein, a federal district judge in Brooklyn, decided last week that there hasn't been enough environmental paperwork—only 4,043 pages—on the sale of federal oil and gas leases off New Jersey last August. So he voided the $1.1 billion deal.

A few days before, Interior Secretary Cecil Andrus, an Idaho environmentalist, canceled the sale, scheduled for tomorrow, of oil and gas leases in the lower Cook Inlet of Alaska. He plans an environmental and geological "review" of this and five other lease sales scheduled by the previous administration.

If we go back a little further, there is the injunction granted against completion of a $116 million TVA hydroelectric project on the Little Tennessee River by a federal judge in Cincinnati on grounds that it threatened a little fish called the Tennessee snail darter.

And before that there was the $2 billion Seabrook nuclear power project in New Hampshire, first announced by the government and then held up by an EPA man in Boston over some implied threat to clam larvae, and still pending in Washington.

Then there was the proposed $700 million Dickey-Lincoln hydroelectric project on Maine's Upper St. John River, stalled by a controversy over environmentalist claims that it would threaten the Furbish lousewort. And before that, Appalachian Power's proposed New River hydroelectric project in Virginia and North Carolina, was scotched when the U.S. declared the river a "wilderness" area.

Then there are those oil shale projects in Utah and Colorado. They may not have panned out economically, but it will be sometime before we know for sure, because they too are stalled on environmental grounds. Finally, there was that famous Kaiparowits coal fired electric plant in Utah, scrapped last year by the utilities that had proposed to build it. During the 13 years the project was being considered, estimated costs increased sevenfold to a prohibitive $3.5 billion and the utilities spent $5 million on paperwork alone. In that case, it was the black-footed ferret, the kangaroo rat and several other species in the vicinity of the project that supposedly would have been threatened.

The ideas that man should never again disturb the environment for his economic ends, that after eons evolution shall end and even the most insignificant species shall never again vanish, that nothing shall go forward until the most remote danger to the environment is resolved through endless judicial processes, are responsible for the billions in economic losses represented in the above projects. It may be time to ask if that is truly a rational way to address the future.

It is certainly time to ask whether anyone can honestly believe that the energy shortages now besetting the nation are the result of a lack of natural resources. And time to ask whether the heroes of the environmentalist movement—the men and women who blithely damage the future prospects for millions of American workers and their families on dubious grounds—are as heroic as their admirers think.[1]

Under the seemingly unemotional statement of facts in the editorial, a good deal of passion is smoldering. To one who is accustomed to thinking in terms of cost curves or benefit-cost analysis (or any other specific kind of economic value), the enormous expenditure of money on environmental skirmishes represents one of the great financial catastrophes of the modern age. Rockefeller and Carnegie certainly did not have these problems, and because they did not, they were able to "rationalize" their industries out of chaos within a generation.

Much has already been said in this book about why environmentalists use whatever tools are available in order to effect environmental change. Without attempting to answer or agree with the writer's well-chosen examples on a case-by-case basis or to repeat what has been explained about the variety of environmental traditions and values, it is possible to discuss major issues raised in the editorial which transcend individual cases. It is certainly "time to ask if [economic loss because of environmental conflicts] is truly a rational way to

[1] *Wall Street Journal*, February 22, 1977, p. 22.

address the future"; the need is even more pressing to clarify the basis of regional and national rationality.

Goals and Values

One can establish principles of rationality only after a group settles on goals. Then it can sometimes be proved that some methods are more efficient or rational to reach those particular goals than are other methods. So long as unchecked economic growth represented a consensus in American society, many social and environmental side effects (that is, "evils") could be ignored. Now other goals and values have been pushed into the public consciousness—many precipitated by environmental struggles. Eventually these other goals and values have found their way into the directives of public policy. The process appears irrational to the *Wall Street Journal* writer because there seems to be no institution to iron out the contradictions of the conflicting goals and values.

The alternative goals—unfettered economic growth or environmental quality with a minimum of risk—and their respective means appear to be rational in themselves, because they carry their own sets of assumptions and values with them. It is a common trait to characterize those outside the logic of one's own perspective as irrational, particularly if the proponent tends to stress both goals and means which are defined solely in terms of economic efficiency. Efficiency is a capitalist value. It is possible to prefer "irrationality" to goals associated with capitalist or material accumulation or to set environmental goals not based on efficiency and still to attempt (efficiently) to achieve alternative results.

It can also be noted that the complaints registered in the editorial tend to discredit certain theories that the capitalist elite dominate the democratic process in the United States.[2] If in fact environmen-

[2] T. R. Dye and H. Zeigler, *The Irony of Democracy* (Belmont, Calif.: Wadsworth, 1970). Dye and Zeigler give an extended explanation of elite theory. See also T. R. Dye, *Understanding a Public Policy* (Englewood Cliffs, N.J.: Prentice-Hall, 1972), pp. 17–37. This source gives a summary of other political models. See also W. R. Burch, "Who Participates—A Sociological Interpretation of Natural Resource Decisions," *Natural Resources Journal* 16 (1976): 41–54.

talism is costing an elite group billions of dollars—which it is—perhaps discarded theories of pluralism should be reviewed and rethought. Environmentalists also constitute a minority group, but in the main they have not encouraged the goals of those captains of industry who in the past have contributed representatives of the economic elite to government (despite the charges of Richard Neuhaus, in *In Defense of People* [1971], which flew in all directions). And although some wilderness advocates, scientists, and economists might accept some of the goals of the middle- or upper-class consensus, the movement as a whole espouses qualitatively different goals. Even President Carter himself did not hesitate to challenge the strongest of the lobbies, the oil companies, while defending his conservationist energy plan.

It would be naive to assume, of course, that the upper economic groups do not command enough financial power to control in large measure the direction of American resource exploitation. Yet countervailing environmental forces with a different kind of power—traditional or quasi-religious and intellectual (which are needed by capital as well for continued expansion)—have been able successfully to challenge the ability of the elite groups to control America's environmental destiny completely. Furthermore, almost a dozen federal agencies and similar ones in all of the states exist to oversee environmental interests. These cannot all be dominated by monied interests, although that might often seem to be the case. The question remains, When and under what circumstances do they block environmental controls?

The variety of environmental battles among conflict groups discussed in this book has indicated that the powerful groups do not always determine the outcome of the struggle. No one group enjoys the power needed for complete domination, nationally, regionally, or locally. Nor are single groups necessarily interested in all decisions made in government. Therefore, the conservation groups are able to elicit support from economic interests on special issues at particular periods of time and at particular places. All the while the special interests of environmentalism itself have been expanding as a new power group, the environmental technicians, has arisen to write impact statements and to staff new government agencies.

As historian Samuel Hayes has pointed out, both government and industry have profited from *conservation's* emphasis on efficiency at the turn of the century. This kind of "rationality," along with government cooperation with industry, has given the large corporation the stability which has enabled it to expand and control markets in the utilities, steel, oil, and other industries. More recently, the chemical industry, while suffering attacks by environmentalists for toxic or carcinogenic chemicals, has moved into profitable areas of pollution control. To repeat, it is not easy to separate environmental interests from antienvironmental ones.

The rationality to which the *Wall Street Journal* aspires is less than pure. On one hand, agencies, bureaus, and governments can be dominated or coopted by special economic interests. On the other hand, the agencies and environmental groups like to use power games borrowed from the establishment to stop development in behalf of environmental causes. But whereas in the past conservation people have often supported and furthered the aims of powerful interests, the issues of growth and risk seem to have frustrated their purposes in recent times.

At bottom it might be that the *Journal* was irritated or alarmed at the influence of environmentalists, at their successes, and at their access to decision makers. No doubt the *Journal* was upset by the unwonted environmental values of even the president. The decades of environmental struggle may have seemed to pay off before environmentalism deserved such recognition. In any case, a rational public policy, on which the *Journal* is insisting, demands that the policy makers must

1. Know all of the society's value preferences and their relative weights
2. Know all of the policy alternatives available
3. Know all of the consequences of each policy alternative
4. Calculate the ratio of achieved to sacrificed societal values for each policy alternative
5. Select the most efficient policy alternative.[3]

[3] Dye, *Understanding a Public Policy*, p. 27.

These conditions assume that *all* the value preferences of society can be known and weighed with a predictive capacity to foresee consequences of policy alternatives. As we have seen, conflicting values are difficult to compare—the apples and oranges problem—and policy makers have not in the past been noted for a rational weighing of alternatives even when thousands of pages of scientific data have been available for an assessment of *present* social, economic, and environmental impacts.

Environmental Policy Decisions

Each faction struggles to achieve short-range goals with very limited tools, as the editorial implies. The environmental impact statement is a good example of a policy instrument which has cost a great deal of money and has been used to the advantage of both growth and antigrowth forces. Very often local development projects are rubber-stamped and sanctioned with a predisposed or inadequate impact report which is supposed to prove the project's environmental purity. At other times federal agencies determine that a specific project does not "significantly" affect the natural environment. In such situations projects do not even require a statement. Development interest groups often have found allies in the new middle-class professionals in charge of overseeing impact reports.

On the other hand, some highways, dams, airports, industrial sites, and nuclear waste disposal sites have been cancelled or postponed, if not because of an environmental impact statement, at least as a result of the litigation that stemmed from a controversy over the report. More often the developers have been required to modify some aspect of the project to bring it into line with environmental standards. The Alaskan pipeline is an example of one such proposal that was changed after environmental assessment but not completely stopped.

Most projects are decided upon, especially by government officials, long before the impact report is filed.[4] And despite the clear

---

[4] R. Odell, "NEPA—It's Still a Hard Act to Follow," *Environmental Action* (July, 1976): 4–8. See also B. A. Ackerman, S. A. Ackerman, J. W. Sawyer, and D. W. Henderson, *The Uncertain Search for Environmental Quality*

intent of the National Environmental Policy Act, no governmental agency is required to follow the recommendations of the impact statement, even if it suggests specific environmental provisions. Nor are there built-in enforcement procedures. All is left to the "irrational" vigilance of nearby environmentalists, who will sue if need be. Long-term goals are necessarily transformed into short-range tactical maneuvers.

The Tocks Island Dam Project, referred to in chapter 1, suggests the structural problems of environmental planning when many kinds of interest groups battle over their rights in the public arena. Another study which looks at the attempt to clean up the Delaware River underlines the myriad of difficulties in the implementation of a "rational" public policy regarding public goods (in this case, unpolluted water).[5]

First a study group was commissioned by the U.S. Public Health Service to provide an analysis, called the Delaware Estuary Comprehensive Study (DECS). Antipollution decisions were then to be made on the basis of the study by the Delaware River Basin Commission (DRBC), which included the governors of the affected states and the secretary of the interior. Much ado was made of this cooperative venture in policy making, but local interests and competing governmental units blocked both quick, effective bargaining and hoped-for action. The DECS analysis itself was laden with the value assumptions of its writers, giving decision makers extra reasons to upbraid the report. The very separation of the "thinking agency" (DECS) and the "acting agency" (DRCB) contributed largely to confusion and impasse. "Cooperative federalism" or decentralization of decision making did not facilitate "rational" or fair policy implementation. On the other hand, more centralization might have put so much power into the hands of the decision makers that it would have tempted them to ignore those who did not share their own values. Less importance is given to discussion and bargaining when one authority has all the power.

(New York: The Free Press, 1974). This source contains an extremely informative case study (and policy analysis) of efforts by local and regional agencies to clean up the Delaware River.

[5] Ackerman, et al., *Uncertain Search*.

Clean Air Policy

The same kinds of goal conflicts and value conflicts have followed the less-than-rational application of the Clean Air Act. In 1970 Congress imposed a strict schedule on car manufacturers for reducing pollutants, and the EPA was required to establish nationwide air pollution standards to protect human health. The states were to file implementation plans with the EPA by the middle of 1975. Not one state had complied with EPA air pollution guidelines by that date, though all had begun to implement their own less stringent programs. Neither had the thirty-one major metropolitan areas begun to implement plans to lower pollution levels by reducing, rescheduling, or redistributing traffic.

One reason for the lack of compliance was the 1973 oil crisis, which led to Project Independence and the increase of coal burning, clearly a change in national goals and a lessening of earlier interest. Even though the power plants which were required to switch from oil- to coal-burning facilities were also bound by strict air pollution requirements, none paid much attention to the clean air rules.[6] Environmental purposes were uneconomic, and no teeth were put into the new requirements. Perhaps the shift in national purposes led to that tactic.

Neither did environmental considerations play a role in a new Department of Energy policy in 1979 to encourage the burning of natural gas instead of coal. When the Natural Gas Policy Act of 1978, a key bill of President Carter's energy package, became law, gradual deregulation of natural gas encouraged stepped-up development of old and new fields. Almost immediately a surplus of natural gas developed because intrastate gas could be marketed to consumer states at higher prices. Thus, in early 1979 Energy Secretary James R. Schlesinger urged electric utilities and industrial users to return to natural gas as an energy source and assured them that they would "be

---

[6] This fact was emphasized by a utilities industry spokesman in April, 1977, on a special "Meet the Press" program discussing President Carter's energy program. His point was that the air-pollution rules were unrealistic and uneconomic. Another industrial spokesman candidly admitted that he believed that corporations would put off pollution control equipment for as long as possible since they would save money for capital expenditure and maintenance for every year they did not utilize the equipment.

provided every encouragement to burn gas instead of oil." Coal was at the moment to be deemphasized.

State and local agencies set up to monitor and enforce pollution standards often follow the values of locals, or at least the local representatives. Texas and Oklahoma have different values and norms from those of New York and California. Local industry can pressure regional agencies more effectively than federal environmental staff people can. Sometimes monitoring is done by a local health department which is understaffed and lacking in proper equipment. Since it is not mandatory to use "in-stack" monitoring devices, it is not always possible to identify the offender. When proved guilty, large industries will pay insignificant fines and contest verdicts when they feel harassed.

Although the Clean Air Act states, "the prevention and control of air pollution at its source is the primary responsibility of States and local Governments . . . ," the EPA sets standards for certain pollutants and prosecutes single cases. Furthermore, the Federal Water Pollution Act of 1972 authorizes the EPA to bring actions and seek orders against polluters and fine them. However, the EPA is also hampered by a shortage of lawyers, the length of time each case requires, and resentment from state and local authorities when the agency moves on a case. Often EPA activity is publicly attacked by industry and local and state agencies together, which makes enforcement a difficult political matter.

Even when the EPA set new guidelines in 1973 for construction projects which would attract auto traffic, the local uproar was spread across the country. One southern California paper headlined, "Hard Hats Damn EPA"; Senator Goldwater spoke for many politicians when he wrote to President Nixon: "I resent it very much for some Washington, San Francisco, or any other bureaucrat telling my state how to run [its] affairs and ramming impractical and unreasonable regulations down [its] throat."[7]

Nationally, EPA guidelines have fluctuated with changing policy goals or technological fixes and enforcement. On the one hand, during the first two years of its existence after 1970, when standards and

[7] J. Quarles, *Cleaning Up America* (Boston: Houghton-Mifflin, 1976), pp. 47ff., 209.

requirements had not yet been set, the agency was able to initiate over one thousand enforcement actions, and in the following two years it fined one thousand more. On the other hand, the EPA exempted eight steel plants in Ohio's Mahoning Valley because "severe economic and employment disruptions" might have resulted if the plants had been forced to clean up water discharges into the Mahoning River.

Another EPA requirement, one for the automobile industry to install catalytic converters in new models to break down emissions of dangerous compounds, was lifted in 1975 because a study (later discredited) indicated that the converters seemed to be producing other potentially dangerous sulfates which could interact with water vapor in the atmosphere. Congress mandated that final pollution standards for autos be reached by the time the 1978 models were marketed. Rather than enforce desulfurization of gasoline at a time of rising prices, EPA Administrator Russell Train lifted the requirement, though such decisions were to be made only by Congress. Many of those who lived in large metropolitan regions cursed the decision for its effect on them, but those in less populous areas cheered, and the oil and auto industries breathed, if not cleaner air, at least a sigh of relief.

In 1977, under heavy lobbying from the auto industry, which claimed that requirements were unmeetable (though about one-half dozen independent analyses indicated that the standards originally set by the Clean Air Act could have been met and were met by several foreign auto makers), Congress relaxed auto emissions standards which were to have gone into effect that year.

Then in early 1979 the EPA decreed that the permissible amount of ozone in the air may rise to 0.12 part ozone per million parts of air from 0.08 part per million, the earlier standard. EPA Administrator Douglas Costle said that the change was "based on a careful evaluation of medical and scientific evidence." Immediately the American Petroleum Institute filed a suit contending that the rule was still more stringent than necessary, and the Environmental Defense Fund and other environmental groups claimed that the new standard would seriously affect the health of people with asthma.

The most recent episode in the conflicts between environmentalists and foes has been the use of traditional environmentalist weapons—the lawsuit and the impact report—against the environmentalists themselves.[8] Developers, landowners, dam supporters, and others have begun to serve summonses on environmental groups on a range of charges from trespassing and defamation of character to property loss. Partly as a result of the rising number of lawsuits in recent years, the cost of liability insurance for large environmental groups has greatly increased. In one case, a citizen of southern California served a summons on a Sierra Club president because a mountain lion attacked his horse.

In another suit, four of the largest oil companies won a ruling that the Federal Trade Commission would be required to prepare an environmental impact statement before proceeding with its antitrust complaint against the eight largest oil companies. The presumption of the oil companies and the judge is that large firms would cause less damage to the environment than many small firms; as the judge put it, "in the rare case where the FTC determines that the severity of the offense doesn't justify the environmental cost of remedying it, no doubt we all will be better off bearing the noncompetitive effects rather than paying for competition with our natural resources."

Thus, if changing values and conflicting goals on the federal, regional, and local levels have brought messy and costly confusion in public policy, it is also true that the time-honored traditions of American governance have contributed their share of problems. The system of legal advocacy whereby the "truth" is discovered in an adversary relationship instead of rational discussion and establishing of priorities and goals has in fact been one of the few ways that any party can get a hearing for its case. This is not the place to question the worth of an institution of such long standing, but a few of the results of the process should be examined.

---

[8] B. Stall, "Ecologists' Big Weapon Being Used Against Them," *Los Angeles Times*, February 15, 1977, p. 7. See also R. Lindsey, "Tax-Exempt Foundations Formed to Help Business Fight Regulation," *New York Times*, February 12, 1978.

The Adversary Relationship

In most of the adversary relationships discussed throughout this book, private legal actions by conservationists were employed to achieve environmental ends, sometimes against developers or industries and sometimes against governmental agencies. The federal government itself has used its powers over natural resources both in a regulatory function and in civil suits. The EPA has become involved in the largest number of disputes over air and water requirements. For example, Du Pont and seven other chemical companies claimed in court that Congress had given the EPA the power only to issue guidelines, not to issue mandatory regulations over industrial discharges; they took the case all the way to the Supreme Court, which rejected their arguments.

The EPA has also had a long-standing dispute with U.S. Steel in Pittsburgh.[9] The battle has been particularly significant because basic issues of health, jobs, quality of life, environmental degradation, and industrial exigencies all have been raised within the volatile context of an adversary relationship. Industrial leader and former U.S. Steel Chairman Edward Speer unofficially represented a number of lesser firms in his complaints about environmental rules and job safety regulations, alleged stifling of production, threatening of jobs and curtailing of economic growth. The EPA, on its side, has been a source of inspiration to local environmentalists for the values it has upheld in the long struggle.

In early 1976 in a speech before a business research group, deputy EPA Administrator John Quarles chided U.S. Steel for a "record of environmental recalcitrance . . . and being more willing to enter into confrontation with the government than almost any other company," and he cited the following examples:

1. U.S. Steel refused to slow down production during a serious air-pollution alert in Birmingham in 1971.
2. It refused to comply with a water pollution permit program under

[9] K. P. Maise, "Can EPA Clean up U.S. Steel?" *Environmental Action*, September, 1976, pp. 4–8. See also E. Morgenthaler, "U.S. Steel, EPA Fight Long Running Battles over Plant Pollution," *Wall Street Journal*, August 6, 1976; and Quarles, *Cleaning Up America*, pp. 53–57, 116, 230–231.

the 1899 Refuse Act until the EPA threatened Justice Department prosecution.

3. It received delays year after year from 1965 on to replace heavily polluting open-hearth furnaces in Gary, Indiana, and then closed them at the end of 1974, claiming that twenty-five hundred jobs would be affected, but actually laying off about five hundred and blaming the EPA for causing unemployment. (In late 1978 the EPA sued for "long-standing air pollution" violations at the Gary mill.)

4. U.S. Steel violated a similar compliance schedule in Alabama in 1974, where furnaces were emitting three thousand tons of pollutants a year.

5. The company continually violates water pollution regulations in Gary and other places. (In late 1978 the EPA sued for the company's failure to install a water treatment system for blast furnace wastes at the Lorain, Ohio, plant.)

U.S. Steel denied most of the charges.

U.S. Steel owns the Clairton Coke Works near Pittsburgh, where vegetation around the plant has all but vanished. During negotiations with the EPA and local agencies over increased concentrations of soot and dirt emissions in 1977, the confrontation became more intense. Attorney Anthony Picadio, who was advising a county official, reflected (in a *Wall Street Journal* report) on the behavior of the U.S. Steel representative: "It was incredible. Every time you would offend him, he'd grab his papers, throw them in his briefcase and say, 'We're just not going to negotiate.'" U.S. Steel eventually agreed to clean up the Clairton plant by the late 1980s, but the company rarely keeps a court consent decree on time.

Is such an adversary relationship the "rational" way to solve serious problems of health and the environment?

The U.S. Labor Department has known for many years and has reported that "men employed at coke ovens have an excessive risk of lung cancer," and those at the top of the ovens are five times more susceptible to that disease than are other steelworkers, who suffer from abnormally high rates of it as well. Finally, in 1975 the department proposed emission rules for coke ovens to lessen health hazards

from the emissions. Next, the Ford administration Wage-Price Council opposed the rules because of the high costs of installation. The
industry's American Iron and Steel Institute then claimed that the
proposed standards were unattainable, and the United Steelworkers'
Union produced studies which showed that the rules were not stringent enough to safeguard the health of the workers. The steel industry
took the matter to court, where after a few years and millions of dollars in legal fees the Labor Department's coke-oven emissions standards were upheld.

There are many more examples of suits by private groups against
government agencies and industry, by agencies against industry, and
by industry against private groups and government agencies, as the
editorial opening the chapter indicates. In each case the *de facto*
planning was done by opposing parties representing conflicting values
in an adversary situation. The government agencies themselves sometimes represent qualitatively different values of commercial development or environmental protection; in other words, the Department
of Commerce, Bureau of Reclamation, Army Corps of Engineers,
Department of Transportation, and the Department of Energy have
not represented the same values as those of the Environmental Protection Agency. The irrationality of conflict should not be laid at
the feet of the "heroes of the movement," who, after all, have been
loyal and committed to those values which have directed their purposes, but instead should be ascribed to the difficulty of planning in
a socially diverse and complex social system. A single rational goal,
or goals supported by similar values, can no longer be applied to the
American nation, if it ever could. More specifically, not everyone now
accepts the desirability of unchecked growth or undue risk.

Environmentalists have resorted to the adversary process mostly
because it has been their most successful tactic to achieve their purposes, especially when the movement was more wilderness-oriented.
Environmental lawyers have even defended the process as the most
equitable and the most nearly certain to reach the "truth" when reasonable and unreasonable parties differ.[10] There are many priorities,

[10] J. Sax, *Defending the Environment* (New York: Vintage, 1971); and
D. Sive, "The Role of Litigation in Environmental Policy," *Natural Resources
Journal* 11 (1971): 470–477.

however, where more is at stake than differing opinions about whether the law is protecting environmental quality. Furthermore, only those with the financial resources to protect their health or environment can do so. The Sierra Club or the Environmental Defense Fund or any other group must make decisions about which legal battles are most important, for their treasuries do not stretch very far, and some cases cost millions of dollars. Although legal victories do make a difference in many areas, it seems as though environmentalists are running in all directions at once, rushing to plug a myriad of new holes in the dike.

There are other difficulties connected with court settlement of environmental issues, particularly cases implementing the National Environmental Policy Act (NEPA).[11] Lower courts can be overruled by each other and by the Supreme Court, and Congress can override them all by changing legislation. Courts are notoriously influenced by the political environment in which they exist when criticisms mount against them. Furthermore, environmental litigants must battle against prevailing power and popular attitudes fostered by commercial, industrial, and agency interests as well as procedural rules which are stacked against litigants. A loss on any technical ground can throw out a case. Long-term environmental goals and objectives are submerged in libraries full of procedural minutiae and ten-thousand-page environmental impact statements which intimidate ordinary citizens concerned about the environment.

Growth (Sprawl) or Land-Use Planning

The adversary relationship has also settled the issues of suburban sprawl—truly irrational development around the nation's urban areas. Environmentalists have found themselves in the middle of all kinds of land-use and settlement questions, not only with industrial fights or wilderness-protection issues. The problems of population distribution and industrial development, of course, are quite complex. To leave their resolution to market forces or adversary litigation seems to assure the pattern of irrationality.

[11] H. J. Courtner, "A Case Analysis of Policy Implementation NEPA," *Natural Resources Journal* 16 (1976): 334–336.

Historically, for example, suburban sprawl occurred because land was cheaper in rural areas, cheap government loans were available, and highways were subsidized by the federal, local, and state governments. Rate payers in the cities paid for new utilities in the suburbs. Cheap gasoline, ever-extending highways, and relative quiet in the country spurred land developers to buy up cheap land in undeveloped areas—land that was cheap a generation ago. Since they were interested in cutting expenses rather than efficient and orderly development of facilities, land developers bought where they could in leapfrog fashion, and local governments tied the pieces together with roads and utilities. In the meantime, the cities, where the utilities and transportation already existed, were disintegrating. Pollution and sprawl were increasing. Prime agricultural land was taken out of production because it brought in more money from developers than from food production. City limits and metropolitan expansion were chaotically planned; often the land itself spread over six times the amount actually used.

Suburban shopping centers and malls, increasingly popular in the 1960s and 1970s, have also contributed significantly to the waste and inefficient use of land and energy resources. The mall is a regional shopping center built usually on the outskirts of a medium to large city near a freeway. In 1977 more than eight hundred new shopping centers were opened, with 118 million square feet of retail space covering formerly rural lands. One mall south of Dayton, Ohio, is typical of hundreds around the country.[12] Like most shopping centers, the Dayton Mall was once thousands of acres of fields, pastures, and woodlands. These are now transformed into a gigantic complex of buildings and parking lots large enough for almost 7,000 cars. An average of 15,800 autos go into the mall every day (31,600 one-way trips) despite the availability of shopping facilities nearer to the average shopper. Shopping expeditions to the mall from as far away as thirty miles are reported quite common.

Because of the unprecedented drawing power of the mall (it is

[12] *NDRC Newsletter* 6 (1977): 213, 218–219. See also U.S. Transportation Research Bureau, *Transportation and Land Development Policy* (Washington, D.C.: Government Printing Office, 1976), no. 565. See also P. H. Glassman and D. G. Sisler, "Highways, Changing Land Use and Impacts on Rural Life," *Growth and Change* 7 (April, 1976): 3–8.

completely "climate controlled" within its futuristic dome), hundreds of other enterprises line the freeway and other roads on the way to and from it: discount and amusement centers, fast-food chains, housing developments, and industries, for example. Since the design of the area, as is the case with most shopping centers, has been made dependent on auto traffic (it is nearly impossible to walk to most malls), the air quality of the entire region has deteriorated dramatically. Civic leaders fear that the city itself will suffer economic loss as the Dayton Mall draws more and more business from the downtown commercial center.

There as elsewhere, suburban roads and freeways have been initially responsible for opening up land for haphazard sprawling development. A typical pattern is established in the suburbs as traffic congestion justifies road expansion, which accelerates further development. Because of the Clean Air Act provisions, which limit the amount of pollution in a metropolitan region, road building that precipitates further development is increasingly viewed by planners and local air quality board members as a key to environmental degradation. Furthermore, the act gives the EPA implicit power to oversee the implementation of land use and transportation controls when local agencies ignore pollution standards.

The structural difficulty throughout the country comes from the lack of state or federal provisions to coordinate land use and transportation plans on a statewide or regional level. Most states and counties have not placed curbs on road building or on sewer hookups or even water development schemes in the West, all of which encourage spread-out, inefficient growth (and pollution) while the Clean Air Act has mandated less pollution. The inevitable contradiction in public policies seems to have been lost on public officials.

Neither has President Carter's energy plan included enough provisions which would point up the necessity of continued development of mass transit as energy and land conservation measures. Positive encouragement with financial incentives must be used to lure people out of cars and into energy-saving, less polluting public transportation. Higher taxes on gasoline by themselves cannot solve the problem of land and transportation planning around cities.

Public Response to Sprawl

Local residents in some areas of the country have begun to fight the effects of sprawl in a number of its aspects—freeway construction, open-space disruption, coastline degradation, air and water pollution —in the public forum through court litigation, lobbying, petition, and the initiative process.

Many citizens of California were the first in the nation to revolt against the consequences of uncontrolled growth.[13] The coalition which was formed in many local areas included a mix far more diverse than only environmentalist types. Freeway opposition started in 1964 in San Francisco, where citizen groups pressured the Board of Supervisors to reject a state plan for an eight-lane highway through Golden Gate Park. Later in the same year local groups stopped a freeway near the west shore of Lake Tahoe. As more citizen activity threatened continued freeway construction, a group to "save" the freeways was formed to "fight the propaganda of a small but vociferous, anti-automobile anti-freeway group that is threatening to stop construction of vitally needed thoroughfares."

Nevertheless, by the mid-1970s the antifreeway forces managed to stop construction of over half of the state's proposed 12,500-mile freeway network, especially in the Los Angeles area, where freeways already go almost everywhere, and in the San Francisco Bay Area. Poverty groups have joined environmentalists in a number of these battles because the homes and neighborhoods of the poor were the first to be destroyed in freeway construction, and in those days no one had the responsibility to see to it that minorities had other homes to move to.

During the same time period, several dozen California cities and counties made some move toward growth stabilization. The arguments of antigrowth groups often fell back on studies which proved that it would be less expensive for local governments to buy the land for open space than to subsidize the new developments with sewers, schools, roads, water, trees, fire and police protection, and other community services. Developers had their own studies which demon-

[13] T. Harris, "Californians Are Saying 'No' to Growth in a Spreading Revolt That Makes Strange Allies," *California Journal* (July, 1973): 224–229.

strated that the broadened tax base would actually increase revenues for city and county. Most people had their minds made up long before the studies were presented.

The case of the small town of Petaluma, forty miles north of San Francisco, is significant both because the Supreme Court upheld the constitutionality of their plan to regulate multiple-housing construction and because of the unusual alignment of forces represented in the contest for and against growth.[14] At least three distinct viewpoints exerted pressure on local decision makers and eventually were presented in the courts:

1. That of a group of residents who wanted to protect themselves against encroachments from the people working in San Francisco who had begun to settle in the small town about 1970, when the population was 24,870, raising it to 30,500 in two years.
2. That of environmentalists who saw the quick disintegration of the outlying natural environments where developments were springing up.
3. That of low-income people as well as developers, bankers, and others who wanted more new housing.

The city developed a plan to limit future growth in 1972 and was taken to court almost immediately to argue its right to make such a plan. The district court ruled against Petaluma, saying that the city inhibited the rights of those who wanted and needed housing. The Supreme Court eventually upheld the city's right to impose slow-growth regulations, but that decision did not solve the problems of regional planning, the protection of the natural environment, or the economics of regional housing. Only a regional agency could do that.

Those who did not get housing in Petaluma, including minorities, were shunted to nearby communities which seem to be less well equipped than Petaluma to handle the newcomers and which did not enjoy the luxury of no-growth agitation. Nor was the regional environment much better off, since some land is better for housing than

[14] N. F. Litterman, "Three Forces in Coalition and Conflict," *IDS 10 Reader: S.F. Bay Environment* (Berkeley: University of California Department of Conservation and Resource Studies, 1976). See also H. M. Franklin, "Controlling Urban Growth, but for Whom?" in *Management and Control of Growth*, vol. 2, ed. R. W. Scott (Washington, D.C.: The Urban Land Institute, 1975), pp. 78–101.

other land, some is better for agriculture, some has fragile ecosystems, and some does not. As the Court of Appeals noted in favor of Petaluma, "The reasonableness, not the wisdom, of the Petaluma Plan is at issue in this suit." That is, the question that was decided dealt only with those specific points over which there was a fight, not whether an adversary situation is the best way to do land-use planning.

Although the environmentalists seem to have won a victory in Petaluma with the city's annual ceiling of five hundred building permits, the direct effect of the ceiling has been the increase of the price of land and housing (because of the scarcity of permits) and the consequent exclusion of families without such financial resources. Similar kinds of exclusionary zoning with similar effects occurred in Santa Barbara, California; Ramapo, New York; Fairfax County, Virginia; and Boca Raton, Florida. The problem looms larger than local efforts to protect its environment.

Thus, though land-use planning seems to be the most "rational" approach to these problems, there has been much opposition to a perennial land-use bill in Congress. The bill simply provides the states with money to regulate planning of major construction projects such as subdivisions, airports, power plants, oil refineries, and industrial complexes on the condition that environmental quality is safe-guarded.[15] States would have to establish land-use accounting programs, which would take an inventory of natural resources, urban and industrial development, and wilderness areas in order to prepare the states to designate critical environmental regions as protected regions. At the same time, the states would provide major regional development plans for industry, recreation, energy, airports, highways, water, agriculture, and environmental protection. The bill has many features in common with those of the national coastline protection bill. Most developers and the housing industry oppose the legislation, even though the alternative seems to have worked so poorly for various parties in recent years.

[15] L. Gapay, "Land Use Is an Emotional Issue," *Wall Street Journal*, July 3, 1975, p. 20. See also M. McCloskey, "Preservation of America's Open Space: Proposal for a National Land Use Commission," *Michigan Law Review* 68 (1970): 1167; A. B. Bishop et al., *Carrying Capacity and Regional Environmental Management: A Feasibility Study* (Washington, D.C.: Office of Research and Management, U.S. Environmental Protection Agency, 1974).

Despite legislative roadblocks to a national land-use bill, dissatisfaction with the established notion of unlimited rights over private property through free-market bargaining has been mounting because of social and environmental consequences.[16] Not only does the traditional marketplace tend to segregate and separate rich settlements from the poor, but it also leads to progressive deterioration of the landscape and destruction of natural watersheds and fragile ecosystems such as coastlines. The loss of quality in the natural environments in and outside urban areas and leapfrog suburban growth are linked in the inefficiency (irrationality) of the marketplace. As unplanned sales are made, access roads, utilities, water lines, and other features must be extended over larger and larger areas. In short, the market system does not include rational social and environmental objectives within its own purposes of unfettered expansion.

Regional Environmental Conflicts

Growth also often means that some states or regions gain material benefits while others suffer environmental damage. One example cited above, the construction of shopping malls, offers an illustration of the phenomenon. Malls are usually built near county lines, drawing business from both counties but paying various kinds of tax revenues only to the county in which the malls are situated. The adjacent county, in the meantime, suffers traffic congestion, air pollution, and drainage or flood problems if it happens to lie in the downstream side of the large, impervious surface of the mall. (Parking lots destroy the natural flow of water into and out of the soil.)

States also battle over similar environmental "externalities."[17] For example, an industry association in Connecticut developed a good court case against New York and New Jersey because its members had to pay for air pollution generated and blown from industrial

[16] Task Force on Land Use and Urban Growth, Rockefeller Brothers Fund, *The Use of Land: A Citizen's Policy Guide to Urban Growth* (New York: Crowell, 1973). See also A. P. Solomon, "The Effect of Land Use and Environmental Controls on Housing," Working Paper No. 34, Joint Center for Urban Studies of MIT and Harvard University, February, 1976.

[17] D. Lewis, "Skirmishes in the War Between the States," *New York Times*, July 23, 1978.

sources in their neighboring states. In another court case, New Jersey sued New York and Pennsylvania to stop dumping their garbage on its land, and though it lost its case, the state made a strong point nationally.

Other cases are made with increasing regularity. Brookhaven National Laboratory on Long Island had to bury its radioactive wastes beneath its own nuclear reactor because New York City and New London, Connecticut, where the wastes could have been shipped by ferry, both stopped the wastes from passing through their jurisdictions.

And when residents of a region manage to stop heavy trucks from passing through their cities, the rigs bypass those areas and go into other towns. This happened in New York, causing truckers to detour into Bergen County, New Jersey, when New York set up restrictions on heavy trucks. Finally, the Tocks Island Dam project was complicated by state conflicts. Governor Shapp of Pennsylvania wanted the dam for the security of Philadelphia's water supply. New York and New Jersey were opposed to the dam for a variety of reasons.

Thus, to infer that environmentalists are to blame for irrationalities associated with environmental problems and economic growth, as the editorialist cited at the beginning of the chapter seems to do, is an oversimplification. For political answers to complex environmental questions, a good place to start is a statement of basic democratic principles instead of what seems to be the economic imperative.

The next step is to set up planning agencies that reflect real rather than political constraints. These agencies must draw their charters from the statements of basic democratic principles.

Therefore, the people themselves must have direct access to whatever centralized authority is given power to approve and implement land-use plans. That is, they must be able to help set priorities, goals, and methods to implement land-use or other environmental plans. Centralized agencies are necessary because environmental and land-use questions reach beyond the immediate vicinities of proposed developments. Pollution can extend for hundreds or thousands of miles, and even in the case of open space, city dwellers far from rural development projects are deprived of landscapes and wilderness areas which surround their industrial pockets. It was mainly because of wide support and a national interest in the preservation of rural environments that British lawmakers passed a national Town and Country Planning Act to protect rural areas from commercial development.

If central planning is important, citizen access, participation, and monitoring are just as necessary. The process assumes free access to information and interchange among value (conflict) groups and the opportunity of these groups to assist each agency in hammering out a working agreement. The assumptions and democratic goals of the propositions made above include the following:[18]

1. A citizen has a right and legal standing to environmental quality, for which there is solid legal precedent.

2. A citizen has statutory rights of access to information before, during, and after public or private proposals and when any policy which affects the environment has been implemented.

3. The media must be given the public charge of thoroughly investigating and reporting environmental issues before, during, and after the policy-making process in order to facilitate public communication and discussion of the issues.

4. Schools on every level must promote awareness of environmental protection with the same kind of priority given to other aspects of democratic education, such as civil rights, religious freedom, and freedom of speech, so that citizens come to expect the right to a decent environment as they do other basic rights.

5. All types of social, economic, and political activities must be used to achieve a rational, equitable, and environmentally sound resource allocation and management program with wide citizen participation. Alternatives include permit systems from administrative agencies for any proposed industrial or commercial use of land,

[18] W. R. Sewell and T. O. Riordan, "The Culture of Participation in Environmental Decisionmaking," *Symposium on Public Participation in Resource Decisionmaking*, pp. 15–16. See also "Symposium on Public Participation in Resource Decisionmaking," *Natural Resources Journal* 16 (1976). See also D. T. Savage et al., *The Economics of Environmental Improvement* (Boston: Houghton-Mifflin, 1974); and R. T. Green and G. D. Bruce, "The Assessment of Community Attitudes toward Industrial Development," *Growth and Change* 7 (1974): 28–33.

[19] G. Neustadter, "The Role of the Judiciary in the Confrontation with the Problems of Environmental Quality," *UCLA Law Review* 17 (1970): 1072.

water, minerals, timber, and other natural resources, and, of course, the more traditional participation methods, including hearings, public opinion polls, workshops, and citizen task forces.

It is inevitable that the courts will be involved in the protection of citizens' environmental rights as well as in the interpretation of congressional mandates in this area of the law. G. Neustadter writes: "The rule of the judiciary in confronting problems of environmental quality must be to insure that other decision-making bodies of the government make the best possible decisions about environmental quality. The assurance comes only when those decisions represent a conscious and informed societal choice of public policy—a type of choice which is, after all, a presumed foundation of the democratic system."[19]

Regional decision-making systems would differ for diverse environmental issues—air and water pollution, coastline protection, flood control, highway or power plant construction, industrial development, airports, natural-resource exploitation, and recreation among others. Different problems in different geographic locations require different decision-making jurisdictions. Local, regional, state, and federal agencies are often involved in complex decision-making processes because different environmental problems carry with them "spill-over" effects. All the issues, however, seem to involve an inherent difficulty both in assuring people the right of access to the decision-making body and also in interesting them in exercising their rights, both because the problems do extend beyond local jurisdictions and because the various jurisdictions of government are not inclined to cooperate with one another.

A case study on the Tocks Island Dam Project looked not only at intergovernmental cooperation but also into the attitudes and participation of individual citizens toward the local and regional decision-making systems.[20] The researcher found that each level of government tended to communicate and cooperate with other members of that level, that participation was dominated by federal and regional officials, that responsibility and authority overlapped or were in conflict, and that citizens themselves (the "nonexperts") tended to feel power-

[20] A. R. Gitelson, "The Tocks Island Project: A Case Study of Participation and Interaction Patterns in an Intergovernmental Decision-Making System," *Publius* 6 (Winter, 1976): 21–47.

less in the face of complex bureaucracies. It was on the basis of this and similar studies that the five assumptions and democratic goals listed above were developed. Institutions and procedures have not yet been worked out to solve the problems of cooperation and participation in decision-making systems, especially since only the most powerful interest groups seem to have the most impact on political decisions.

One regional agency, the Association of (San Francisco) Bay Area Governments (ABAG), invited (with a push from the EPA) interest groups, politicians, and specialized regional agencies to work with it to produce a comprehensive environmental management plan particularly designed to solve problems of air and water pollution and solid waste disposal.[21] ABAG formed a technical staff to make recommendations to a task force made up of elected officials from Bay Area cities and counties; from local and regional air and water pollution, water supply, transportation, and solid waste boards; and from thirteen major interest groups representing business, environmentalists, labor minorities, senior citizens, the lung association, and others. Groups in the task force were to alert their constituencies as the plan evolved, and decisions were to be made over a two-year period before the final stages involving public hearings.

By the time agreement was reached on the management plan, over twenty thousand people were directly involved in the process of providing input for or voting on it. The plan represented a step toward more direct representation through possible future elected regional boards and at least better regional environmental quality and a more environmentally aware general public, even if the final provisions of the plan did not meet the expectations of many environmental advocates.

The Rule of Reason

This chapter began with a *Wall Street Journal* editorial which lamented environmental legal activities which its author perceived

[21] O. Huth, "Managing the Bay Area's Environment: An Experiment in Collaborative Planning," *Public Affairs Report* 18 (1976): 2. This publication is produced by the Institute of Governmental Studies, University of California, Berkeley.

as "irrational" obstructionism. Many examples presented throughout this book would tend to reinforce the notion that the conflicts among environmentalists and their opponents at bottom are questions of value where no middle position seems to be acceptable to either side. Thus, the antagonists fight it out in the courts, where adversaries win some and lose some.

Yet any true "rule of reason," whether advocated by the *Wall Street Journal* or the *Sierra Club Bulletin*, must be established with an understanding that the other party's value system is open to broader visions, not closed and dogmatized forever. Conventional lawsuits and the adversary system of challenges do not ordinarily lend themselves to the possibility of new insights derived from the give and take of critical discussion.

Law professor Milton Wessel, in his book *The Rule of Reason*, maintains that conventional courtroom practices of withholding information, deceit, procedural delays, *ad hominem* attacks, and the win-at-any-cost legal mentality are not appropriate for environmental and consumer cases. Wessel says that the adversary system does not incorporate the potential arguments, needs, and values of an important third party, the public, in its deliberations. What is at issue is the right of society at large to find out the facts of an issue and to be included in the process of important societal decisions. As we have seen, contemporary courtroom procedures and the usual legal "games" work against these goals.[22]

Wessel urges that "socio-scientific" cases be argued under the rule-of-reason principle associated with antitrust litigation. A rule-of-reason principle would admit the primacy of the common societal good over the good of conflicting parties, which is to say, the necessity of presenting all the important data of the case in good faith, even admitting personal interests and biases. Whether implementing such a proposal is an impossible dream in the present age of dogmatism, economic concentration and power, and individualist struggles, the idea addresses the important issue of the public good in the national environmental debate.

It should not be considered unusual or strange that a book

[22] M. Wessel, *The Rule of Reason* (Reading, Mass.: Addison-Wesley, 1976).

which traces the paradoxical and variegated ideologies and values of environmental groups and their opposition should insist on citizen participation as well as planning in the interests of the future public good. Centralized control without citizen access and monitoring leads to self-satisfied or unresponsive bureaucratic paternalism. Without a central authority, local units would fight endlessly among themselves, and the natural environment would come out no better than with no participation at all. Although the combination of democracy joined with centralized planning seems contradictory, it really also seems to be the only rational choice.

Preconditions of such systems are the right and ability to understand the issues and the interests and values of the participants. Therein the question of environmental ethics is highlighted.

10

Environmental Ethics

THE term *environmental ethics* usually refers to Aldo Leopold's "land ethic," which prescribes that nature should be granted rights on an equal status with humans. Writers on the environmental crisis have often taken their cue from Leopold, who deprecated the human "failure to accord to all life and to the environment itself an ethical status comparable to that which he normally accords to his fellow man. It follows that any meaningful long-term corrective to environmental abuse depends on ethical evolution. People have to grow up, ethically, to a realization that the concepts of right and wrong do not end with man-to-man relationships."[1]

Leopold attempted to illustrate that ethics has evolved from rights given by individuals to one another and step by step expanded to include one's family, tribe, region, nation, race, all races, some animals (SPCA), and thence all life (Schweitzer); his point was that ethics should continue to include the entire natural world, including plants and rocks. Although Leopold's perspective is, from an environmentalist point of view, beyond reproach, the argument breaks down at many stages. Tribal morality, for example, undoubtedly pre-

---

[1] R. Nash, "Environmental Ethics," in *Environmental Spectrum*, ed. R. O. Clark and P. C. List (New York: Van Nostrand, 1974), pp. 142–143, quoted in R. E. Dunlap and K. D. Van Liere, "Land Ethics or Golden Rule," *Journal of Social Issues* 33 (1977): 1–11. See also I. Barbour, ed., *Western Man and Environmental Ethics* (Reading, Mass.: Addison-Wesley, 1973); and D. H. Strong and E. S. Rosenfield, "Ethics or Expediency: An Environmental Question," *Environmental Affairs* 5 (1976): 255–270.

ceded individual morality, and aboriginals, primitive peoples from around the world (while supposedly in the tribal stage), seemed to have little difficulty accepting those outside their race almost as soon as they encountered Europeans. Furthermore, it seems clear that nature was not only accorded rights in primitive times, but it was even worshiped and revered (albeit for reasons of fear and for purposes of control). From this standpoint Leopold seems to have gotten his sequence backward; at least the evolution of ethics does not seem to have progressed along the lines he has suggested, whether or not the next stage will include both the entire biotic community and rocks as well.

Those who appeal to Leopold for support in calling for a new environmental ethic tend to draw on the biocentric tradition which places high value on the untouched state of nature in and for itself. These advocates enjoy enough philosophical and religious reasons supporting their viewpoint without having to appeal to the evolution of ethics. Understanding the position as a fundamentally religious one neither demeans it nor causes a mitigation in the force of its argument. For example, the rationale for a new Ministry of Ecology attests:

a. A new sense of the earth is arising in the believing community place.
b. A numinous integration phase of the earth process is taking place.
c. Humanity may now be defined as the latest expression of the cosmic-earth process, as that being in whom the cosmic-earth human process becomes conscious of itself.
d. The earth will not be ignored, nor will it long endure being despised, neglected, or mistreated.
e. To harm the earth is to harm humanity; to ruin the earth is to ruin humanity.[2]

These statements manifest the growing influence of the French Jesuit Teilhard de Chardin, a scientist and philosopher whose evolutionary religion proclaims "the divine in the heart of matter" and

[2] *Ecology and Religion Newsletter*, no. 47, November, 1977, edited by D. G. Kuby. The quotation comes from T. Barry of the Riverdale Center of Religious Research.

whose faith sees God working through nature to reveal Himself
progressively in each epoch.[3] Chardin's writings express similiar
sentiments of cosmic-earth consciousness and process but do not go
so far as to warn that mistreatment of the earth will surely result
in disaster (a natural-law type of argument). But both the Ministry
of Ecology and Chardin's proclamations are unabashedly religious,
both of them grounded in faith commitments. And they would also
recognize that their ethical program stems as much from a "new
sense of a believing community" as from their personal rational convictions.

Natural Law and Puritan Traditions

The rational side of an environmentalist's religious sensitivity
might very well come from the ecological tradition, derived ultimately
from natural-law discussions or theories of the ancients and the
medieval scholastics. Law and morality have been viewed for
centuries by people in this tradition, from the Stoics and Aristotle
through Thomas Aquinas at least as far as Enlightenment leaders
and thinkers as late as John Locke and Montesquieu, as founded in
nature and its physical laws. The natural world and human reason
were understood as governed by a common unitary principle of the
Eternal Law. As people begin to understand the universal laws of
nature, they become bound to obey them, according to natural-law
theorists.

The move toward scientific experiment which pointed to the
final conquest of nature through understanding led also to empirical
studies which proved to be an "ignorant disregard of the laws of
nature," as George Perkins Marsh lamented in *Man and Nature*.
Such wanton disregard for balances in nature can lead only to evils
for nature and man alike, for "she avenges herself on the intruder."
In fact, her own laws require such vengeance. Later ecologists like
Barry Commoner ("nature knows best"), Garrett Hardin (limited
space and resources of the "commons"), and dozens more illustrate
the same kind of natural-law principles which, if unobeyed, threaten

[3] T. de Chardin, *The Divine Milieu* (New York: Harper and Row, 1960);
T. de Chardin, *Hymns of the Universe* (New York: Harper and Row, 1965).

disaster. Their ethics seem more forceful than the simple application of religious principles; they rest on a model of science which is not infallible. That is, natural law or ecological models of ethics are not necessarily more convincing in themselves than biocentric, religious codes.

Again, Aldo Leopold's ethical principle ("A thing is right when it tends to preserve the integrity, stability, and beauty of the biotic community. It is wrong when it tends otherwise.") implies principles of natural law, but as he admitted in the *Sand County Almanac*, it is difficult to understand the laws of ecology and biology and next to impossible to know them all.[4] Even if one were to agree with the fact that we do know many specific facts about environmental pollution and disruption,[5] it is quite another problem to establish generalized norms and principles from which nature would guide ethical behavior in many different circumstances or select those aspects and laws of nature which could legitimately guide moral behavior.

The third tradition comes from an economic perspective and embraces the puritan virtues of thrift, neatness, conservation, efficiency, providence for the future, and the eschewing of wasteful habits. The morals of Calvin contained the seeds of capital accumulation for profitable production as well as for the scientific management of those industries (forests, too) and even the impetus toward conservation and scientific planning—industrial or governmental, economic or architectural. Since planning and management are neat and economic, that is, efficient and nonwasteful, the tradition is an ethic in itself, at once scientific, good, and wholesome. (Conversely, "It is a sin to waste.") Even the modern environmental economists profit from the almost self-evident clarity of the ethic.

Few will openly object to the "waste is evil" ethic, a principle which Barry Commoner uses to his advantage in *The Poverty of Power*. One of his basic complaints against the capitalist economy is that it cannot structure natural resource development in the most efficient channels, in the "thermodynamic" sense of energy—the

[4] A. Leopold, *Sand County Almanac* (New York: Oxford University Press, 1949), pp. 185–187.
[5] Strong and Rosenfield, "Ethics or Expediency," pp. 365–266.

ability to do work in the most efficient manner possible. Even Robert Heilbroner's apocalyptic *Inquiry into the Human Prospect* prescribes authoritarian management based on old-fashioned thrift, parsimony, and efficiency as the way out of the world environmental crisis.

On a more mundane level, T. A. Heberline claimed that the public was gradually adopting Leopold's land ethic by pointing to evidence that people were doing less littering and more conserving of energy even before the energy crisis of 1973.[6] The author showed that environmental awareness helped to inculcate a sense of responsibility which led to changes in behavior. It would appear, however, judging from his data, that the awareness triggered a traditional morality which is more tied in with conservation-mindedness and nonwastefulness than with the Leopold land ethic, which expresses a biocentric kind of ethic.

All of the traditions have led to an interest in developing a new environmental ethic. The success of these efforts is mixed, for reasons alluded to in chapter 1 as much as for reasons of outright conflict with opposing groups. Many people cannot relate to the new ethic personally because legal, social, economic, and political institutions do not support it and furthermore because they do not share the religious conviction or scientific viewpoint of environmentalists. Their common-sense experience about the way the world acts does not confirm the latter. Nonwasteful behavior can be adopted quite independently of environmentalism and has a great deal to do with whether a commodity like gasoline is scarce and how much it costs. The ethical traditions of environmentalism present sound insights and directions, but they must embrace wider implications of the contemporary world.

Ethics in the Public Forum

The question of environmental ethics should not be construed as a problem of rights of nature versus rights of people but at least

---

[6] T. A. Heberline, "The Land Ethic Realized: Some Social Psychological Explanations for Changing Environmental Attitudes," *Journal of Social Issues* 28 (1972): 79–87.

partially as interest groups competing for wider support over particular issues. Even Christopher Stone's proposition that legal rights be granted to natural objects necessarily includes a guardian for the natural environment. It is the environmental perspectives and commitments of the group in question which would come into legal conflict with perspectives of other interest groups. This is what has happened in the recent history of the environmental movement.

In the process of the practical struggle among groups, legal and administrative precedent (in the executive agencies, the legislature, or the judiciary) begins to establish the foundations of a practical ethic. Of course, law and morality are not identical. Laws or administrative procedure are born of practical necessity and known circumstances; ethical norms are general, often coming from untraceable origins and liable to widely divergent interpretations.

Yet in societal and legal discourse and interaction an ethic develops imperceptibly as rules are established for social and environmental behavior.[7] Since conflicting groups usually seek to influence legislative or judicial decisions, their "moral" perspectives become part of the inevitable compromises. Furthermore, as the wider populace accepts or rejects the laws, new procedures (say of public participation), or decisions in question, the basis for a wider ethic emerges.

Gradually, then, ethical norms become more generalized, more socialized, so that they rest on a common perception of the truth accepted by a large body of people who share a common conception of right and wrong. The perception comes from a historical process of acceptance of certain beliefs, principles, behavior, and traits of character. It is the societal expression and answer to the perennial question of how one should live a good life. It is both an expression of the law and an influence on new laws .

In former days the common conception of the truth disallowed a dissenting opinion. The basis of democratic society is supposed to be just the opposite, with a presumption of the extraordinary importance of public discussion where interested parties present

---

[7] S. E. Stumpf, *Morality and the Law* (Nashville: Vanderbilt University Press, 1966). See also A. L. Goodhart, *English Law and the Moral Law* (London: Stevens, 1953).

their views in good faith. Spokesmen of different values use the public forum to explain, to persuade, and to advocate their position in dialogue with those holding other opinions. Democratic truth results from the interchange—a tentative, changing truth.

Honesty is taken for granted in the discussion. The medieval scholastic philosophers considered deliberate deception a sin against the natural law because truthful social relations are a precondition for society itself. That is, if people cannot count on their fellow humans to tell the truth, a secure social system becomes impossible. Deliberate deception, coverup, lawbreaking for economic advantage, and dissemination of misleading propaganda by the media are a few examples of unethical behavior among those groups which have concerned themselves and the public over matters of environmental importance.

Honest discussion among groups conflicting over environmental matters is an essential component of environmental ethics. The opposite has been the case in just about every environmental battle of the past decade. The combatants have considered themselves to be in some kind of holy war; at worst, however, they carefully calculate the best means by which they can woo and propagandize—everything short of force—the uncommitted voter to their side.

For example, during 1976 a number of states prepared ballot measures for the people to decide whether construction of nuclear power plants should be halted until the respective legislatures were satisfied that safety and waste disposal problems had been solved. Long before the first election ballot was cast, the Atomic Industrial Forum, a trade association with 625 members, including 56 utility firms, set out to raise over ten million dollars for a media blitz to warn electric-power users of the dangers of brownouts, economic recessions, and other problems if controls were to be put on the nuclear industry.[8]

The nuclear industry hired public-opinion expert Patrick Caddell (later a pollster for President Carter) to do a study on costs and the thrust of a pro-nuclear campaign and received his report at the

[8] This news story, written by Bill Richards, was syndicated by the Washington Post Service in March, 1976, and carried by dozens of papers throughout the country for over a month.

annual meeting of the forum, where Caddell recommended an immediate attack: "Just as the antinuclear, antigrowth, antitechnology forces have sold fear, the industry needs to find a lever with equal emotional intensity—massive unemployment, no growth, poorer living standards, runaway costs, and foreign dominance."

The tone of Caddell's remarks represents a combination of locker-room exhortation, expensive public relations knowhow, and out-and-out scare tactics, certainly not honest public discussion. Perhaps Caddell spoke that way because he actually felt that the antinuclear forces had the edge on emotional argument and that his side needed a wedge just as powerful. Perhaps he wanted to convince his listeners of the importance of the media battle, where they would hold a four- or five-to-one edge on financial resources. Perhaps he took that approach because the adversary, win-at-any-cost mentality is so ingrained in the national psyche that it is blatantly naive to suggest rational discussion of any important public question.

It is true that environmentalists stressed (maybe even overplayed) the risk factor to their advantage. That, after all, *is* their major concern about nuclear power. The nuclear industry, for their part, pulled out the stops—lights going out on television screens, dire warnings about brownout and unemployment, and accusations that environmentalists were leading the country to ruin. Everyone spent a lot of money; few citizens received much unmuddled information.

Neither did the public receive unvarnished information after the notorious Three Mile Island nuclear reactor broke down and released radiation in 1979. The plant's public relations officials met with a group from a large public relations firm in a motel near the disaster site. Outside the motel room two reporters from the *Philadelphia Inquirer*—Jonathon Neumann and Julia Cass—listened and took notes.

The plant officials suggested that "experts" be called in immediately to assure the public that the accident was not serious (they did not seem as interested in whether or not the accident actually *was* serious as they were in the image of Metropolitan Edison Co.). "Press kits" and telephone numbers were to be given to reporters who wanted interviews with executives or further information. Phones were to be taken off the hook. Perhaps the reason these suggestions were not implemented was the article "A Secret Utility Meeting About Public Relations" printed on the following Sunday in the *Philadelphia Inquirer*.

Much earlier than the nuclear campaign, some environmentalists termed corporate environmental advertising "ecological pornography," not because industry was fighting environmentalism, but because so many firms used interest in environmental problems to sell their products.[9] The implication or explicit message of many corporate ads about the environment and their products is either that with good technology they can easily solve problems of the environment or that the corporations actually leave nature in better shape after they exploit its resources.

According to a report of the Council on Economic Priorities, ecological advertising by large corporations ranges from outright lying to subtle deception. It may cost far more than any actual efforts to reduce pollution. In the article cited above on "ecological pornography," the authors argue that environmental groups can make a case to the Federal Communications Commission for equal time to reply to Standard Oil's famous multimillion-dollar media campaign which was intended to sell their antipollution additive F–310. Many environmentalists at the time complained because Standard Oil was misleading television viewers on a number of counts by implying that the actual pollution problem comes from the gasoline instead of from large engines or the automobile culture. There were also many questions about F–310 itself.

The flak Standard Oil took from environmentalists, however, did not stop Phillips Petroleum from hiring out two tame cougars, a tame deer, and a trained golden eagle for a television commercial and then filming them as if they lived in harmony with the oil rigs and nature in northern Utah.[10] Exxon has done dozens of similar

---

[9] A. F. Neckritz and L. B. Ordower, "Ecological Pornography and the Mass Media," *Ecology Law Quarterly* 1 (1971): 374–399. See also "A Proposed Statutory Right to Respond to Environmental Advertisements: Access to the Airways after CBS v. Democratic National Committee," *Northwestern University Law Review* 69 (1974): 34–36.

[10] *Los Angeles Times*, March 1, 1976, p. 12.

shots with their offshore oil rigs, emphasizing wildlife; crisp, clear sea; and other positive visual images. Reclamation of strip-mined lands is another favorite scene that has been embellished for the television cameras.

The marketing strategies of many corporations seem to be directed to convincing consumers that their companies are different from other "less responsible" firms and that their brands therefore must be better. Most people now realize, for example, that there is no real difference between most products sold under different labels; thus, new kinds of tactics have been devised to make them seem different. Competition makes sense only if the producer can convince the buyer that his products are cheaper or better than those of other producers. Since the prices of similar products are usually nearly equal, the sales pitch has to emphasize other reasons to buy the goods, such as the contention that they cause less environmental damage than others. Gasoline was one of the first products marketed in this manner, followed by biodegradable detergents when non-biodegradable detergents were found to pollute lakes and rivers. Now the approach appears quite often, particularly on the television screen, where it is best suited to show off landscapes and wildlife.

Environmental ethics first of all should be distinguished from traditional ethics only in their frames of reference. Since an important aspect of this book has been exploration of the kinds of relationships which various environmental and other interest groups have developed over matters of the human and natural environment, it is important to underline what norms are most appropriate for these kinds of interactions. The notion presented above (and that informs much of what comes below) is John Rawls's "justice as fairness" doctrine, as applied to environmental concerns.[11] Rawls's fairness principles are applied to the basic structure of society. They are principles which he believes most people would come to through free and rational discourse. In his *A Theory of Justice* he presents principles and applications that would regulate a society in which everyone acted justly. Here, the ideas are applied to questions of environmental matters.

[11] J. Rawls, *A Theory of Justice* (Cambridge, Mass.: Harvard University Press, 1972).

Justice applies especially to the quality of corporate responsibility and ethical behavior; that is, what an industry does to prevent accidents and disease, to curb pollution, to advertise fairly, to guarantee products, to represent itself publicly with honesty, and so on.

Can unemployment be construed as primarily a problem of environment, or should it be more precisely linked to social and political goals? Construction and factory workers have suffered a high degree of unemployment at regular intervals in all western countries for over two hundred years, mostly because resource and other industries have chosen to automate in order to achieve greater profits and higher productivity. Why should environmental considerations be blamed for unemployment when they are responsible for at least as many new jobs as are lost (over a million jobs to implement water quality programs alone)? The problem lies more in social and political priorities and the will to implement new job programs than in the corporate perception of why environmental restraints should be removed, more in the duty of a society toward all its citizens than in the efforts of industry to evade social and environmental responsibility.

The implication of the question, "Should priority be given jobs or the environment?" is that of mutual incompatibility. Many business groups tend to phrase the question that way through the media when they are faced with pollution or land-use controls in order to generate public support for themselves. But as former United Auto Workers President Leonard Woodcock has stated: "The idea that business will be driven to bankruptcy and massive numbers of jobs will be lost if strict environmental and safety standards are adopted is the same tired line that has been brought up again and again through the years. They tried when the minimum wage was introduced, when Social Security and unemployment insurance were developed. . . ."[12]

Dozens of industries have claimed that safety regulations will cost hundreds of millions of dollars. For example, when the federal government proposed restrictions on the widely used plastic vinyl

[12] W. Anderson, "Jobs vs. Environment: The Fight Nobody Can Win," *Cry California*, Summer, 1977, p. 4.

chloride, industry spokesmen claimed that at least two million jobs would be lost as well as sixty-five billion dollars' worth of production. Four years later in 1977, after the enforcement of stricter standards, production was up 8 percent with no workers laid off.

Proof of compatibility of environmental and economic goals abounds as long as corporate managers feel secure about margins of profitability. For example, employment usually is linked with increased growth rates, which in turn are perceived as dependent on increased use of energy, which tends to discharge more and more waste heat and pollutants into the environment. If we want high employment, the argument goes, we must either accept more pollution or be willing to pay to have it cleaned up because economic growth necessarily entails more energy use.

Yet after national priorities were established by President Carter's 1978 energy proposals, which emphasized conservation through more efficient energy use, it was discovered that energy consumption could be cut substantially by efficiency and energy-saving devices and still allow economic growth. When the 1978 study sponsored by the National Academy of Sciences and the National Academy of Engineers confirmed that moderate economic growth could easily be sustained while energy growth was cut in half, the "jobs versus environment" arguments were forgotten as corporate spokesmen applauded tax incentives to assist them with the costs of modernization (costs which in some cases had already been realized by tax depreciation allowances).

Thus "fairness" refers to a wide range of public discourse regarding environmental or any other type of activity. It should also regulate questions of health of workers and of people living in polluted environments. The poorer sections of urban environments have traditionally borne the most severe impacts of pollution. According to figures reported to the California assembly in 1979 by the Western Institute for Occupational/Environmental Science, farm workers in low-paying migratory jobs suffer most from the effects of pesticides; three thousand of them are hospitalized each year because of exposure. To paraphrase Rawls, justice has not regulated environmental questions because, for reasons of social and economic inequalities, environmental health and quality are not "reasonably expected to be to everyone's advantage."[13]

Ethics of Environmental Health

Ethical considerations, as we have seen, apply to responsibility regarding toxic substances. A history of disregard for worker health and safety (even if not malicious) as well as of industrial use of the natural environment as a free garbage disposal area has unfolded in the United States from colonial times to the present. One of the worst examples occurred recently in Hopewell, Virginia, at a small, makeshift pesticide plant that turned out Kepone, a chlorinated hydrocarbon related to mirex. Kepone was developed by Allied Chemical in the 1950s and found to be effective against banana pests.[14] Allied Chemical and government agencies ran tests of the chemical in the early 1960s and found, among other things, that rats developed tremors, fish died, and pheasant reproduction was reduced sharply when minuscule amounts of Kepone—less than one to fifty parts per million—were added to their diets.

Employees working at the Hopewell plant were found to have 7.5 to 72 parts per million of the chemical in their blood streams. (*Parts per million* indicates the proportion between the chemical and all other substances in a given part of the body. For example, one crystal of salt in a four-ounce jar of water—about one hundred grams—is one part per million. Some substances, such as plutonium, are so toxic that one part per million can cause serious sickness and even death.)

Employees of the pesticide factory regularly complained to their superiors about dizziness, violent trembling, chest pains, and vision problems, but they were assured that Kepone is not a health hazard. Those who persisted in complaining were told that they were liable to be laid off. Finally, one Virginia health official, Dr. Robert Jackson, closed the plant and tested past and present employees.

[13] Rawls, *Theory of Justice*, p. 60.
[14] T. J. Bray, "Chemical Firm's Story Underscores Problem of Cleaning Up Plants," *Wall Street Journal*, December 2, 1975. See also T. J .Bray's editorial, "Kepone and the Toxic Control Bill," *Wall Street Journal*, September 29, 1976.

Over half had high levels of Kepone in their blood; thirteen were hospitalized for more severe problems such as memory loss, tremors, and liver damage. Some were found to be sterile. (The National Cancer Institute found Kepone's effect on rats to be statistically significant for liver cancer.)

Allied Chemical was later indicted by a federal grand jury on 1,094 criminal counts of dumping Kepone into the James River, which was closed to fishing because of the discharges, and for failing to report massive discharges of the chemical into the sewage treatment plant. Kepone was also found in large amounts all the way down the James to Chesapeake Bay.

Yet in its 1975 annual statement, Allied reported, "It is believed on the basis of . . . insurance coverage and the speculative nature of damages alleged, that any loss ultimately sustained . . . will not materially affect the company's material position."[15] The report seemed to reflect the situation accurately, for in 1976 Allied was fined $13.24 million for polluting the James River, an amount equaling about two days' average revenue for Allied Chemical, as A. V. Krebs has pointed out.[16] But even this amount was reduced to $5 million because Allied Chemical gave a (tax-deductible) donation to the Virginia Environment Endowment. No one went to jail for the offenses committed in the Kepone affair.

Similar effects on workers were reported at the Velsicol Chemical Corporation's plant in Baytown, Texas, where dozens of workers were disabled because of the highly toxic chemical leptophos (Phosvel), prohibited for use in the United States but sold outside the country. Another case occurred at the Occidental Chemical Corporation in Lathrop, California, where workers were made sterile by exposure to DBCP (dibromochloropropane), a soil fumigant, and at Dow Chemical's plant at Magnolia, Arkansas, where DBCP caused sterility and cancer.[17]

Velsicol has been charged with a crime for allegedly concealing damaging information by conspiring to suppress test results that

[15] Quoted in Bray, "Kepone and the Toxic Control Bill."

[16] A. V. Krebs, *AgBiz Tiller* 1 (1977): 6.

[17] R. D. Lyons, "Pesticide: Boon and Possible Bane," *New York Times*, December 11, 1977, p. 1. Also F. C. Klein, "Small Chemical Firm Has Massive Problems with Toxic Products," *Wall Street Journal*, February, 13, 1978.

tended to show that the pesticides heptachlor and chlordane caused cancer in laboratory animals. In the investigation which followed the allegation, a staff report of the Senate Judiciary Committee noted that the firm was informed of a variety of illnesses suffered by employees but neglected to report the incidences to the EPA or begin neurological examinations until five months after it received the report of the first medical consultant.

The chemicals, related to DDT, were banned by the EPA for most purposes in 1975 after tests showed they could cause cancer in laboratory animals. The federal regulations follow a scientific principle that anything that causes cancer in animals is very likely to do the same in humans over a period of time as minute amounts accumulate or have synergistic reactions with other pollutants.

For twenty years DBCP has been connected with sterility in laboratory research with test animals. Workers in half a dozen plants producing DBCP had no training to handle the chemical, and at least one hundred of them became sterile. Legal action is pending against companies manufacturing DBCP, but a more serious concern deals with possible future manifestations of cancer.

Responsibility for public health and property applies as much to the disposal of toxic substances as to conditions in the workplace. The company which disposed of the dangerous chemicals at Niagara Falls' Love Canal, the Hooker Chemicals and Plastics Corporation, knew about the seeping of chemicals into local neighborhoods there at least twenty years before the New York Health Department investigated serious health problems, according to the testimony of a former company executive at a congressional subcommittee hearing. The firm kept the problem a secret because it feared legal liability.

Beginning in 1978, the EPA found out about dozens of cases of illegal dumping of toxic substances. Many "scavengers" who contract with producers employ a variety of illegal methods to dispose of toxic wastes, from dumping them on roads or open fields to feeding them into pipes which empty into water systems. In New Jersey, for example, where large amounts of chemicals are produced and dumped, a firm called Iron Oxide routinely (and illegally) piped hazardous materials into Newark Bay. Hundreds of other "midnight haulers" around the country dump wastes into swamps, sewers, pits, and abandoned wells to avoid paying for disposal at approved sites. Very often their activities are well known to the middle managers of the corporations that hire them, but corporate executives can avoid responsibility and ethical questions by finding legal loopholes or by hiding in a complicated organizational bureaucracy.

Corporate Ethics

Christopher Stone, whose influential articles on the legal rights of natural objects have raised important environmental questions, has also pointed out problems of corporate ethics in the aptly titled article, "The Kepone Affair Reveals a Deadly Shell Game." He asks: "When the wrongdoer is a corporation whose employees are hidden in the shadows of a vast bureaucratic latticework, are the present laws and institutions adequate? Can they really daunt companies into setting up appropriate ways to monitor their compliance with the law? Can the rules make themselves felt in the lives of individual workers, staying the hand of the individual employee who finds himself on the edge of a reckless act?"[18]

None of the wrongdoers at Allied Chemical were punished by the firm or even fined or censured. Stone's questions carry further implications. Who, for example, should be held ethically responsible for a chemical known to be toxic or carcinogenic, for a factory that dozens of investigators found "alarmingly unsafe," for the destruction of much life in a river, and for many other environmental problems nearer the plant? Top management? Middle managers, eager to increase productivity at the expense of the workers and the environment, to say nothing of the people of the small community who also breathed much of the pesticide? In environmental matters many individuals besides industry people are required to make judgments on many levels. One state official, for example,

[18] C. Stone, "The Kepone Affair Reveals a Deadly Shell Game," *New York Times*, December 11, 1977, part 4, p. 3. Another version of the article appeared in *Business and Society* 18 (1977): 1. See also C. Stone, *Where the Law Ends: The Social Control of Corporate Behavior* (New York: Harper and Row, 1975).

refused to refer Kepone health problems to OSHA because, "You don't talk to federal people unless you absolutely have to." Ethical concerns might start with corporate behavior, but they certainly do not end there.

As a starter, Christopher Stone, among others, would hold the top executive of a company that violates environmental laws responsible in cases of corporate criminal negligence.[19] Agencies and courts are increasingly agreeing with this opinion. Rather than attempting to prove criminal intent to show guilt, prosecutors have been demonstrating that criminal liability stems from the defendant's responsible position in the corporation, whether or not he or she either knew about the criminal activity or was directly involved in it. In 1976 five corporate executives were jailed for various types of corporate crime, perhaps because of a 1975 Supreme Court decision which upheld the conviction of the president of a Baltimore food warehouse with unsanitary conditions because he was the responsible officer of the company, not because he personally condoned the activity.

This moral and legal concept of responsibility can be traced at least as far back as the medieval canon law notions (embodied in English common law) of culpable ignorance and of virtual intention —that a person is responsible for not knowing what he or she should know and intends to be the natural and probable consequences of his or her actions.[20] That is, a person can be considered criminally negligent (in past ages, immoral) when harm or evil effects are (were) caused by actions which the person could have anticipated even though he or she might not have directly intended them. In the past, executives of both corporations and governments have let their subordinates know that they were not to be informed of unseemly activities. This ploy might not work in the future.

For some time it has been recognized that fining corporations is an ineffective deterrent to criminal activity. The new approach

[19] S. P. Sethi, "One Way to Punish a Corporation: Jail the Boss," *New York Times*, February 12, 1978.
[20] S. G. Kuttner, *Kanonistische Shuldlehre von Gratian bis auf die Dekreten Gregos IX* (Rome: Vatican Press, 1935).

proposes to pressure the topranking official to influence lower employees in behalf of higher stages of legal or ethical morality. S. P. Sethi calls the proposal "a kind of trickle-down theory of top-to-bottom ethics." The same standards of ethics could rightfully be applied to agency officials who know about illegal activity but who do not cooperate with other enforcement agencies, as noted above. The legal device has hardly proved itself at this stage, however.

Corporations and Public Agencies

The institutional environmental "recalcitrance" of U.S. Steel and other corporations should be looked on even moreso as a problem of ethics (environmental ethics, if you will), because many firms are gigantic. They have monumental financial and physical means to pollute the natural environment and its residents. U.S. Steel employs a predictable set of tactics, according to officials from local, state, and federal agencies, which are designed to delay the inevitable installation of pollution control equipment, and only when forced does the firm put in the least acceptable equipment.[21]

First, the company "negotiates" with environmental agencies until the talks break down. Then the agencies file court suits and obtain consent decrees along with more long-term bargaining. Next, the company fails to meet the terms of the decrees and applies for variances and postponements. At the same time, at the cost of tens of thousands of dollars, as the former chairman of the firm, Edgar B. Speer, used to do, the company takes out full-page advertisements threatening local communities with loss of jobs "if we're asked to go beyond what is economically practical in pollution controls—or held to unreasonable timetables."

Neither does the company take a leadership role in developing the necessary technology to control pollution, particularly in its coke works, according to EPA officials. It consistently chooses the cheapest, least effective technology for new facilities as well as old, even

---

[21] E. W. Kenworthy, "U.S. Steel under Fire As Problem Polluter," *New York Times*, July 13, 1975, sec. 3, p. 11. See also D. Clippinger, "U.S. Steel Threatens Pittsburgh," *Philadelphia Inquirer*, June 27, 1976, p. 7-C.

when smaller firms like Jones and Laughlin or Inland Steel have proven the value of certain more expensive technologies like the closed pipeline system in their coke works.

The problem can be identified as an ethical one: a lack of commitment to a national goal and a waste of resources and money to divert and confuse rather than attempting intelligent planning with representatives of agencies and the community.

U.S. Steel is not an isolated example. Media and court battles are waged every day over some aspect of environmental protection. All the players come in on cue—researchers, industry, government agencies, environmentalists—and the drama begins. The sequence of events that occurred after Congress passed a law requiring selected utilities to switch from oil and gas burners to coal-burning facilities indicates how messy the relationships can get.

After the Federal Energy Administration had served notice to the utility companies to change to coal, the EPA was asked to determine at what level sulfur dioxide emissions from the power plants would be considered a threat to human health. The EPA had sponsored research on this subject—twenty-two million dollars' worth—for several years and had concluded that sulfates from sulfur dioxide pollution were most likely to cause adverse health effects. Sulfates are produced in the atmosphere from coal combustion in a complex series of reactions. Utilities attempt to control sulfur dioxide pollution by building tall power-plant stacks and switching to cleaner fuels when pollution gets excessive. However, the EPA has argued that the tall stacks enable air drafts to take the pollution farther downwind away from monitoring equipment and allow more time for the conversion process of the sulfur dioxides to the more deadly sulfates to take place.

Thus, in order to make his case stronger for sulfur-trapping devices called scrubbers to be required in the converted power plants, Dr. John F. Finkea of the EPA rewrote the agency report on the health consequences of sulfur oxides, exaggerating the evils of sulfates and downplaying qualifiers or contradictory evidence.[22]

22 W. B. Rood, "EPA Study—The Findings Got Changed," *Los Angeles Times*, February 29, 1976.

The utilities industry, and especially the American Electric Power Company, which was already balking at EPA pollution control requirements, expressed its horror through a $3.1 million media campaign to turn public opinion against the EPA. The industry published over thirty full-page ads in such newspapers and magazines as the *New York Times*, the *Wall Street Journal*, the *Washington Post*, *Time,* and *Newsweek* as well as just about all the local dailies in the Midwest. They quoted scientists who questioned Finkea's report, complained about the EPA's "unnecessarily restrictive regulations," and warned that the agency would cost consumers billions of extra dollars in their electric bills (despite the fact that coal is cheaper than oil).

The Federal Energy Administration and the Federal Power Commission joined the utilities in attacking the EPA study, hiring consultants of their own. After many months of expensive media infighting, consultants' reports, a congressional investigation, and further research—with untold millions spent on it all—congressional investigators concluded that the research was "useless for determining what precise levels of specific pollutants represent a health hazard." The EPA continued to maintain that sulfates are significantly harmful, though at not statistically exact levels, and that the utilities are still required to install scrubbers. Few of the utilities have complied with the order, calling it unreasonable, and the situation remains what it was in 1970 when the original sulfur study was begun.

If federal agencies often engage in conflicts over goals and methods, so are there disagreements between federal and state agencies and between state and local agencies. As was previously suggested, local agencies are more likely to succumb to industry lobbying and even to their threats about job losses. In California in 1976 an environmentalist State Air Resources Board took the offensive against one local southern California board which it accused of moving too slowly against oil refineries for "massive" violations of pollution control laws.[23] The state board seized some local enforce-

---

[23] W. B. Rood, "State Air Board to Enforce Pollution Rules in County," *Los Angeles Times*, April 13, 1976. See also W. B. Rood, "Report Backs State on Oil Refinery Leaks," *Los Angeles Times*, April 22, 1976.

ment powers, the local board threatened to take the matter to the courts, and the Los Angeles Board of Supervisors called for a grand jury investigation. The jury upheld the charges made by the state board but condemned the state for publicly embarrassing the local board after "using speculative and questionable scientific techniques." Thence followed a flutter of public protestations, accusations, and self-righteous pronouncements. Government falls to the media when government by purposeful planning fails.

Ethics of Environmental Discourse

Very often discussions about environmental ethics get bogged down in controversies over the rights of people and the "rights" of nature to be left undisturbed or untouched. It is more accurate, and more honest, to attempt to clarify the variety of viewpoints than it is to accuse opposing viewpoints of not caring about people or about the natural environment. Only a group of people can recognize the importance of an undisturbed ecosystem or appreciate the fact that nature is pristine and understand the possible consequences of both. By the same token, highly defined economic interests often take it upon themselves to speak in behalf of people who need jobs and their rights or those who want recreation and so on.

The perspective of this book has been that most value orientations about environmental matters have been rooted in historical experience, with each enjoying importance and validity in different circumstances. Such an approach does not mean that a relativist kind of ethics is proposed or that it ultimately matters little what kind of perspective is accepted as public policy. The approach does assume that it is better for people to be involved in the choices—environmental or social—which face them than for those choices to be made by irrational forces of the marketplace or by an authoritarian government.

Therefore, the assumption here is that it is in the many areas of the workplace, the academic community, the business world, and the public forum that the ethics of environmental concerns first of all pertain. Because uncommitted, often disinterested groups hold the balance of political power in elections, those who do have an interest in the outcome of those elections exert pressure to gain the groups' support. The problem is compounded because each group tends to identify its own position with the summation of all truth, goodness, and national interest. At the same time it is unwilling to accept the validity of other people's understanding of the issues. Thus it has become almost a national tradition to use whatever Machiavellian tactics are necessary to win. Unthinkable amounts of money are collected and spent on media propaganda, lobbying, pressuring, and winning over the unknown voter to the righteous cause.

Of course, ethics extends beyond the processes of consensual democracy, but in a society where the consensus is uncertain, even fragile, clarification of goals and means through fair, honest, and open discourse is a fundamental obligation. Only in such a social environment is it possible to think and converse about the special rights of all beings in nature.

These ethical considerations might appear naive and idealistic when one considers the balance of power among conflicting groups in the environmental arena. Workers, especially the 70 percent who do not belong to unions, and consumers are in an inherently weaker position than large corporations, which have easy access to politicians and huge financial resources by which they can present their viewpoints through the mass media.

Charles E. Lindblom has concluded that the "close but uneasy relationship between private enterprise and democracy" has threatened the very existence of democratic society. That is, the passive controls of electoral government cannot match the pervasive system of market rewards, values, and imperatives of power. At the same time, Lindblom's careful study of contemporary socialist societies implies that the market system appears superior to socialist bureaucracy, "moral incentives," and rationing. Yet the market system assumes that private business will seek its own advantage as it decides what goods will be produced, where it will build factories, what kinds of technology will be used, and so on. Corporate boards are institutionally pressured by stockholders to bring a good return on their investments, lower executives are pressured by higher executives, and the same pressures are passed down the line. Even seamy activities can be rationalized within such a system (as was the Watergate break-in). Social and environmental responsibility assumes that everyone from stockholder to efficiency manager can be convinced of the importance of ethical concerns.[24]

Yet, as has been pointed out repeatedly throughout this text, business and other interests do not perceive the natural environment in the manner that environmentalists do. Neither do they underestimate the potential political power of their environmentalist foes. They have even borrowed their adversaries' tactic of using tax-exempt foundations to fight environmental restrictions.[25]

The Pacific Legal Foundation of Sacramento, California (organized in 1974), was the first of about a dozen such groups spread around the country. Those groups fight consumer and environmental organizations like the Sierra Club, the Environmental Defense Fund, and the Natural Resources Defense Council. The Pacific group has a staff of fifteen lawyers. It enjoys a budget of over $1.2 million (contributed by businesses, corporations, and "private charitable" foundations). It has initiated or joined more than one hundred major court battles, and according to its assistant legal director, the group and its clients "have prevailed in 80% of the cases that reached final judgment."[26]

Other legal foundations claim similar success stories. The Atlanta group won a court decision which upheld a factory owner who refused to allow an OSHA inspector to enter his plant without a search warrant. The Washington Legal Foundation successfully defended a mine owner who claimed that he had been harassed by a federal mine safety inspector who charged him with safety violations. Dozens more lawsuits are pending, including one brought by the Denver group against the EPA's strip-mining and resource development restrictions.

As Mark Green observed in a *New York Times* article, the wealth of the corporate world also contributes to the manipulation of the mass media.[27] In some cases corporations simply buy their

[24] C. E. Lindblom, *Politics and Markets: The World's Political Economic Systems* (New York: Basic Books, 1977).
[25] R. Lindsey, "Tax-Exempt Foundations Formed to Help Business Fight Regulation," *New York Times*, February 12, 1978.
[26] Ibid.
[27] M. Green, "How Business is Misusing the Media," *New York Times*, December 18, 1977.

own journals, as the Atlantic Richfield Company has done with the London *Observer* or as ITT has attempted to do (although it was later thwarted by the Justice Department) with American Broadcasting Company television stations. Mostly, however, the media are influenced by the massive amounts of money controlled by business. Over and above the thirty-three billion dollars spent on advertising every year, business adds almost another billion dollars toward advocating its point of view on energy, free enterprise, tobacco, pesticides, and other controversial subjects through editorials, newspaper supplements, cartoons, and other devices by means of thousands of radio stations, television stations, and newspapers around the country, which often use their materials without citing the corporate source. Obviously groups which object to the business point of view do not have the money to reply, particularly on such a wide-spread scale. Thomas Mechling, a former public relations official at IBM and later at Xerox Corp., contends that many large firms believe that "by sheer weight of money and words they can build a credibility that their actions don't warrant."[28]

Mark Green concludes his *New York Times* article: "We would all be better off if companies abandoned their small army of canned editorialists, editorial censors, advocacy advertising and media acquisition agents and focused instead on obeying the law and telling the truth. In the long run, candor is preferable to manipulation, strategically as well as ethically."[29]

It is astounding that in the face of such economic power so much environmental counteractivity should exist at all. The phenomenon tends to support the belief that the germination of a healthy environmental ethic is ultimately possible.

Environmental Justice

The final area of environmental ethics would deal with matters of equity and fairness not only for workers in an industrial environment but also for all who are subjected to pollution and the con-

---

[28] "When Disaster Comes, Public Relations Men Won't Be Far Behind," *Wall Street Journal*, August 23, 1979.

[29] Green, "How Business is Misusing the Media."

sequences of the degradation of the regional natural environments. Here, traditional concern for justice under the law would coincide with recent research showing damage to health and the environment. Such sources of ethical norms already reside in the moral conscience of the larger society. They can be supported by a growing body of scientific evidence indicating patent harm done to large segments of society, such as the urban poor living in heavily polluted inner-city areas, children who suffer higher incidences of infection while residing in districts with excessive ozone pollution, workers in steel and chemical factories, and all the communities surrounding such sources of pollution.

The notion of justice has been further developed by many environmentalists and applied to questions of the scarcity of natural resources and the distribution of wealth, in and out of the United States.[30] The idea's most popular spokesperson is Barry Commoner, who in *The Closing Circle* pointed out that the earth's resources will be depleted long before enough economic wealth from growth could pile up and "trickle down" to the millions living in poverty, especially since in the meantime rich nations are increasingly resorting to highly capital-intensive, polluting technology in order to increase profits. The poor stay poor while the natural environment is degraded and disrupted and resources are depleted. The argument equates excessive maldistribution of wealth and an ethical problem of social justice with environmental degradation. Pursuit of this line of thought has led many in the environmental movement, especially Commoner himself, to a more radical critique of economic and social institutions surrounding energy and other environmental questions.

According to Commoner's *The Poverty of Power*, the waste of energy supposed to do productive work not only is a sin against the natural environment in the objective depletion of natural resources and the degradation of the environment, but it also increases social costs of a debilitated population from pollution-induced sickness; it furthermore devastates landscapes (lowering aesthetic values) and

---

[30] J. N. Smith, ed., *Environmental Quality and Social Justice in Urban America* (Washington, D.C.: Conservation Foundation, 1974). See also A. Crosland, *A Social Democratic Britain* (London: Fabian Society, 1971); and H. E. Daly, ed., *Toward a Steady-State Economy* (San Francisco: W. H. Freeman, 1973).

leads to unemployment as energy production becomes more capital intensive (instead of labor intensive) to make up for the energy inefficiency.[31] Questions here are raised about injustices in the social sphere which are connected to issues that have long been recognized as environmental problems.

Tired of being accused of not caring about people or jobs, one group of environmentalists set up an organization in Washington, D.C., called Environmentalists for Full Employment. In one of their first newsletters they outlined their assumptions and political program:

Modern technologies that are excessively capital intensive and energy wasteful simultaneously destroy the environment, deplete resources and cause structural unemployment. These problems must be attacked concurrently, and such technologies must be rejected.

U.S. economic history is a parade of innovations using more and more capital, energy, and resources. In a world of increasing population and diminishing resources, it is more efficient to fully employ human resources while conserving capital and natural resources. But most economic analyses have not yet grasped this new reality.

U.S. policy makers have consistently failed to internalize all the costs of our economic system—including pollution, unemployment and other social costs—in their accounting procedures. We must follow the principles of ecology that state that nothing is "free," nothing is "thrown away," and that everything must be accounted for on a closed-loop basis.

National leadership naively assumed that material satisfaction for everyone can be obtained through a policy of undifferentiated growth. Since this policy has clearly failed both the environmentalist and the worker, we must strive for a fairer redistribution of the nation's resources rather than a continued expansion of resource-intensive production, the fruits of which are inequitably shared.

Therefore, environmentalists have been taken into a new arena of ethical judgments about the direction of American society: "Why are we so dependent on the production of goods in the private sector to maintain employment, goods that are ill-matched with such new human needs as mass transit and clean sources of power? Why, in fact, can we not restructure our corporate and governmental institutions to meet new and future needs instead of continuing to address

[31] B. Commoner, *The Poverty of Power* (New York: Knopf, 1976).

past conditions?"[32] Or, "Why do people produce junk and cajole other people into buying it? Not out of any innate love for junk or hatred for the environment, but simply to *earn an income*."[33]

If (inefficient) energy and capital-intensive industry lead to environmental decay or resource depletion, and if they result either in employment to manufacture frivolous commodities for which billions are expended on advertising or in unstable employment and unemployment, then a new ecological ethic based on a human-service-oriented society should be placed on the agenda of American public policy. As Arthur Pearl writes:

> It is only in a human service society, which is labor intensive rather than capital intensive, that the resources of the earth will be conserved and human resources be expended for the benefit of human beings. Such a society is less likely to breed war, racism, and poverty; these are necessary concomitants of a capital-intensive society.
>
> In essence, we have a surplus of human beings and a shortage of nonrenewable materials; thus we have to reverse our historical view of efficiency. Heretofore, efficiency has been calculated by the introduction of labor-saving, capital-intensive activity. Now we must have ecological efficiency, replacing machines wherever possible with human beings and, at the same time, offering the worker a gratifying experience, a feeling of competence, belonging, and usefulness, which once again leads us back to a human services society that is labor intensive and environment saving. . . .
>
> The two crucial variables are quality of life and environment. Our cost-benefit analysis must ask how much nonreplenishable nature is expended in relation to the benefit side of improved quality of life. . . .
>
> It is important to recognize the crunch that the blue-collar worker is in. The environmentalists by and large have asked him to sacrifice for conservation by paying increasing taxes for cleaning up the society and surrendering employment and comfort. He is also asked to pay for the human services, but these in no way serve his needs. He has reason to be unhappy with the education his children receive and his low-quality and expensive health services. A true environmental approach would offer quality services and place the burden of cost on those most able to pay.[34]

---

[32] H. Henderson, "Ecologists vs. Economists," *Harvard Business Review* 51 (July–August, 1973): 34.

[33] Daly, *Toward a Steady-State Economy*, p. 14.

[34] A. Pearl, "An Ecological Rationale for a Human Services Society," *Social Policy* 2 (September–October, 1971): 3, 40–41.

This perspective of environmental ethics in which social justice and environment are closely linked is gaining more and more adherents. Herman E. Daley's anthology on a steady-state economy, cited above, contains similar suggestions, as do the works of Barbara Ward, E. F. Schumacher, E. J. Mishan, K. William Kapp, Kenneth Boulding, John Kenneth Galbraith, and others. They can be linked with the most recent energy-efficient studies, which apply to automobiles as well as factories, as long as the "service economy" does not encourage increased automobile use as it creates more leisure-time activities.

These are issues of environmental ethics which include and transform Leopold's land ethic, natural-law ethical theories, and old-fashioned efficiency and conservation ethics. Since they embrace traditional moral norms of justice and equity, they can absorb environmental biocentric, ecologic, and economic traditions into established legal structures. That is, the approach is rooted in an ethic which follows an established political-legal tradition, a carefully defined political philosophy directed at cultivating what Daniel Bell calls *civitas*, the ability of individuals and groups to forego their short-term interests and "diverse private wants" for the demonstrable public needs and good of the larger society.[35]

It is apparent that the goal of a firmly established environmental ethic will be achieved only if efforts are made through many institutions on many fronts: courses in educational curricula, of course, undergirded with price mechanisms, legal decisions and environmental legislation, prosecutions for criminal negligence in the workplace and community, institutional arrangements which guarantee public participation in environmental decision making, and public discussion of ethical systems regarding environmental justice. Through these processes *civitas* may one day become a commonplace public virtue. When this happens we will know that the three traditions of environmentalism have been transformed from isolated ethical enclaves into informing virtues of a new social/environmental system.

[35] D. Bell, *The Cultural Contradictions of Capitalism* (New York: Basic Books, 1975).

Epilogue
Sincerity and Authenticity

It is obvious that environmentalists have been concerned to develop an environmental ethic because of their perception of the environmental crisis. They believe that new norms need to be generated immediately so that people may be moved to action quickly in order to save the natural environment, and indeed the world, from ecological disaster.

A major thesis of this book has been that the special imperatives and environmental ethics which are proposed by biocentric advocates, ecological scientists, and efficiency economists are derived from powerful but limited traditions and often are not intelligible within an institutional context. Worse, the directives are framed in such a generalized or unbelievable mode that when applied concretely in special situations, the prescriptions seem either meaningless, impossible to fulfill, or creative of undue economic hardships.

Of course, those who accept the traditions from which the dicta are taken understand their meaning and find them congenial to follow. It is difficult for these sometimes sectarian apologists to comprehend why, in the face of such impressive evidence, others do not share their morality, their classically imposed categorical imperatives. Their commitment comes from reasons they perceive to be overriding despite the incomprehension of outsiders. The latter, as has been emphasized throughout the book, have their own value systems.

It can be assumed that conflicting parties are sincere about their personal viewpoints. Most advocates of a sectarian position, from revolutionary terrorists to fascistic Nazis and Klansmen, seem to be loyal to personal convictions and values. In democratic societies, confrontation tends to grow among viewpoints, and commentators gravely speak of irreconcilable conflicts of value.

For these and other historical reasons, "sincerity" has fallen from favor as a virtue in the past two centuries. It has been replaced with the more impressive-sounding "authenticity," which refers to the willingness and capacity of a person to respond to the demands placed on him or her by any particular historical and moral situation.[1] Authenticity, then, seemingly takes a person out of the realm of abstract ethics of his or her own interior consciousness in the attainment of virtue and demands an ability to respond (called "responsibility") to the needs and moral imperatives of the external world. Thus, the authentic person is necessarily an activist.

But according to our account, each group claims that its viewpoint represents the most authentic response to crises of the world and that its activity and policy suggestions represent the best possible solution to a more environmentally sound world. (Similarly, various sectarian leftist groups claim that their positions and politics are best suited to lead the world to a humane socialist society.) The accent of every group is on authenticity along with a proper dogma and code of ethics.

Ethical responsibility is ultimately personal; that is, it is the individual who accepts or rejects societal tradition, who forms values and ideals to which he or she is loyal, who responds to what is perceived to be justice/injustice or environmental sanity/insanity. Therefore, sincerity or honesty of purpose is important but surely is not the whole story. H. Richard Niebuhr posed the question as "To whom or what am I responsible and in what community of interaction am I myself?"[2]

It is easy to understand the latter half of the question, especially in the context of this book's premises; the problem would refer to

---

[1] The distinction is made by Lionel Trilling, *Sincerity and Authenticity* (Oxford: Oxford University Press, 1972). My version is closer to that of Brian Wicker, "Sincerity, Authenticity and God," *New Blackfriars* 57 (May, 1976): 196–203.

[2] H. Niebuhr, *The Responsible Self* (New York: Harper and Row, 1963), p. 68.

whether or not the community of interaction is open or closed. If closed, the community would tend to generate an inbred, defensive (albeit sincere) code of ethics. The defensiveness breaks down in proportion to the openness of the tradition or community.

The answer to the first part of Niebuhr's question depends on a personal or group understanding of the world and furthermore on the credibility of those who interpret the world in the name of environmentalism (or natural or social science). If the condition of authenticity is responsiveness to the moral imperatives of the world, then it behooves those who present those imperatives (that is, environmental activists and spokespersons) to get their goals and facts straight, to know what values are defining the imperatives, and to decide what is negotiable and nonnegotiable before appealing to others for support (and for their "authentic" response). Here we could return to the preface and begin our exposition all over again.

If the philosophical, scientific, and economic truths of environmentalism became static, reified, truncated, or closed; if they are not able to be associated with the wider realities of the societal system; if environmentalism remains outside of and unconnected to the rapidly changing forces of history; and if environmentalists interpret reality within an incomplete or skewed framework, then their failure will ultimately be uncovered by those who might otherwise follow their lead.

Yet transparent goals, even purified values, are just the start of an authentic ethical morality, which by definition generates norms *for action*, and are refined and clarified by the struggles of that activity itself. Enlightened action, in turn, needs goals and ideals. An environmental ethic looks to a heretofore unrealized goal—justice among people living in the natural world. This goal goes beyond a defensive posture, either protecting a piece of wilderness against intruders or defending some abstract ecological principle or decrying economic waste. In the end an environmental ethic must focus on a democratic ideal, and environmentalism must gear itself to pursue that ethic.

Index